Ideas of History

RONALD H. NASH is Professor of Philosophy and Head of the Department of Philosophy and Religion at Western Kentucky University, Bowling Green, Kentucky. A native of Cleveland, Ohio, Nash received his M. A. from Brown University and his Ph. D. from Syracuse University. He has also taught philosophy at Syracuse University, Houghton College and Barrington College. Professor Nash is the author or editor of six books including *The Light of the Mind: St. Augustine's Theory of Knowledge* (1969).

IDEAS OF

Edited by Ronald H. Nash

Volume

HISTORY

E. P. Dutton & Co., Inc. New York 1969

Speculative Approaches to History

FIRST EDITION

Copyright © 1969 by Ronald H. Nash
All rights reserved. Printed in the U.S.A.

No part of this publication may be reproduced or transmitted in any form or by any means, electronic or mechanical, including photocopy, recording, or any information storage and retrieval system now known or to be invented, without permission in writing from the publishers, except by a reviewer who wishes to quote brief passages in connection with a review written for inclusion in a magazine, newspaper or broadcast.

Published simultaneously in Canada by
Clarke, Irwin & Company Limited, Toronto and Vancouver.

Library of Congress Catalog Card Number: 69-17929

Designed by The Etheredges

To Betty Jane, Jeffrey, and Jennifer

Contents

VOLUME I:
SPECULATIVE APPROACHES TO HISTORY

PREFACE: WHAT IS HISTORY? *xiii*

1. ST. AUGUSTINE *3*
   Introduction *3*
   Augustine: The City of God *7*
   Bibliography *23*

2. GIAMBATTISTA VICO *25*
   Introduction *25*
   Vico: The New Science *30*
   Bibliography *46*

3. IMMANUEL KANT 48
Introduction 48
Kant: *Idea of a Universal History from a Cosmopolitan Point of View* 50
Bibliography 66

4. JOHANN GOTTFRIED HERDER 68
Introduction 68
Herder: *Outlines of a Philosophy of the History of Man* 71
Bibliography 83

5. G. W. F. HEGEL 85
Introduction 85
Hegel: *The Philosophy of History* 89
Bibliography 107

6. KARL MARX AND FRIEDRICH ENGELS 108
Introduction 108
Marx: *Historical Materialism* 114
Marx and Engels: *The Communist Manifesto* 116
Engels: *Idealism and Materialism* 122
Discussion—Sidney Hook: *An Evaluation of Marx's View of History* 130
Bibliography 138

7. OSWALD SPENGLER 140
Introduction 140
Spengler: *The Decline of the West* 142
Discussion—R. G. Collingwood: *Spengler's Theory of Historical Cycles* 157
Bibliography 173

8. ARNOLD TOYNBEE 175
Introduction 175
Pitirim A. Sorokin: *Toynbee's Philosophy of History* 178
Pitirim A. Sorokin: *Comments on Volumes VII–X of Toynbee's A Study of History* 197
Toynbee: *A Study of History* 200
Bibliography 219

9. THE CHRISTIAN UNDERSTANDING OF HISTORY 221
Introduction 221
Kenneth Scott Latourette: *The Christian Understanding of History* 224
Reinhold Niebuhr: *Faith and History* 245

Bibliography 263

10. **HISTORY AND HISTORICISM** 265
   Introduction 265
   Maurice Mandelbaum: Speculative Philosophy of History: A Critique 268
   M. C. D'Arcy, S.J.: History and Historicism 278
   Bibliography 290

VOLUME II:
THE CRITICAL PHILOSOPHY OF HISTORY

PREFACE *xi*

11. **POSITIVISM AND IDEALISM: THE PROBLEM OF HISTORICAL UNDERSTANDING** 3
    Introduction 3
    Positivism: Auguste Comte 8
    Positivism: John Stuart Mill: Ethology—The Science of the Formation of Character 12
    Idealism: Wilhelm Dilthey 25
    Idealism: R. G. Collingwood: Human Nature and Human History 35
    W. H. Walsh: Positivist and Idealist Approaches to the Philosophy of History 56
    Bibliography 71

12. **THE PROBLEM OF HISTORICAL EXPLANATION** 75
    Introduction 75
    Carl G. Hempel: Explanation in Science and in History 79
    William Dray: The Historical Explanation of Actions Reconsidered 106
    Maurice Mandelbaum: Historical Explanation: The Problem of "Covering Laws" 124
    Rudolph H. Weingartner: The Quarrel About Historical Explanation 140
    Bibliography 157

13. **THE PROBLEM OF HISTORICAL OBJECTIVITY** 159
    Introduction 159
    Charles A. Beard: The Case for Historical Relativism 162
    Carl L. Becker: What Are Historical Facts? 177

A. I. Melden: *Historical Objectivity, a "Noble Dream"?*   193
Ernest Nagel: An Evaluation of Historical Relativism   205
William Dray: The Historian's Problem of Selection   216
Bibliography   227

14. **THE PROBLEM OF HISTORICAL CAUSATION**   228
    Introduction   228
    W. H. Walsh: Historical Causation   234
    Raymond Aron: Evidence and Inference in History   252
    Raphael Demos: The Language of History   279
    Bibliography   299

15. **HISTORICAL DETERMINISM**   300
    Introduction   300
    Sidney Hook: The Hero in History   302
    Isaiah Berlin: Historical Inevitability   312
    Ernest Nagel: Determinism in History   319
    Bibliography   350

16. **CONCLUSION**   351
    Georges Florovsky: The Study of the Past   351

Preface: What Is History?

The word "history" is ambiguous. It may mean either the *study* of certain events that happened in the past or else it can be used to refer to those events themselves. For example,

> We call Cromwell a "maker of history" although he never wrote a line of it. We even say that the historian merely records the history which kings and statesmen produce. History in such instances is obviously not the narrative but the thing that awaits narration. The same name is given to both the object of the study and the study itself.[1]

[1] James T. Shotwell, *An Introduction to the History of History* (New York: Columbia University Press, 1922), pp. 2, 3.

The distinction between these two meanings of history is more readily apparent in German than it is in English. The Germans distinguish handily between *Historie* (the process of events) and *Geschichte* (the narrative that connects and makes the events intelligible).

This book is concerned primarily with the historian's record of the past—with written history—although we recognize, of course, that the events of history provide a necessary foundation for written history.

No historian is interested in everything that belongs to the past, e.g., the prehuman past. His primary concern is with the past of the human race. But even a recognition of *what* the historian studies is not sufficient to delimit history; one must also notice *how* the historian deals with the human past. Benedetto Croce once drew a helpful distinction between chronicle and history. A chronicle gives what W. H. Walsh calls "a simple narrative" while history is concerned to provide "a significant narrative." In Walsh's words,

> The historian is not content to tell us merely what happened; he wishes to make us see why it happened, too. In other words, he aims . . . at a reconstruction of the past which is both intelligent and intelligible.[2]

WHAT IS THE PHILOSOPHY OF HISTORY?

C. D. Broad once distinguished two types of philosophy — speculative and critical philosophy.[3] Critical philosophy, according to Broad, performs the necessary tasks of analyzing the concepts we use and criticizing our basic beliefs. Speculative philosophy, on the other hand, begins with what science tells us about the world and ourselves, adds whatever man's religious and ethical experiences may imply, and then attempts to construct a view of the whole of reality. Speculative philosphy is illustrated by the

[2] W. H. Walsh, *An Introduction to the Philosophy of History* (London: Hutchinson and Co., 1958), p. 32. See the selection from Walsh in Volume Two.

[3] C. D. Broad, *Scientific Thought* (New York: Harcourt, Brace and Co., 1923), Ch. I.

grandiose metaphysical systems one finds in the writings of Spinoza, Leibniz, and Hegel. Examples of critical philosophy can be found in the careful analysis of philosophical concepts found in the dialogues of Plato and, more recently, in the writings of a number of British analytical philosophers.

Corresponding to these two branches of philosophy, there are two divisions of the philosophy of history. Critical philosophy of history, which is similar in many respects to the philosophy of science, attempts to clarify the nature of the historian's own inquiry. It criticizes the fundamental beliefs of the historian and analyzes the basic concepts he uses, e.g., the concepts of cause, explanation, fact, etc. The critical philosophy of history asks such questions as: How does the historian come to understand the past? Is the historian's method of inquiry significantly different from the kind of inquiry found in the natural sciences? What is the nature of historical explanation and does it differ from explanation in the natural sciences? Can the historian be objective? Many contemporary philosophers are convinced that questions like these are the only legitimate problems left for the philosopher of history and that all attempts at formulating speculative theories about history must be abandoned. The critical philosophy of history will be examined in more detail in Volume Two.

The writings of most of the classical philosophers of history (e.g., Augustine, Vico, Kant, Herder, Hegel) exemplify the speculative philosophy of history. Their work was an attempt to discover if there is any pattern or meaning to history as a whole. William H. Dray has drawn attention to three major questions that have concerned speculative thinkers in the philosophy of history.[4]

1. *What is the pattern of history?* Several major types of answer have been given. Some like St. Augustine and Immanuel Kant have proposed a *linear* pattern, that is, history has a goal or end toward which it is moving. Others like the ancient Stoics have advanced a *cyclical* theory of history. Nietzsche's doctrine of eternal recurrence is a more recent statement of the view that history continually repeats itself.

---

[4] William H. Dray, *Philosophy of History* (Englewood Cliffs, New Jersey: Prentice-Hall, 1964), pp. 63 ff.

> This life, as thou livest it now, as thou hast lived it, thou needst must live it again, and an infinite number of times; and there will be in it nothing new; but every grief and every joy, every thought and every sigh, all the infinitely great and the infinitely little in thy life must return for thee, and all this in the same sequence and the same order. And also this spider and the moonlight through the trees, and also this moment and myself.[5]

Still others like Vico and Spengler combined the linear and cyclical views and offered what might be called a *spiral* theory of history. In their views, while there is a certain repetition in history, there is also progress toward some goal. Finally, a few thinkers have advanced what might be called a *chaotic* view of history, that is, history has no pattern or meaning.

2. *What is the mechanism of history?* Speculative philosophers of history have not been content simply to offer patterns of history; they have also attempted to explain how changes in history take place. Among the interesting theories that will be proposed in Part One of this volume are Hegel's World Hero, Vico's Divine Providence, Marx's Economic Determinism, Toynbee's formula of Challenge and Response, and Spengler's suggestion that each culture follows a determined biological course of birth, growth, and decay.

3. *What is the purpose or value of history?* The more recent volumes of Arnold Toynbee's *A Study of History* illustrate an attempt to answer this question. For Toynbee, the end of history (viz., the attainment of a universal religion) justifies and explains everything that has happened in the past.

Volume One of this work contains selections from most of the important speculative philosophers of history. For the most part, these selections contain their authors' answers to the three major questions of the speculative philosophy of history. In addition, the chapters on Marx, Spengler, and Toynbee (perhaps the three philosophers of history who have most influenced twentieth-century thought) contain critical discussions on their thought. Volume One concludes with two essays that examine both critically and sympathetically the speculative approach to history.

---

[5] F. Nietzsche, *The Gay Science*, #341.

Volume **I** *Speculative Approaches to History*

1 St. Augustine (354–430)

A survey of the speculative philosophers of history could conveniently begin with Giambattista Vico (1668–1744) who without doubt is the modern father of the philosophy of history, with St. Augustine, or with the classical Greek writers. To be sure, the Greek historians [1] and philosophers did have a speculative philosophy of history. Most of them, however, thought of history as proceeding in terms of eternally recurring cycles.[2]

[1] The major historians of classical Greece and Rome were Herodotus (5th c., B.C.), Thucydides (5th c., B.C), Polybius (2nd c., B.C.), Livy (59 B.C.–A.D. 17) and Tacitus (c. A.D. 54–A.D. 116).
[2] See Heraclitus, *Frags.* 30, 31, 51; Empedocles, *Frag.* 115; Aristotle, *Met.* XII, 8; Marcus Aurelius xi, 1; Seneca, *Ep. ad Lucilium* 24.

But there are good reasons for passing over the Greek view of history and beginning with St. Augustine. The cyclical theory of history found among the Greeks (and Romans, as well) actually tended to depreciate history. If history goes round and round, never getting anywhere, forever repeating itself, there can be no goal either for man as an individual or for the species. Whatever happens to man will happen again; whatever man accomplishes, he must accomplish again and again—forever. It was Christianity, and in particular St. Augustine, that sought to counter the pessimistic view of history found in pagan philosophy with a theory that lent meaning and significance to history. As one historian explains,

> The importance of the Biblical conception [of history] cannot be overstressed. Here for the first time Western man was presented with a purposive, goal-directed interpretation of history. The Classical doctrine of recurrence had been able to give a "substantiality" to history, but it had not given it any aim or direction. It is not strange that Classical man lost interest in history when it represented for him no more than eternally repetitious events. But for the "people of God" in Israel and in the Church, history was definitely "going somewhere." All our modern conceptions of historical progress—whether religious or materialistic, Christian or Marxist—take their origin ultimately from the Biblical idea of history.[3]

St. Augustine's philosophy of history is spelled out in his monumental work, *The City of God* (written between A.D. 413 and 426). The immediate occasion for Augustine's writing this book was the sack of Rome by Alaric in A.D. 410. Non-Christians throughout the Roman Empire charged that Rome's catastrophe was a result of the city's turning from its pagan deities to Christianity. Augustine began *The City of God* for the express purpose of answering these charges. Before he finished, however, he

---

[3] John Warwick Montgomery, *The Shape of the Past: An Introduction to Philosophical Historiography* (Ann Arbor, Michigan: Edwards Bros., 1962), p. 42. Cf. George P. Grant: "What must be insisted is that the very spirit of progress takes its form and depends for its origin on the Judeo-Christian idea of history." *Philosophy in the Mass Age* (Vancouver: Copp Clark, 1959), p. 49.

found himself involved in discussions of numerous other topics including what amounted to a Christian philosophy of history.

The first ten books of *The City of God* contain Augustine's answers to the pagan accusations. Among other things, he argued that Rome had been victim to other catastrophes before Christianity. In fact, he maintained, Rome was sacked not because it had turned to Christianity but because it had not become Christian enough. He presents a catalogue of the vices of Rome sufficient to make it clear that there was no justification whatsoever for regarding the eternal city as a Christian metropolis.

The most interesting philosophical passages occur in the last half of the work (Books XI through XXII) where he turns to the major theme of his study, the existence within the world of two cities or societies—The City of God and The City of Man. "Two cities have been formed by two loves, the earthly by the love of self, even to the contempt of God; the heavenly by the love of God, even to the contempt of self." (XIV, 28) Men belong to the City of God by virtue of their love of God. Augustine never identified the City of God with the Church. He knew only too well the depths of insincerity and hypocrisy to be found within professing Christendom. Alluding to Jesus' parable of the wheat and the tares (Matthew 13), Augustine explained that the two cities will coexist throughout human history. Only at the final resurrection and judgment which will bring human history to an end will the two cities finally be separated in order that they may share radically different destinies—heaven and hell.

Augustine distinguished six major periods of history corresponding to the six days of creation. These six periods encompassed respectively the times from Adam to Noah and the flood, from Noah to Abraham, from Abraham to David, from David to the Exile, from the Exile to the birth of Christ. The sixth day is the age of the Church which will last until the final judgment. The seventh day, like the Sabbath of God, will be the age of rest when the redeemed rest in the Lord for eternity. The event around which all history pivots, of course, is the coming of Christ.

One rather common objection to Augustine's philosophy of history is that he derives it, not from history itself, but rather from the Christian Scriptures. While it is true that Augustine does superimpose the Biblical view of history upon human history, this in itself may not make his theory less plausible than later speculative systems. One thing that will become clear as we proceed is that no speculative philosopher of history (no matter how many and how loud his claims to the contrary) derives his pattern of history solely from the historical data. No matter how much data Hegel, Marx, Spengler, Toynbee, and the rest may appeal to, their theories, in the final analysis, are *imposed upon* history, not *derived from* it. If this judgment is sound, God (or rather, a revelation from God) is as good a source for a theory of history as any one man's reflection on the matter. At least, this is how Augustine would have looked at it. If nothing else, perhaps Augustine should be given some credit for being more conscious than many of those who followed him that no philosophical principles of history can be abstracted from human experience.

History itself exhibits no meaningful pattern for Augustine. The only thing he can discern in human history is the presence of human sin. In this, he anticipates (or perhaps influences) later thinkers like Kant and Hegel who admit to the overabundance of carnage, bloodshed, and greed in history. Augustine became aware of God's presence in history through divine revelation. Through the same source, he learned of God's plan which makes history significant and meaningful.

The following selections from *The City of God* begin with Augustine's critical observations about the Greco-Roman cyclical view of time. He attacks the moral implications of this theory of eternal recurrence. If life is to have meaning, there must be at least the possibility of hope and progress. And there can be progress only when one is going somewhere. Therefore, in order for life to have any value, history must have a goal and the cyclical view of history must be false.

Later selections present samples of Augustine's discussions about the two cities. An interesting corollary of his position is his theory of the state.[4] Just as the City of God is not the Church, so the City of Man should not be identified with the State. The State, therefore, is not completely evil. On the contrary, it is

---

[4] See H. A. Deane, *The Political and Social Ideas of St. Augustine* (New York: Columbia University Press, 1963).

God's instrument on earth to facilitate the temporal good of all men and to punish the evildoer. Because man is evil, he needs civil government to keep him in check. The State then is necessary to preserve the peace and all Christians are obliged to obey their rulers except when those leaders command acts contrary to God's will. Augustine is not blind to the fact that not all states are just. He draws a comparison between unjust kingdoms and robber bands or pirate ships. (IV, 4) He defines a government as a people united in a general agreement on those things it respects. (XIX, 24) Both the earthly and heavenly cities aim at peace. But the peace of the City of Man is a temporal peace consisting of order among men. The City of God aims at an eternal peace of heavenly blessedness.

ST. AUGUSTINE
THE CITY OF GOD[*]

Augustine's critique of cyclical views of history. This controversy some philosophers have seen no other approved means of solving than by introducing cycles of time, in which there should be a constant renewal and repetition of the order of nature;[1] and they have therefore asserted that these cycles will ceaselessly recur, one passing away and another coming, though they are not agreed as to whether one permanent world shall pass through all these cycles, or whether the world shall at fixed intervals die out, and be renewed so as to exhibit a recurrence of the same phenomena—the things which have been, and those which are to be, coinciding. And from this fantastic vicissitude they exempt not even the immortal soul that has attained wisdom, consigning it to a ceaseless transmigration between delusive blessedness and real misery. For how can that be truly called blessed which has no assurance of being so eternally, and is either in ignorance of the truth, and blind to the misery that is approaching or, knowing it, is in misery and fear? Or if it passes to bliss, and leaves miseries

---
[*] Reprinted from Marcus Dods's translation of *The City of God* (Edinburgh: 1881).
[1] i.e., the orthodox Stoic position.

forever, then there happens in time a new thing which time shall not end. Why not, then, the world also? Why may not man, too, be a similar thing? So that, by following the straight path of sound doctrine, we escape, I know not what circuitous paths, discovered by deceiving and deceived sages.

Some, too, in advocating these recurring cycles that restore all things to their original cite in favor of their supposition what Solomon says in the book of Ecclesiastes: "What is that which hath been? It is that which shall be. And what is that which is done? It is that which shall be done: and there is no new thing under the sun. Who can speak and say, See, this is new? It hath been already of old time, which was before us." [2] This he said either of those things of which he had been speaking—the succession of generations, the orbit of the sun, the course of rivers —or else of all kinds of creatures that are born and die. For men were before us, are with us, and shall be after us; and so all living things and all plants. Even monstrous and irregular productions, though differing from one another, and though some are reported as solitary instances, yet resemble one another generally, in so far as they are miraculous and monstrous, and, in this sense, have been, and shall be, and are no new and recent things under the sun. However, some would understand these words as meaning that in the predestination of God all things have already existed, and that thus there is no new thing under the sun. At all events, far be it from any true believer to suppose that by these words of Solomon those cycles are meant, in which, according to those philosophers, the same periods and events of time are repeated; as if, for example, the philosopher Plato, having taught in the school at Athens which is called the Academy, so, numberless ages before, at long but certain intervals, this same Plato and the same school, and the same disciples existed, and so also are to be repeated during the countless cycles that are yet to be—far be it, I say, from us to believe this. For once Christ died for our sins; and, rising from the dead, He dieth no more. "Death hath no more dominion over Him"; [3] and we ourselves after the resurrection shall be ever with the Lord, [4] to

[2] Eccles. 1:9, 10.
[3] Romans. 6:9.
[4] I Thess. 4:16.

whom we now say, as the sacred Psalmist dictates, "Thou shalt keep us, O Lord, Thou shalt preserve us from this generation."[5] And that too which follows, is, I think, appropriate enough: "The wicked walk *in a circle*"; not because their life is to recur by means of these circles, which these philosophers imagine, but because the path in which their false doctrine now runs is circuitous. (XII, 13)

The city of God and the city of man. The city of God we speak of is the same to which testimony is borne by that Scripture, which excels all the writings of all nations by its divine authority, and has brought under its influence all kinds of minds, and this not by a casual intellectual movement, but obviously by an express providential arrangement. For there it is written, "Glorious things are spoken of thee, O city of God."[6] And in another psalm we read, "Great is the Lord, and increasing the joy of the whole earth."[7] And, a little after, in the same psalm, "As we have heard, so have we seen in the city of the Lord of hosts, in the city of our God. God has established it for ever." And in another, the holy place of the tabernacles of the Most High. "God is in the midst of her, she shall not be moved."[8] From these and similar testimonies, all of which it were tedious to cite, we have learned that there is a city of God, and its Founder has inspired us with a love which makes us covet its citizenship. To this Founder of the holy city the citizens of the earthly city prefer their own gods, not knowing that He is the God of gods, not of false, i.e., of impious and proud gods, who, being deprived of His unchangeable and freely communicated light, and so reduced to a kind of poverty-stricken power, eagerly grasp at their own private privileges, and seek divine honors from their deluded subjects; but of the pious and holy gods, who are better pleased to submit themselves to one, than to subject many to themselves, and who would rather worship God than be worshiped as God. But to the enemies of this city we have replied in the ten preceding books, according to our ability and help afforded by our Lord and King. Now recog-

[5] Ps. 12:7.
[6] Ps. 87:3.
[7] Ps. 48:1.
[8] Ps. 46:4.

nizing what is expected of me, and not unmindful of my promise, and relying, too, on the same succor, I will endeavor to treat of the origin, and progress, and deserved destinies of the two cities (the earthly and the heavenly, to wit), which, as we said, are in this present world commingled, and as it were entangled together. And, first, I will explain how the foundations of these two cities were originally laid, in the difference that arose among the angels. (XI, 1)

We have already stated in the preceding books that God, desiring not only that the human race might be able by their similarity of nature to associate with one another, but also that they might be bound together in harmony and peace by the ties of relationship, was pleased to derive all men from one individual, and created man with such a nature that the members of the race should not have died, had not the two first (of whom the one was created out of nothing, and the other out of him) merited this by their disobedience; for by them so great a sin was committed, that by it human nature was altered for the worse, and was transmitted also to their posterity, liable to sin and subject to death. And the kingdom of death so reigned over men, that the deserved penalty of sin would have hurled all headlong even into the second death, of which there is no end, had not the undeserved grace of God saved some therefrom. And thus it has come to pass, that though there are very many and great nations all over the earth, whose rites and customs, speech, arms, and dress, are distinguished by marked differences, yet there are no more than two kinds of human society, which we may justly call two cities, according to the language of our Scriptures. The one consists of those who wish to live after the flesh, the other of those who wish to live after the spirit; and when they severally achieve what they wish, they live in peace, each after their kind. (XIV, 1)

Accordingly, two cities have been formed by two loves: the earthly by the love of self, even to the contempt of God; the heavenly by the love of God, even to the contempt of self. The former, in a word, glories in itself, the latter in the Lord. For the one seeks glory from men; but the greatest glory of the other is God, the witness of conscience. The one lifts up its head in its own glory; the other says to its God, "Thou art my glory, and the lifter up of mine head." [9] In the one, the princes and the nations it subdues are ruled by the love of ruling; in the other, the princes and the subjects serve one another in love, the latter obeying, while the former take thought for all. The one delights in its own strength, represented in the persons of its rulers; the other says to its God, "I will love Thee, O Lord, my strength." [10] And therefore the wise men of the one city, living according to man, have sought for profit to their own bodies or souls, or both, and those who have known God "glorified Him not as God, neither were thankful, but became vain in their imaginations, and their foolish heart was darkened; professing themselves to be wise"— that is, glorying in their own wisdom, and being possessed by pride—"they became fools, and changed the glory of the incorruptible God into an image made like to corruptible man, and to birds, and four-footed beasts, and creeping things." For they were either leaders or followers of the people in adoring images, "and worshiped and served the creature more than the Creator, Who is blessed forever." [11] But in the other city there is no human wisdom, but only godliness, which offers due worship to the true God, and looks for its reward in the society of the saints, of holy angels as well as holy men, that God may be all in all.[12] (XIV, 28)

This race we have distributed into two parts, the one consisting of those who live according to man, the other of those who live according to God. And these we also mystically call the two cities, or the two communities of men, of which the one is predestined to reign eternally with God, and the other to suffer eternal punishment with the devil. This, however, is their end, and of it we are to speak afterward. At present, as we have said enough about their origin, whether among the angels, whose numbers we know not, or in the two first human beings, it seems suitable to attempt an account of their career, from the time when our two first parents began to propagate the race until all human generation shall cease. For this whole time or world age, in which the

[9] Ps. 3:3.
[10] Ps. 18:1.
[11] Rom. 1:21–25.
[12] I Cor. 15:28.

dying give place and those who are born succeed, is the career of these two cities concerning which we treat.

Of these two first parents of the human race, then, Cain was the firstborn, and he belonged to the city of men; after him was born Abel, who belonged to the city of God. For as in the individual the truth of the apostle's statement is discerned, "that is not first which is spiritual, but that which is natural, and afterward that which is spiritual," [13] whence it comes to pass that each man, being derived from a condemned stock, is first of all born of Adam evil and carnal, and becomes good and spiritual only afterward, as a whole. When these two cities began to run their course by a series of deaths and births, the citizen of this world was the firstborn, and after him the stranger in this world, the citizen of the city of God, predestined by grace, elected by grace, by grace a stranger below, and by grace a citizen above. By grace—for as far as regards himself he is sprung from the same mass, all of which is condemned in its origin; but God, like a potter (for this comparison is introduced by the apostle judiciously, and not without thought) of the same lump made one vessel to honor, another to dishonor.[14] But first the vessel to dishonor was made, and after it another to honor. For in each individual, as I have already said, there is first of all that which is reprobate, that from which we must begin, but in which we need not necessarily remain; afterward is that which is well-approved, to which we may by advancing attain, and in which, when we have reached it, we may abide. Not, indeed, that every wicked man shall be good, but that no one will be good who was not first of all wicked; but the sooner anyone becomes a good man, the more speedily does he receive this title, and abolish the old name in the new. Accordingly, it is recorded of Cain that he built a city,[15] but Abel, being a sojourner, built none. For the city of the saints is above, although here below it begets citizens, in whom it sojourns till the time of its reign arrives, when it shall gather together all in the day of the resurrection; and then shall the promised kingdom be given to them, in which they shall reign with their Prince, the King of the ages, time without end. (XV, 1)

[13] I Cor. 15:46.
[14] Rom. 9:21.
[15] Gen. 4:17.

I promised to write of the rise, progress, and appointed end of the two cities, one of which is God's, the other this world's, in which, as far as mankind is concerned, the former is now a stranger. But first of all I undertook, as far as His grace should enable me, to refute the enemies of the city of God, who prefer their gods to Christ its founder, and fiercely hate Christians with the most deadly malice. And this I have done in the first ten books. Then, as regards my threefold promise which I have just mentioned, I have treated distinctly, in the four books which follow the tenth, of the rise of both cities. After that, I have proceeded from the first man down to the flood in one book, which is the fifteenth of this work; and from that again down to Abraham our work has followed both in chronological order. From the patriarch Abraham down to the time of the Israelite kings, at which we close our sixteenth book, and thence down to the advent of Christ Himself in the flesh, to which period the seventeenth book reaches, the city of God appears from my way of writing to have run its course alone; whereas it did not run its course alone in this age, for both cities, in their course amid mankind, certainly experienced checkered times together just as from the beginning. But I did this in order that, first of all, from the time when the promises of God began to be more clear, down to the virgin birth of Him in whom those things promised from the first were to be fulfilled, the course of that city which is God's might be made more distinctly apparent, without interpolation of foreign matter from the history of the other city, although down to the revelation of the new covenant it ran its course, not in light, but in shadow. Now, therefore, I think fit to do what I passed by, and show, as far as seems necessary, how that other city ran its course from the times of Abraham, so that attentive readers may compare the two. (XVIII, 1)

[Augustine then traces the parallel courses of the two cities to the end of the world.]

Peace and happiness belong to the heavenly city, both now and in eternity. But not even the saints and faithful worshipers of the one true and most high God are safe from the manifold temptations and deceits of the demons. For in this abode of weakness, and in these wicked days, this state of anxiety has also its use, stimulating us to seek with keener longing for that security where peace is complete and unassailable. There we shall enjoy the gifts of nature, that is to say, all that God the Creator of all natures has bestowed upon ours—gifts not only good, but eternal—not only of the spirit, healed now by wisdom, but also of the body renewed by the resurrection. There the virtues shall no longer be struggling against any vice or evil, but shall enjoy the reward of victory, the eternal peace which no adversary shall disturb. This is the final blessedness, this the ultimate consummation, the unending end. Here, indeed, we are said to be blessed when we have such peace as can be enjoyed in a good life; but such blessedness is mere misery compared to that final felicity. . . . (XIX, 10)

And thus we may say of peace, as we have said of eternal life, that it is the end of our good. . . . As the word peace is employed in connection with things in this world in which certainly life eternal has no place, we have preferred to call the end or supreme good of this city life eternal rather than peace. . . . The end or supreme good of this city is either peace in eternal life, or eternal life in peace. For peace is a good so great, that even in this earthly and mortal life there is no word we hear with such pleasure, nothing we desire with such zest, or find to be more thoroughly gratifying. . . . (XIX, 11)

The nature and value of peace. Whoever gives even moderate attention to human affairs and to our common nature, will recognize that if there is no man who does not wish to be joyful, neither is there any one who does not wish to have peace. For even they who make war desire nothing but victory—desire, that is to say, to attain to peace with glory. For what else is victory than the conquest of those who resist us? and when this is done there is peace. It is therefore with the desire for peace that wars are waged, even by those who take pleasure in exercising their warlike nature in command and battle. And hence it is obvious that peace is the end sought for by war. For every man seeks peace by waging war, but no man seeks war by making peace. For even they who intentionally interrupt the peace in which they are living have no hatred of peace, but only wish it changed into a peace that suits them better. They do not, therefore, wish to have no peace, but only one more to their mind. And in the case of sedition, when men have separated themselves from the community, they yet do not effect what they wish, unless they maintain some kind of peace with their fellow conspirators. And therefore even robbers take care to maintain peace with their comrades, that they may with greater effect and greater safety invade the peace of other men. And if an individual happen to be of such unrivaled strength, and to be so jealous of plots, and commits depredations and murders on his own account, yet he maintains some shadow of peace with such persons as he is unable to kill, and from whom he wishes to conceal his deeds. In his own home, too, he makes it his aim to be at peace with his wife and children, and any other members of his household; for unquestionably their prompt obedience to his every look is a source of pleasure to him. And if this be not rendered, he is angry, he chides and punishes; and even by this storm he secures the calm peace of his own home, as occasion demands. For he sees that peace cannot be maintained unless all the members of the same domestic circle be subject to one head, such as he himself is in his own house. And therefore if a city or nation offered to submit itself to him, to serve him in the same style as he had made his household serve him, he would no longer lurk in a brigand's hidingplaces, but lift his head in open day as a king, though the same covetousness and wickedness should remain in him. And thus all men desire to have peace with their own circle whom they wish to govern as suits themselves. For even those whom they make war against they wish to make their own, and impose on them the laws of their own peace. . . . (XIX, 12)

The peace of the body then consists in the duly proportioned arrangement of its parts. The peace of the irrational soul is the harmonious repose of the appetites, and that of the rational soul the harmony of knowledge and action. The peace of body and soul is the well-ordered and harmonious life and health of the living creature. Peace between man and God is the well-ordered obedience of faith to eternal law. Peace between man and man is well-ordered concord. Domestic peace is the well-ordered concord between those of the family who rule and those who obey. Civil peace is a similar concord among the citizens. The peace of the celestial city is the perfectly ordered and harmonious enjoyment of God, and of one another in God. The peace of all things is the tranquillity of order. Order is the distribution which allots things equal and unequal, each to its own place. And hence, though the miserable, in so far as they are such, do certainly not enjoy peace, but are severed from that tranquillity of order in which there is no disturbance, nevertheless, inasmuch as they are deservedly and justly miserable, they are by their very misery connected with order. . . . God, then, the most wise Creator and most just Ordainer of all natures, Who placed the human race upon earth as its greatest ornament, imparted to men some good things adapted to this life, to wit, temporal peace, such as we can enjoy in this life from health and safety and human fellowship, and all things needful for the preservation and recovery of this peace, such as the objects which are accommodated to our outward senses, light, night, the air, and waters suitable for us, and everything the body requires to sustain, shelter, heal, or beautify it: and all under this most equitable condition, that every man who made a good use of these advantages suited to the peace of this mortal condition, should receive ampler and better blessings, namely, the peace of immortality, accompanied by glory and honor in an endless life made fit for the enjoyment of God and of one another in God; but that he who used the present blessings badly should both lose them and should not receive the others. (XIX, 13)

The whole use, then, of things temporal has a reference to this result of earthly peace in the earthly community, while in the city of God it is connected with eternal peace. And therefore, if we were irrational animals, we should desire nothing beyond the proper arrangement of the parts of the body and the satisfaction of the appetites—nothing, therefore, but bodily comfort and abundance of pleasures, that the peace of the body might contribute to the peace of the soul. For if bodily peace be wanting, a bar is put to the peace even of the irrational soul, since it cannot obtain the gratification of its appetites. And these two together help out the mutual peace of soul and body, the peace of harmonious life and health. For as animals, by shunning pain, show that they love bodily peace, and, by pursuing pleasure to gratify their appetites, show that they love peace of soul, so their shrinking from death is a sufficient indication of their intense love of that peace which binds soul and body in close alliance. But, as man has a rational soul, he subordinates all this which he has in common with the beasts to the peace of his rational soul, that his intellect may have free play and may regulate his actions, and that he may thus enjoy the well-ordered harmony of knowledge and action which constitutes, as we have said, the peace of the rational soul. And for this purpose he must desire to be neither molested by pain, nor disturbed by desire, nor extinguished by death, that he may arrive at some useful knowledge by which he may regulate his life and manners. But, owing to the liability of the human mind to fall into mistakes, this very pursuit of knowledge may be a snare to him unless he has a divine Master, whom he may obey without misgiving, and who may at the same time give him such help as to preserve his own freedom. And because, so long as he is in this mortal body, he is a stranger to God, he walks by faith, not by sight; and he therefore refers all peace, bodily or spiritual or both, to that peace which mortal man has with the immortal God, so that he exhibits the well-ordered obedience of faith to eternal law. But as this divine Master inculcates two precepts—the love of God and the love of his neighbor—and as in these precepts a man finds three things he has to love—God, himself, and his neighbor—and that he who loves God loves himself thereby, it follows that he must endeavor to get his neighbor to love God, since he is ordered to love his neighbor as himself. He ought to make this endeavor in behalf of his wife, his children, his household, all within his reach, even as he would wish his neighbor to do the same for him if he needed it; and consequently he will be at peace, or in well-ordered concord, with all men, as far as in him lies. And this is the order of this concord, that a man, in the first place, injure no one, and in the second, do good to every one he can reach. Primarily, therefore, his own household are his care, for the law of nature and of society gives him readier access to them and greater opportunity of serving them. And hence the apostle says, "Now, if any provide not for his own, and specially for those of his own house, he hath denied the faith, and is worse than an infidel." [16] This is the origin of domestic peace, or the well-ordered concord of those in

---

[16] I Tim. 5:8.

the family who rule and those who obey. For they who care for the rest rule—the husband and the wife, the parents, the children, the masters, the servants; and they who are cared for obey—the woman their husbands, the children their parents, the servants their masters. But in the family of the just man who lives by faith and is as yet a pilgrim journeying on to the celestial city, even those who rule serve those whom they seem to command; for they rule not from a love of power, but from a sense of the duty they owe to others—not because they are proud of authority, but because they love mercy. (XIX, 14)

But the families which do not live by faith seek their peace in the earthly advantages of this life; while the families which live by faith look for those eternal blessings which are promised, and use as pilgrims such advantages of time and of earth as do not fascinate and divert them from God, but rather aid them to endure with greater ease, and to keep down the number of those burdens of the corruptible body which weigh upon the soul. Thus the things necessary for this mortal life are used by both kinds of men and families alike, but each has its own peculiar and widely different aim in using them. The earthly city, which does not live by faith, seeks an earthly peace, and the end it proposes, in the well-ordered concord of civic obedience and rule, is the combination of men's wills to attain the things which are helpful to this life. The heavenly city, or rather the part of it which sojourns on earth and lives by faith, makes use of this peace only because it must, until this mortal condition which necessitates it shall pass away. Consequently, so long as it lives like a captive and a stranger in the earthly city, though it has already received the promise of redemption, and the gift of the Spirit as the earnest of it, it makes no scruple to obey the laws of the earthly city, whereby the things necessary for the maintenance of this mortal life are administered: and thus, as this life is common to both cities, so there is harmony between them in regard to what belongs to it. But, as the earthly city has had some philosophers whose doctrine is condemned by the divine teaching, and who, being deceived either by their own conjectures or by demons, supposed that many gods must be invited to take an interest in human affairs, and assigned to each a separate function and a separate department—to one the body, to another the soul; and in the body itself, to one the head, to another the neck, and each of the other members to one of the gods; and in like manner, in the soul, to one god the natural capacity was assigned, to another education, to another anger, to another lust; and so the various affairs of life were assigned—cattle to one, corn to another, wine to another, oil to another, the woods to another, money to another, navigation to another, wars and victories to another, marriages to another, births and fecundity to another, and other things to other gods; and as the celestial city, on the other hand, knew that one God only was to be worshiped, and that to Him alone was due that service which the Greeks call *latreia* [worship] and which can be given only to a god, it has come to pass that the two cities could not have common laws of religion and that the heavenly city has been compelled in this matter to dissent, and to become obnoxious to those who think differently, and to stand the brunt of their anger and hatred and persecutions, except in so far as the minds of their enemies have been alarmed by the multitude of the Christians and quelled by the manifest protection of God accorded to them. This heavenly city, then, while it sojourns on earth, calls citizens out of all nations, and gathers together a society of pilgrims of all languages, not scrupling about diversities in the manners, laws, and institutions whereby earthly peace is secured and maintained, but recognizing that, however various these are, they all tend to one and the same end of earthly peace. It therefore is so far from rescinding and abolishing these diversities, that it even preserves and adopts them, so long as no hindrance to the worship of the one supreme and true God is thus introduced. Even the heavenly city, therefore, while in its state of pilgrimage, avails itself of the peace of earth, and, as far as it can without injuring faith and godliness, desires and maintains a common agreement among men regarding the acquisition of the necessaries of life, and makes this earthly peace bear upon the peace of heaven; for this alone can be truly called and esteemed the peace of the reasonable creatures, consisting as it does in the perfectly ordered and harmonious enjoyment of God and of one another in God. When we shall have reached that peace, this mortal life shall give place to one that is eternal, and our body shall be no more this animal body which by its corruption weighs down the soul, but a sp. :-

ual body feeling no want, and in all its members subjected to the will. In its pilgrim state the heavenly city possesses this peace by faith; and by this faith it lives righteously when it refers to the attainment of that peace every good action toward God and man; for the life of the city is a social life. (XIX, 17)

On social and political justice in the city of man. Justice being taken away, then, what are kingdoms but great robberies? For what are robberies themselves, but little kingdoms? The band itself is made up of men; it is ruled by the authority of a prince, it is knit together by the pact of the confederacy; the booty is divided by the law agreed on. If, by the admittance of abandoned men, this evil increases to such a degree that it holds places, fixes abodes, takes possession of cities, and subdues peoples, it assumes the more plainly the name of a kingdom, because the reality is now manifestly conferred on it, not by the removal of covetousness, but by the addition of impunity. Indeed, that was an apt and true reply which was given to Alexander the Great by a pirate who had been seized. For when that king had asked the man what he meant by keeping hostile possession of the sea, he answered with bold pride, "What thou meanest by seizing the whole earth; but because I do it with a petty ship, I am called a robber, whilst thou who dost it with a great fleet are styled emperor." [17] (IV, 4)

This, then, is the place where I should fulfill the promise I gave in the second book of this work, and explain, as briefly and clearly as possible, that if we are to accept the definitions laid down by Scipio in Cicero's *De Republica,* there never was a Roman republic; for he briefly defines a republic as the weal of the people. And if this definition be true, there never was a Roman republic, for the people's weal was never attained among the Romans. For the people, according to his definition, is an assemblage associated by a common acknowledgment of right and by a community of interests. And what he means by a common acknowledgment of right he explains at large, showing that a republic cannot be administered without justice. Where, therefore, there is no true justice there can be no right. For that which is done by right is justly done, and what is unjustly done cannot be

[17] Cicero, *De Republica,* III.

done by right. For the unjust inventions of men are neither to be considered nor spoken of as rights; for even they themselves say that right is that which flows from the fountain of justice, and deny the definition which is commonly given by those who misconceive the matter, that right is that which is useful to the stronger party. Thus, where there is not true justice there can be no assemblage of men associated by a common acknowledgment of right, and therefore there can be no people, as defined by Scipio or Cicero; and if no people, then no weal of the people, but only of some promiscuous multitude unworthy of the name of the people. Consequently, if the republic is the weal of the people, and there is no people if it be not associated by a common acknowledgment of right, and if there is no right where there is no justice, then most certainly it follows that there is no republic where there is no justice. Further, justice is that virtue which gives every one his due. Where, then, is the justice of man, when he deserts the true God and yields himself to impure demons? Is this to give every one his due? Or is he who keeps back a piece of ground from the purchaser, and gives it to a man who has no right to it, unjust, while he who keeps back himself from the God who made him, and serves wicked spirits, is just? (XIX, 21)

But if we discard this definition of a people, and, assuming another, say that a people is an assemblage of reasonable beings bound together by a common agreement as to the objects of their love, then, in order to discover the character of any people, we have only to observe what it loves. Yet whatever it loves, if only it is an assemblage of reasonable beings and not of beasts, and is bound together by an agreement as to the objects of love, it is reasonably called a people; and it will be a superior people in proportion as it is bound together by higher interests, inferior in proportion as it is bound together by lower. According to this definition of ours, the Roman people is a people, and its weal is without doubt a commonwealth or republic. But what its tastes were in its early and subsequent days, and how it declined into sanguinary seditions and then to social and civil wars, and so burst asunder or rotted off the bond of concord in which the health of a people consists, history shows, and in the preceding books I have related at large. And yet I would not on this account say either that it was not a people, or that its administration was not a republic, so long as there remains an assemblage of reasonable beings bound together by a common agreement as to the objects of love. But what I say of this people and of this republic I must be understood to think and say of the Athenians or any Greek state, of the Egyptians, of the early Assyrian Babylon, and of every other nation, great or small, which had a public government. For, in general, the city of the ungodly, which did not obey the command of God that it should offer no sacrifice save to Him alone, and which, therefore, could not give to the soul its proper command over the body, nor to the reason its just authority over the vices, is void of true justice. (XIX, 24)

The ultimate destinies of the two cities. But, on the other hand, they who do not belong to this city of God shall inherit eternal misery, which is also called the second death, because the soul shall then be separated from God its life, and therefore cannot be said to live, and the body shall be subjected to eternal pains. And consequently this second death shall be the more severe, because no death shall terminate it. But war being contrary to peace, as misery to happiness, and life to death, it is not without reason asked what kind of war can be found in the end of the wicked answering to the peace which is declared to be the end of the righteous? The person who puts this question has only to observe what it is in war that is hurtful and destructive, and he shall see that it is nothing else than the mutual opposition and conflict of things. And can he conceive a more grievous and bitter war than that in which the will is so opposed to passion, and passion to the will, that their hostility can never be terminated by the victory of either, and in which the violence of pain so conflicts with the nature of the body, that neither yields to the other? For in this life, when this conflict has arisen, either pain conquers and death expels the feeling of it, or nature conquers and health expels the pain. But in the world to come the pain continues that it may torment, and the nature endures that it may be sensible of it; and neither ceases to exist, lest punishment also should cease. Now, it is through the last judgment that men pass to these ends, the good to the supreme good, the evil to the supreme evil. . . . (XIX, 28)

In this, then, consists the righteousness of a man, that he submit himself to God, his body to his soul, and his vices, even when they rebel, to his reason, which either defeats or at least resists them; and also that he beg from God grace to do his duty, and the pardon of his sins, and that he render to God thanks for all the blessings he receives. But, in that final peace to which all our righteousness has reference, and for the sake of which it is maintained, as our nature shall enjoy a sound immortality and incorruption, and shall have no more vices, and as we shall experience no resistance either from ourselves or from others, it will not be necessary that reason should rule vices which no longer exist, but God shall rule the man, and the soul shall rule the body, with a sweetness and facility suitable to the felicity of a life which is done with bondage. And this condition shall there be eternal, and we shall be assured of its eternity; and thus the peace of this blessedness and the blessedness of this peace shall be the supreme good. (XIX, 27)

I think I have now, by God's help, discharged my obligation in writing this large work. Let those who think I have said too little, or those who think I have said too much, forgive me; and let those who think I have said just enough give thanks, not to me, but rather join me in giving thanks to God. Amen. (XXII, 30)

BIBLIOGRAPHY

St. Augustine's *City of God* can be found in several translations. Inexpensive editions are published by Dutton (Everyman's Library), Hafner (Hafner Library of Classics), and Random House (Modern Library).

BARROW, R. H. *Introduction to St. Augustine. The City of God.* London, n.d.

BATTENHOUSE, ROY, (ed.). *A Companion to the Study of St. Augustine.* New York: 1955.

BURLEIGH, J. *The City of God: A Study of St. Augustine's Philosophy.* London: 1949.

CLARK, GORDON H. "Augustine of Hippo," *The Encyclopedia of Christianity,* Vol. I. Wilmington, Delaware: 1964.

COCHRANE, C. N. *Christianity and Classical Culture: A Study of*

Thought and Action from Augustus to Augustine. London: 1944.

DAWSON, CHRISTOPHER. *The Dynamics of World History.* New York: 1956.

DEANE, H. A. *The Political and Social Ideas of St. Augustine.* New York: 1963.

FIGGIS, J. N. *The Political Aspects of St. Augustine's City of God.* Gloucester, Mass.: 1921.

GILSON, E. *The Christian Philosophy of Saint Augustine.* New York: 1960.

KEYES, G. L. *Christian Faith and the Interpretation of History.* Lincoln, Nebraska: 1966.

LOETSCHER, F. W. "Augustine's City of God," *Theology Today,* 1944.

LÖWITH, KARL. *Meaning in History.* Chicago: 1949.

MARROU, H. *St. Augustine and His Influence Through the Ages.* New York: 1957.

MOMMSEN, T. E. "St Augustine and the Christian Idea of Progress: The Background of the City of God," *Journal of the History of Ideas,* 1951.

MOURANT, J. A. *Introduction to the Philosophy of St. Augustine.* University Park, Pa.: 1964.

NASH, RONALD H. *St. Augustine's Theory of Knowledge.* Lexington, Ky.: 1969.

OSMUN, G. W. *Augustine: The Thinker.* New York: 1906.

PEGIS, A. C. "The Mind of St. Augustine," *Medieval Studies,* 1944.

PORTALIE, E. A. *A Guide to the Thought of Saint Augustine.* Chicago: 1960.

VERSFIELD, M. *A Guide to the City of God.* New York: 1958.

2 Giambattista Vico (1668–1744)

During the thirteen hundred years between St. Augustine and Giambattista Vico, there were several attempts to construct theories of history. Most of these (at least those systems formulated by Christians) were modeled after the work of Augustine and need not be noticed here. With Giambattista Vico, a man who has been called Italy's greatest philosopher, the modern philosophy of history begins. If one forgets that Vico antedated Herder, Kant, and Hegel, it is easy to overlook his contributions to the philosophy of history. When these thinkers are studied in chronological sequence, however, one begins to appreciate the momentous influence Vico's views had on later philosophers. In

25

fact, Vico's influence was reserved almost exclusively for such later thinkers; his contemporaries were unable to appreciate the genius and originality of his work.

Vico was the first to attempt a construction of universal history on empirical grounds. He thought he had discovered within history an eternal law of development. His pattern was neither cyclical like that of the Greeks nor strictly linear like Augustine's. It was more of a spiral pattern that combined the recurrence of the cyclical view and the progress of the linear.

Vico also made the first attempt to justify history as an autonomous body of knowledge separate from science. In his emphasis upon the importance of the inner life of man for history, he anticipated such twentieth-century idealists as Croce and Collingwood. In addition, Vico made several contributions to the critical philosophy of history. He warned historians about a number of prejudices that could detract from the quality of their work: [1] (1) the error of exaggerating the wealth, power and grandeur of the period of history being studied; (2) the conceit that many historians have for the past of their own nation as seen, for example, in the practice of many historians of describing the history of their own nation as favorably as possible; (3) the prejudice of thinking that the people the historian is studying were as learned and cultured as he himself is; (4) the fallacy of thinking that simply because two nations share a similar idea or institution, one must have borrowed it from the other; (5) the error of thinking that people in the past knew more about their own times than we can know today.

In addition to these warnings, Vico also made some positive contributions to historiography. He pointed out the value of linguistics, mythology, and tradition for a reconstruction of the past. While mythology, for example, should not be taken literally, it can be a valuable supplement to our other sources about the life, beliefs, and practices of an ancient people.

René Descartes (1596–1650) set the stage for Vico's great contribution to the philosophy of history. Descartes had observed that too much time spent in studying history usurps time that might otherwise be spent on the present. He objected to the

---

[1] See sections 119–146 of Vico's *New Science* which follow.

THE NEW SCIENCE

general unreliability of historical accounts of the past and to the relative uselessness of history for present-day living. In Descartes' words,

> The overcurious in the customs of the past are generally ignorant of those of the present. Besides, fictitious narratives lead us to imagine the possibility of many events that are impossible; and even the most faithful histories, if they do not wholly misrepresent matters, or exaggerate their importance to render the account of them more worthy of perusal, omit, at least, almost always the meanest and least striking of the attendant circumstances; hence it happens that the remainder does not represent the truth, and that such as regulate their conduct by examples drawn from this source, are apt to fall into the extravagances of the knights-errant of romance, and to entertain projects that exceed their powers.[2]

While Descartes and his followers glorified the mathematical and physical sciences at the expense of history, Vico countered that history was eminently capable of being understood by man. Vico based his claim upon his principle of *verum factum:* the true and the created are identical.[3] One can know something with certitude only when he has made it.

> Truth and knowledge are for Vico coextensive and convertible terms. What is true to us is all that we know. What we know is all that is true to us. There is no human truth outside of human knowledge, just as there is no divine truth outside of divine knowledge. There is no unknown truth. If there were, there would be unmade or ungenerated truth, and the criterion would not apply. The truth is what is known; to be known it must be made; the knowing and the making of truth are inseparable.[4]

Vico relates his principle of *verum factum* to the case of God's omniscience. Because God has made all things, He knows all things. Vico's application of this principle to history should be clear by now. The Cartesians had exhausted their efforts in trying to know the world which they had not made; at the same

---

[2] René Descartes, *A Discourse on Method,* Part One, trans. John Veitch.
[3] See sections 331 and 332 which follow.
[4] Robert Flint, *Vico* (Edinburgh: William Blackwood, 1884), p. 94.

time, they ignored history which man has authored. Since God is the creator of the world, only He can know it with certainty; but since man is the author of history, it follows that history is one thing that man *can* know. Alan Donagan writes,

> Vico's principle that what men have made, men can hope to know, is the foundation of modern scientific historiography. First, it defines what historians study: namely, whatever survives from past human actions. Secondly, it implicitly specifies their aim: to recover the human thinking, however different from our own it may have been, by which what survives from the past was made.[5]

One of the more important ways in which man comes to know the past is through a study of that which man has created, for example, his language, history, law, religion, and mythology. On this point, Vico clearly anticipates Wilhelm Dilthey's "objective mind" and R. G. Collingwood's view that the historian must try to grasp the thinking of man in the past.

The major source for Vico's philosophy of history is his *Scienza Nuova* (*The New Science*), a work that went through three editions.[6] Vico's views were generations ahead of his time. In fact, his book was not even translated into English until 1948. *The New Science* has two major aims: (1) Vico wishes to discover if there is a universal law of history that governs the past; is there, in other words, a pattern to history? (2) He desires to see how this law is reflected in the history of particular peoples.

Vico uses two methods to accomplish his aims—philosophy and philology. The meaning of these terms is never spelled out but a careful consideration of his use of the terms suggests that philosophy is *reasoning* from axioms, definitions, and postulates while philology is an *empirical* study of the languages, history, and literature of people.[7]

The pattern Vico found in history was a spiral-like movement; there is both repetition and progress in history. There are periods in history that seem to go through a similar development.

---

[5] Alan Donagan, *Philosophy of History* (New York: Macmillan, 1965), p. 7.

[6] 1725, 1730, and 1744. The selections in this volume are taken from the 1744 edition.

[7] See selections 129–140 and 351–360 which follow.

This course of development (*corso*) is then repeated (*ricorso*) in other periods, not in the same events, to be sure, but in the general framework. The general pattern is the same but the particular events will differ. Vico distinguished three stages in the development of any period of history — the age of gods, the age of heroes, and the age of men. The following schema indicates some of the characteristics of these ages.

AGE OF GODS	AGE OF HEROES	AGE OF MEN
An age of sensation	An age of imagination	An age of reason
Man's nature: fierce and cruel	Man's nature: noble and proud	Man's nature: benign and reasonable
Government: Theocratic (Man subordinate to deity)	Government: Warrior Aristocracy (Some men subordinate to others)	Government: Democracy (All men equal)

Corresponding to these three ages, there were three types of human nature (barbarous, proud, and reasonable), three kinds of custom, three kinds of law, religion, etc.

Vico believed he had discovered the movement from an age of gods, to an age of heroes, to an age of men in several periods of history. The history of Greece provides one example of this development. Greece before the times of Homer illustrates the age of the gods. Men were fierce and barbarous and yet the customs of the age were tinged with religion; everything, they believed, was determined by the gods. Moving from the times described by Homer to the period of Homer itself, one finds a marked shift from sensationism to imagination; one can find the beginnings of peculiarly mythical or poetic modes of consciousness; one finds the development of language, law, and culture. During this middle period, agriculture is the basis for economy and a kind of aristocracy arises in which some men assume the role of rulers or leaders. The poetic mode of consciousness during this age of heroes is seen in the myths of Homer; Sparta illustrates the importance of an agricultural economy and a warrior aristocracy. Finally, with the ascendancy of Athens, we come to an age of reason in the history of Greece. Now we find a democratic form of government in which all free citizens are regarded as equal and with this comes a more settled state of affairs. The culture of the times is ruled by the ideal of pure rationality. Man loses some of his barbarity and becomes more benign.

Thus the course of man, Vico maintains, is a movement from a primitive mentality to a religious way of life, and ultimately to an age of reflective rationality. However, each period of human history eventually dissolves into a time of decline, decadence, and barbarism which makes the beginning of a new cycle possible.

That which makes history move, Vico tells us, is the providence of God. To be sure, it is often quite difficult to detect God's providence at work in history. Man is selfish and history records only too clearly the results of man's self-seeking. However, if man were left on his own, he would eventually destroy all of his kind. Divine providence works immanently within history to keep man in check within the orders of the family, the society, and the state. Vico's view of providence bears a number of interesting similarities to Hegel's notion of "the cunning of reason." According to Hegel, God uses the selfish desires of men to work out his own purposes in history. Vico, like Hegel, insists that divine providence always operates indirectly, by secondary means. Providence always realizes its purposes in a natural way. Vico's lack of emphasis on the transcendence of God has led several critics to point out that his position may be unable to avoid a pantheism which he certainly did not intend to espouse.

GIAMBATTISTA VICO
THE NEW SCIENCE [*]

Some principles of historical criticism. 119. . . . We now propose the following axioms, both philosophical and philological, including a few reasonable and proper postulates and clarified definitions. And just as the blood does in animate bodies, so

[*] Reprinted from *The New Science of Giambattista Vico,* trans. Thomas Goddard Bergin and Max Harold Fisch by permission of Cornell University Press. Copyright 1948 by Cornell University; revised edition, ©1968 by Cornell University.

will these elements course through our Science and animate it in all its reasonings about the common nature of nations.

I. 120. Because of the indefinite nature of the human mind, wherever it is lost in ignorance, man makes himself the measure of all things.

121. This axiom explains those two common human traits, on the one hand that rumor grows in its course, on the other that rumor is deflated by the presence [of the thing itself]. In the long course that rumor has run from the beginning of the world it has been the perennial source of all the exaggerated opinions which have hitherto been held concerning remote antiquities unknown to us, by virtue of that property of the human mind noted by Tacitus in his *Life of Agricola,* where he says that everything unknown is taken for something great.

II. 122. It is another property of the human mind that whenever men can form no idea of distant and unknown things, they judge them by what is familiar and at hand.

123. This axiom points to the inexhaustible source of all the errors about the beginnings of humanity that have been adopted by entire nations and by all the scholars. For when the former began to take notice of them and the latter to investigate them, it was on the basis of their own enlightened, cultivated, and magnificent times that they judged the origins of humanity, which must nevertheless by the nature of things have been small, crude, and quite obscure.

124. Under this head are to be recalled two types of conceit we have mentioned above, one of the nations and the other of the scholars.

III. 125. As for the conceit of the nations, we have heard that golden saying of Diodorus Siculus. Every nation, according to him, whether Greek or barbarian, has had the same conceit that it before all other nations invented the comforts of human life and that its remembered history goes back to the very beginning of the world.

IV. 127. To this conceit of the nations there may be added that of the scholars, who will have it that whatever they know is as old as the world.

128. This axiom disposes of all the opinions of the scholars concerning the matchless wisdom of the ancients. It convicts of

fraud the oracles of Zoroaster, the verses of Orpheus, and the golden verses of Pythagoras . . .

V. 144. Uniform ideas originating among entire peoples unknown to each other must have a common ground of truth.

145. This axiom is a great principle which establishes the common sense of the human race as the criterion taught to the nations by Divine Providence to define what is certain in the natural law of nations. And the nations reach this certainty by recognizing the underlying agreements which, despite variations of detail, obtain among them all in respect of this law. Thence issues the mental dictionary for assigning origins to all the diverse articulated languages. By means of this dictionary is conceived the ideal eternal history which determines the histories in time of all the nations . . .

146. This same axiom does away with all the ideas hitherto held concerning the natural law of nations, which has been thought to have originated in one nation and been passed on to others. This error was encouraged by the bad example of the Egyptians and Greeks in vainly boasting that they had spread civilization throughout the world. It was this error that gave rise to the fiction that the Law of the Twelve Tables came to Rome from Greece. If that had been the case, it would have been a civil law communicated to other peoples by human provision and not a law which Divine Providence ordained naturally in all nations along with human customs themselves. Indeed it will be one of our constant labors throughout this book to demonstrate that the natural law of nations originated separately among the various peoples, each in ignorance of the others, and that subsequently, as a result of wars, embassies, alliances, and commerce, it came to be recognized as common to the entire human race.

The philosophical method. 129. To be useful to the human race, philosophy must raise and direct weak and fallen man, not rend his nature or abandon him in his corruption.

130. This axiom dismisses from the school of our Science the Stoics who seek to mortify the senses and the Epicureans who make them the criterion. For both deny Providence, the former chaining themselves to fate, the latter abandoning themselves to chance. The latter moreover affirm that the human soul dies with the body. Both should be called monastic or solitary philoso-

phers. On the other hand [this axiom] admits to our school the political philosophers, and first of all the Platonists, who agree with all the lawgivers on these three main points: that there is Divine Providence, that human passions should be moderated and made into human virtues, and that the human soul is immortal. Thus from this axiom are derived the three principles of this Science.

131. Philosophy considers man as he should be and so can be of service to but very few, who wish to live in the Republic of Plato, not to fall back into the dregs of Romulus.

132. Legislation considers man as he is in order to turn him to good uses in human society. Out of ferocity, avarice, and ambition, the three vices which run throughout the human race, it creates the military, merchant, and governing classes and thus the strength, riches, and wisdom of commonwealths. Out of these three great vices, which could certainly destroy all mankind on the face of the earth, it makes civil happiness.

133. This axiom proves that there is Divine Providence and further that it is divine legislative mind. For out of the passions of men, each bent on his private advantage, for the sake of which they would live like wild beasts in the wilderness, it has made the civil orders by which they may live in human society.

137. Men who do not know the truth of things try to reach certainty about them, so that, if they cannot satisfy their intellects by science, their wills at least may rest on conscience.

138. Philosophy contemplates reason, whence comes knowledge of the true; philology observes the authority of human choice, whence comes consciousness of the certain.

139. This axiom by its second part defines as philologians all the grammarians, historians, critics, who have occupied themselves with the study of the languages and deeds of peoples; both their domestic affairs, such as customs and laws, and their external affairs, such as wars, peaces, alliances, travels, and commerce.

140. This same axiom shows how the philosophers failed by half in not giving certainty to their reasonings by appeal to the authority of the philologians, and likewise how the latter failed by half in not taking care to give their authority the sanction of truth by appeal to the reasoning of the philosophers. If they had both done this, they would have been more useful to their com-

monwealths and they would have anticipated us in conceiving this Science. . . .

The philological method. 351. These are the philosophic proofs our Science will use, and consequently those which are absolutely necessary for pursuing it. The philological proofs must come last. They all reduce to the following kinds:

352. First, that our mythologies agree with the results of our meditations, not by force and distortion, but directly, easily, and naturally; that they will be seen to be civil histories of the first peoples, who are everywhere found to have been naturally poets.

353. Second, that the heroic phrases, as here explained in the full truth of the sentiments and the full propriety of the expressions, also agree.

354. Third, that the etymologies of the native languages also agree, which tell us the histories of the things signified by the words, beginning with their original and proper meanings and pursuing the natural progress of their metaphors according to the order of the ideas, on which the history of languages must proceed. . . .

355. Fourth, the mental vocabulary of human social things, which are the same in substance as felt by all nations but diversely expressed in language according to their diverse manifestations, is exhibited to be such as we conceived it in the axioms.

356. Fifth, truth is sifted from falsehood in everything that has been preserved for us through long centuries by those vulgar traditions which, since they have been preserved for so long a time and by entire peoples, must . . . have had a public ground of truth.

357. Sixth, the great fragments of antiquity, hitherto useless to science because they lay neglected, broken, and scattered, shed great light when cleaned, pieced together, and set in place.

358. Seventh and last, to all these things, as to their necessary causes, are assigned all the effects narrated by certain history.

359. These philological proofs enable us to see in fact the things we have meditated in idea concerning the world of nations, in accordance with Bacon's method of philosophizing, which is "think [and] see" (*cogitare videre*). Thus it is that with the help of the preceding philosophical proofs, the philological

proofs which follow both confirm their own authority by reason and at the same time confirm reason by their authority.

360. From all that has been set forth in general concerning the establishment of the principles of this Science, we conclude that, since its principles are Divine Providence, moderation of the passions by marriage, and immortality of human souls [witnessed] by burial, and since the criterion it uses is that what is felt to be just by all men or by the majority must be the rule of social life (and on these principles and this criterion there is agreement between the vulgar wisdom of all lawgivers and the esoteric wisdom of the philosophers of greatest repute), these must be the bounds of human reason. And let him who would transgress them beware lest he transgress all humanity.

The principle verum factum. 331. But in the night of thick darkness enveloping the earliest antiquity, so remote from ourselves, there shines the eternal and never-failing light of a truth beyond all question: that the world of civil society has certainly been made by men, and that its principles are therefore to be found within the modifications of our own human mind. Whoever reflects on this cannot but marvel that the philosophers should have bent all their energies to the study of the world of nature, which, since God made it, He alone knows; and that they should have neglected the study of the world of nations or civil world, which, since men had made it, men could hope to know. . . .

332. Now since this world of nations has been made by men, let us see in what things all men agree and always have agreed. For these things will be able to give us the universal and eternal principles (such as every science must have) on which all nations were founded and still preserve themselves.

The three customs of all nations. 333. We observe that all nations, barbarous as well as civilized, though separately founded because remote from each other in time and space, keep these three human customs: all have some religion, all contract solemn marriages, all bury their dead. And in no nation, however savage and crude, are any human activities celebrated with more elaborate ceremonies and more sacred solemnity than religion, marriage, and burial. For by the axiom that "uniform ideas, born among peoples unknown to each other, must have a common ground of truth," [144] it must have been dictated to all nations that from these three institutions humanity began among them all, and therefore they must be most devoutly observed by them all, so that the world should not again become a bestial wilderness. For this reason we have taken these three eternal and universal customs as three first principles of this Science.

334. Let not our first principle be accused of falsehood by the modern travelers who narrate that peoples of Brazil, South Africa, and other nations of the new world live in society without any knowledge of God, as Antoine Arnauld believes to be the case also of the inhabitants of the islands called Antilles. Persuaded perhaps by them, Bayle affirms in his treatise on comets that peoples can live in justice without the light of God. This is a bolder statement than Polybius ventured in the dictum for which he has been acclaimed, that if the world had philosophers, living in justice by reason and not by laws, it would have no need of religions. These are travelers' tales, to promote the sale of their books by the narration of portents. . . . For all nations believe in a provident divinity, yet through all the length of years and all the breadth of this civil world it has been possible to find only four primary religions. The first is that of the Hebrews, whence came that of the Christians, both believing in the divinity of an infinite free mind. The third is that of the gentiles, who believe in the divinity of a plurality of gods, each imagined as composed of body and of free mind. Hence, when they wish to signify the divinity that rules and preserves the world, they speak of *deos immortales*. The fourth and last is that of the Mohammedans, who believe in the divinity of one god, an infinite free mind in an infinite body, for they look forward to pleasures of the senses as rewards in the other life. . . .

336. In the second place, the opinion that the sexual unions which certainly take place between free men and free women without solemn matrimony are free of natural wickedness [i.e., do not offend the law of nature], all the nations of the world have branded as false by the human customs with which they all religiously celebrate marriages, thereby determining that this sin is bestial, though in venial degree. And for this reason: such parents, since they are held together by no necessary bond of law,

are bound to abandon their natural children. Since their parents may separate at any time, if they are abandoned by both, the children must lie exposed to be devoured by dogs. If humanity, public or private, does not bring them up, they will have to grow up with no one to teach them religion, language, or any other human custom. . . .

337. Finally, [to realize] what a great principle of humanity burial is, imagine a feral state in which human bodies remain unburied on the surface of the earth as food for crows and dogs. Certainly this bestial custom will be accompanied by uncultivated fields and uninhabited cities. Men will go about like swine eating the acorns found amidst the putrefaction of their dead. And so with good reason burials were characterized by the sublime phrase "compacts of the human race" . . . and with less grandeur were described by Tacitus as "fellowships of humanity." . . .

338. To complete the establishment of the principles which have been adopted for this Science, it remains . . . to discuss the method which it should follow. It must begin where its subject matter began . . . Our treatment of it must take its start from the time these creatures began to think humanly. In their monstrous savagery and unbridled bestial freedom there was no means to tame the former or bridle the latter but the frightful thought of some divinity, the fear of whom . . . is the only powerful means of reducing to duty a liberty gone wild. To discover the way in which this first human thinking arose in the gentile world, we encountered exasperating difficulties which have cost us the research of a good twenty years. [We had] to descend from these human and refined natures of ours to those quite wild and savage natures, which we cannot at all imagine and can apprehend only with great effort.

339. By reason of all this, we must start from some notion of God such as even the most savage, wild, and monstrous men do not lack. That notion we show to be this: that man, fallen into despair of all the succors of nature, desires something superior to save him. But something superior to nature is God, and this is the light that God has shed on all men. Confirmation may be found in a common human custom, that libertines grown old, feeling their natural forces fail, turn naturally to religion. . . .

341. But men because of their corrupted nature are under the tyranny of self-love, which compels them to make private utility their chief guide. Seeking everything useful for themselves and nothing for their companions, they cannot bring their passions under control to direct them toward justice. We thereby establish the fact that man in the bestial state desires only his own welfare; having taken wife and begotten children, he desires his own welfare along with that of his family; having entered upon civil life, he desires his own welfare along with that of his city; when its rule is extended over several peoples, he desires his own welfare along with that of the nation; when the nations are united by wars, treaties of peace, alliances, and commerce, he desires his own welfare along with that of the entire human race. In all these conditions man desires principally his own utility. Therefore it is only by Divine Providence that he can be held within these orders to practice justice as a member of the society of the family, the state, and finally of mankind. Unable to attain all the utilities he wishes, he is constrained by these orders to seek those which are his due; and this is called just. That which regulates all human justice is therefore divine justice, which is administered by Divine Providence to preserve human society.

342. . . . Our new Science must therefore be a demonstration, so to speak, of the historical fact of Providence, for it must be a history of the forms of order which, without human discernment or intent, and often against the designs of men, Providence has given to this great city of the human race. For though this world has been created in time and particular, the orders established therein by Providence are universal and eternal.

The three ages. 173. Two great remnants of Egyptian antiquity have come down to us. . . . One of them is the fact that the Egyptians reduced all preceding world time to three ages, namely, the age of the gods, the age of the heroes, and the age of men. The other is that during these three ages three languages had been spoken, corresponding in order to the three ages: namely, the hieroglyphic or sacred language, the symbolic or figurative (heroic) language, and the epistolary or vulgar language of men employing conventional signs for communicating the common needs of their life. . . .

176. These three axioms established the fact that the world of

THE NEW SCIENCE

peoples began everywhere with religion. This will be the first of the three principles of this Science.

177. Wherever a people has grown savage in arms so that human laws have no longer any place among it, the only powerful means of reducing it is religion.

178. This axiom establishes the fact that Divine Providence initiated the process by which the fierce and violent were brought from their outlaw state to humanity and entered upon national life. It did so by awakening in them a confused idea of divinity, which they in their ignorance attributed to that to which it did not belong. Thus through the terror of this imagined divinity, they began to put themselves in some order. . . .

196. Every gentile nation had its Hercules, who was the son of Jove; and Varro, the most learned of antiquarians, numbered as many as forty of them.

197. This axiom marks the beginning of heroism among the first peoples, which was born of the false opinion that the heroes were of divine origin. . . .

The course of nations. 238. The order of ideas must follow the order of things.

239. This was the order of human things: first the forests, after that the huts, thence the villages, next the cities, and finally the academies. . . .

241. Men first feel necessity, then look for utility, next attend to comfort, still later amuse themselves with pleasure, thence grow dissolute in luxury, and finally go mad and waste their substance.

242. The nature of peoples is first crude, then severe, then benign, then delicate, finally dissolute.

243. In the human race first appear the huge and grotesque, like the cyclopes; then the proud and magnanimous, like Achilles; then the valorous and just, like Aristides and Scipio Africanus; nearer to us, imposing figures with great semblances of virtue accompanied by great vices, who among the vulgar win a name for true glory, like Alexander and Caesar; still later, the melancholy and reflective, like Tiberius; finally the dissolute and shameless madmen, like Caligula, Nero, and Domitian.

244. This axiom shows that the first sort were necessary in order to make one man obey another in the family-state and pre-

pare him to be law-abiding in the city-state that was to come; the second sort, who naturally did not yield to their peers, were necessary to establish the aristocratic commonwealths on the basis of the families; the third sort to open the way for popular liberty; the fourth to bring in the monarchies; the fifth to establish them; the sixth to overthrow them.

245. This with the preceding axioms gives a part of the principles of the ideal eternal history traversed in time by every nation in its rise, development, maturity, decline, and fall. . . .

349. Our Science therefore comes to describe at the same time an ideal eternal history traversed in time by the history of every nation in its rise, progress, maturity, decline, and fall. Indeed we go so far as to assert that whoever meditates this Science tells himself this ideal eternal history only so far as he makes it by that proof "it had, has, and will have to be." For the first indubitable principle above posited is that this world of nations has certainly been made by men, and its guise must therefore be found within the modifications of our own human mind. And history cannot be more certain than when he who creates the things also describes them. Thus our Science proceeds exactly as does geometry, which while it constructs out of its elements or contemplates the world of quantity, itself creates it; but with a reality greater in proportion to that of the orders having to do with human affairs, in which there are neither points, lines, surfaces, nor figures. And this very fact is an argument, O reader, that these proofs are of a kind divine, and should give thee a divine pleasure; since in God knowledge and creation are one and the same thing. . . .

629. We have seen that the generation of commonwealths began in the age of the gods, in which governments were theocratic, that is, divine. Later they developed into the first human, that is, the heroic, governments, here called human to distinguish them from the divine. Within these human governments . . . the age of gods continued to run its course, for that religious way of thinking must still have persisted by which whatever men themselves did was attributed to the agency of the gods. . . . Herein is Divine Providence to be supremely admired, for, when men's intentions were quite otherwise, it brought them in the first place to the fear of divinity (the cult of which is the first fundamental

basis of commonwealths). Their religion in turn led them to remain fixed on the first vacant lands which they occupied before all others. . . . Further, again by means of religion, Providence led them to unite with chosen women for constant and life-long companionship; hence the institution of matrimony, the recognized source of all authority. Later, with these women, they were found to have established the families, which are the seedplot of the commonwealths. And finally, with the opening of the asylums, they discovered that they had founded the clienteles. Thus the elements were prepared from which, with the first agrarian law, the cities were to be born, based upon the two communities of men that composed them, one of nobles to command, the other of plebeians to obey. . . .

915. In virtue of the principles of this Science established in the first book, and of the origins of all the divine and human things of the gentile world which we investigated and discovered in the second book, and the discovery in the third book that the poems of Homer are two great treasure stores of the natural law of the nations of Greece (just as we had already found the Law of the Twelve Tables to be a great monument of the natural law of the nations of Latium) we shall now, by the aid of philosophical and philological illumination, and relying on the axioms above stated concerning the ideal eternal history [241–245] in this fourth book, discuss the course the nations take, proceeding in all their various and diverse customs with constant uniformity upon the division of the three ages which the Egyptians said had elapsed before them in their world, namely, the successive ages of gods, heroes, and men. For the nations will be seen to develop in conformity with this division by a constant and uninterrupted order of causes and effects present in every nation, through three kinds of natures. From these natures arise three kinds of customs; and in virtue of these customs three kinds of natural laws of nations are observed; and in consequence of these laws three kinds of civil states or commonwealths are established. And in order that men, having reached the stage of human society, may on the one hand communicate to each other the aforesaid three most important matters [customs, laws, commonwealths], three kinds of languages and as many of characters are formed; and in order that they may on the other hand justify them, three kinds of

jurisprudence assisted by three kinds of authority and three kinds of reason in as many of judgments. The three kinds of jurisprudence prevail in three sects of times, which the nations profess in the course of their history. These groups of three special unities, with many others that derive from them and will also be enumerated in this book, all lead to one general unity. This is the unity of the religion of a provident divinity, which is the unity of the spirit informing and giving life to this world of nations . . .

[Vico continues by relating the three kinds of natures, natural law, governments, languages, and jurisprudence to the three ages —divine, heroic, and human.]

1004. All that we have had to say in this book is so much evidence to prove that in the course of the entire lifetime of nations they follow this order through these three kinds of commonwealths or civil states, and no more. They all have their roots in their first, which were the divine governments, and from this beginning all nations (by the axioms above posited [241–245] as principles of the ideal eternal history) must proceed through this sequence of human things; first becoming commonwealths of optimates, later free popular commonwealths, and finally monarchies. . . .

Vico's theory of recurrence (ricorso). 1046. In countless passages scattered throughout this work and dealing with countless subjects, we have observed the marvelous correspondence between the first and the returned barbarian times. From these passages we can easily understand the recurrence of human things in the resurgence of the nations. For greater confirmation, however, we wish in this last book to give a special place to this argument. Thus we shall bring more light to bear on the period of the second barbarism, which has remained more obscure than that of the first. . . . And we shall also show how the Best and Greatest God has made the counsels of His Providence, by which He has guided the human things of all nations, serve the ineffable decrees of His grace.

1047. When, working in superhuman ways, God had revealed and confirmed the truth of the Christian religion by opposing the virtue of the martyrs to the power of Rome, and the teaching of the Fathers, together with the miracles, to the empty wisdom of Greece, and when armed nations were about to arise on every hand destined to combat the true divinity of its Founder, He permitted a new order of humanity to emerge among the nations in order that [the true religion] might be firmly established according to the natural course of human affairs.

1048. Following this eternal counsel, He brought back the truly divine times, in which Catholic kings everywhere, in order to defend the Christian religion of which they are protectors, donned the dalmatics of deacons and consecrated their royal persons (whence they preserve the title Sacred Royal Majesty). They assumed ecclesiastical dignities, as Hugh Capet . . . took the title of Count and Abbot of Paris. . . .

1056. But the most striking recurrence of human things in this connection was the resumption in these divine times of the first asylums of the ancient world, within which, as we learned from Livy, all the first cities were founded. For everywhere violence, rapine, and murder were rampant, because of the extreme ferocity and savagery of these most barbarous centuries. Nor . . . was there any efficacious way of restraining men who had shaken off all human laws save by the divine laws dictated by religion. Naturally, therefore, men in fear of being oppressed or destroyed betook themselves to the bishops and abbots of those violent centuries, . . . and put themselves, their families, and their patrimonies under their protection, and were received by them. . . .

1057. These divine times were followed by certain heroic times, in consequence of the return of a certain distinction between almost opposite natures, the heroic and the human. . . .

1089. Today a complete humanity seems to be spread abroad through all nations, for a few great monarchs rule over this world of peoples. If there are still some barbarous peoples surviving, it is because their monarchies have persisted in the vulgar wisdom of imaginative and cruel religions, in some cases with the less balanced nature of their subject nations as an added factor.

1092. But in Europe, where the Christian religion is everywhere professed . . . there are great monarchies most humane in their customs. It is true that those situated in the cold north, although they are monarchic in constitution yet seem to be governed aristocratically; but if the natural course of civil things is not impeded in their case by extraordinary causes they will arrive at perfect monarchies. In this part of the world alone, because it cultivates the sciences, there are furthermore a great number of popular commonwealths, which are not found at all in the other three parts. Indeed, because of the recurrence of the same public utilities and necessities, there has been a revival of the form of the Aetolian and Achaean leagues. Just as the latter were conceived by the Greeks because of the necessity of protecting themselves against the overwhelming power of the Romans, so the Swiss cantons and the united provinces or states of Holland have organized a number of free popular cities into two aristocracies, in which they stand united in a perpetual league of peace and war. And the body of the German empire is a system of many free cities and sovereign princes. Its head is the emperor, and in matters concerning the states of the empire it is governed aristocratically.

1093. We must observe here that sovereign powers uniting in league, whether perpetual or temporary, come of themselves to form aristocratic states into which enter the anxious suspicions characteristic of aristocracies, as shown above. Hence, as this is the last form of civil states (for we cannot conceive in civil nature a state superior to such aristocracies), this same form must have been the first, which, as we have shown by so many proofs in this work, was that of the aristocracies of the fathers, sovereign family kings united in reigning orders in the first cities. For this is the nature of principles, that things begin and end in them.

1096. Now, in the light of the recurrence of human civil things to which we have given particular attention in this [fifth] book, let us reflect on the comparisons we have made throughout this work in a great many respects between the first and last times of the ancient and modern nations. There will then be fully unfolded, not the particular history in time of the laws and deeds of the Romans or the Greeks, but (in virtue of the substantial identity of meaning in the diversity of modes of expression) the ideal of the eternal laws in accordance with which the affairs of all nations proceed in their rise, progress, mature state, decline, and fall, and would do so even if (as is certainly not the case) there were infinite worlds being born from time to time throughout eternity. Hence we could not refrain from giving this work the invidious title of a New Science, for it was too much to defraud it unjustly of the rightful claim it had over an argument so universal as that concerning the common nature of nations, in virtue of that property which belongs to every science that is perfect in its idea . . .

Conclusion. 1108. It is true that men have themselves made this world of nations (and we took this as the first incontestable principle of our Science, since we despaired of finding it from the philosophers and philologists), but this world without doubt has issued from a mind often diverse, at times quite contrary, and always superior to the particular ends that men had proposed to themselves; which narrow ends, made means to serve wider ends, it has always employed to preserve the human race upon this earth. Men mean to gratify their bestial lust and abandon their offspring, and they inaugurate the chastity of marriage from which the families arise. The fathers mean to exercise without restraint their paternal power over their clients, and they subject them to the civil powers from which the cities arise. The reigning orders of nobles mean to abuse their lordly freedom over the plebeians, and they are obliged to submit to the laws which establish popular liberty. The free peoples mean to shake off the yoke of their laws, and they become subject to monarchs. The monarchs mean to strengthen their own positions by debasing their subjects with all the vices of dissoluteness, and they dispose them to endure slavery at the hands of stronger nations. The nations mean to dissolve themselves, and their remnants flee for safety to the wilderness, whence, like the phoenix, they rise again. That which did all this was mind, for men did it with intelligence; it was not fate, for they did it by choice; not chance, for the results of their always so acting are perpetually the same.

1109. Hence Epicurus, who believes in chance, is refuted by the facts, along with his followers Hobbes and Machiavelli; and so are Zeno and Spinoza, who believe in fate. The evidence is clearly in favor of the contrary position of the political philosophers, whose prince is the divine Plato, who affirms that Providence rules the affairs of men. It was therefore with good reason that Cicero refused to discuss laws with Atticus unless the latter would give up his Epicureanism and first concede that Providence governed human affairs. Pufendorf ignored it in his hypothesis, Selden assumed it, and Grotius excluded it; but the Roman jurisconsults established it as the first principle of the natural law of nations. For in this work it has been fully demonstrated that through Providence the first governments of the world had as their entire form religion, on which alone the state of the families was based; and passing thence to the heroic or aristocratic civil governments, religion must have been their principal firm basis. Advancing then to the popular governments, it was again religion that served the peoples as means for attaining them. And coming to rest at last in monarchic governments, this same religion must be the shield of princes. Hence, if religion is lost among the peoples, they have nothing left to enable them to live in society: no shield of defense, nor means of counsel, nor basis of support, nor even a form by which they may exist in the world at all.

1112. To sum up, from all that we have set forth in this work, it is to be finally concluded that this Science carries inseparably with it the study of piety, and that if one be not pious he cannot really be wise.

BIBLIOGRAPHY

Vico's *New Science,* Translated by T. G. Bergin and M. H. Fisch, was published by the Cornell University Press, Ithaca, New York in 1948. This edition is now out of print. However, a paperback edition of the work is published by Doubleday and Co. Another important source for Vico's views is *The Autobiography of Giambattista Vico,* translated by Bergin and Fisch, and published in 1944 by the Cornell University Press.

ADAMS, H. P. *The Life and Writings of Giambattista Vico.* London: 1935.
BARRY, T. *The Historical Theory of G. B. Vico.* Washington: 1949.
BERLIN, I. "The Philosophical Ideas of Giambattista Vico," *Art and Ideas in Eighteenth Century Italy,* Rome: 1960.
CAPONIGRI, A. R. *Time and Idea: The Theory of History in Giambattista Vico,* London: 1935.

BIBLIOGRAPHY

CHILD, A. "Vico in Translation," *Ethics,* 1950.
COPLESTON, F. C. *History of Philosophy,* Vol. VI. Westminster, Md.: 1960.
CROCE, B. *The Philosophy of Giambattista Vico.* New York: 1913.
D'ARCY, M. C. *The Meaning and Matter of History.* New York: 1961.
FLINT, R. *Vico.* London: 1884.
LIFSHITZ, M. "Giambattista Vico," *Philosophy and Phenomenological Review,* 1948.
LÖWITH, K. *Meaning in History.* Chicago: 1949.
GILSON, E. and LANGAN, T. *Modern Philosophy: Descartes to Kant.* New York: 1963.
MAZLISH, B. *The Riddle of History.* New York: 1966.

3 *Immanuel Kant* (1724–1804)

Immanuel Kant wrote several short essays on the philosophy of history.[1] They all represent an approach, typical of the Enlightenment, which regards history as the story of man's progressive development from barbarism and superstition to a life of reason.

As Kant writes in his most important essay on this subject, *Idea of a Universal History:* "The history of the human race, viewed as a whole, may be regarded as the realization of a hidden plan of nature to bring about a political constitution, internally,

[1] These essays along with an excellent introduction by the editor are published in *On History* by Immanuel Kant, ed. Lewis White Beck (New York: Bobbs-Merrill, 1963).

and, for this purpose, also externally perfect, as the only state in which all the capacities implanted by her in mankind can be fully developed." This proposition not only points to a rational constitutional state (actually, a league of nations) as the end of history, it shows that for Kant the real entity of history is not man as an individual but mankind. Nature does nothing in vain, Kant assures us. Therefore, no basic human desires (including the desire for rationality) will be ultimately frustrated. This means, for Kant at least, that the rational capacities of man will be realized.

However, history itself seems to teach, on the contrary, that these desires *are* frustrated. At first glance, history appears to be anything but meaningful. History affords us with a repugnant spectacle; all is chaos; all one can see are the results of man's selfishness. Furthermore, no man manages to achieve perfect rationality. Life is simply too short. Man comes to the end of his life realizing that there is so much more he could and should have learned. Kant proposes to solve this problem by looking not at the individual man but at the species. While it is true that man's rational capacities are not fully realized in individual men, they are being realized in the steady progress of mankind toward an orderly world order.

Kant admits that he cannot prove that history is teleological, that it has a plan. But while it may be impossible to prove that there is purpose in history, the historian must nonetheless presuppose it. If there is no plan to history, we are no longer justified in believing in providence; and without trust in providence, Kant continues, we no longer have any basis for living a moral life. It is imperative then that the historian uncover the plan implicit in history. Given this clue, Kant believes he can discover the universal laws that determine human actions.

What is the mechanism of history? Kant answers, "The means which nature employs to bring about the development of all the capacities implanted in men is their mutual antagonism in society. . . . By this antagonism I mean the unsocial sociability of men; that is, their tendency to enter into society, conjoined, however, with an accompanying resistance which continually threatens to dissolve this society." (Fourth proposition) That which causes history to move, then, are antagonisms in society. Men need to live together yet there is a pull to individualism that threatens to destroy society. The very thing then that makes history appear meaningless turns out to be the instrument used by Nature to bring about the development of man's potentialities.[2] Kant's happy phrase, "unsocial sociability," speaks both of man's tendency to enter into society and his natural inclination to isolate himself from others. Man needs others but he cannot get along with them.

True to his age then Kant presents us with a linear view of history that permits us to look optimistically toward a future in which mankind will progress toward an international state of rational law and peace. The major defect in Kant's view, as some see it, is that Kant, apart from any historical data, proposed to work out the plan of world history a priori.[3] To arrive at conclusions about history through some means other than historical research seems not only arbitrary but, in the words of Flint, "a monstrous paradox."

IMMANUEL KANT
IDEA OF A UNIVERSAL HISTORY
FROM A COSMOPOLITAN POINT OF VIEW [*]

Whatever metaphysical theory may be formed regarding the freedom of the will, it holds equally true that the manifestations of the will in human actions are determined, like all other external events, by universal natural laws. Now history is occupied with the narration of these manifestations as facts, however deeply their causes may lie concealed. Hence in view of this natural principle of regulation, it may be hoped that when the play of the freedom of the human will is examined on the great scale of universal history a regular march will be discovered in its

---

[2] The similarity of this position in Kant to Vico's doctrine of providence should be noted. It should also be compared with Hegel's concept of the "cunning of reason."

[3] This criticism is raised by, among others, Robert Flint in *The Philosophy of History in France and Germany* (London: 1874) and, more recently, by W. H. Walsh in *An Introduction to the Philosophy of History* (London: 1953), pp. 127–130.

[*] Translated by W. Hastie.

movements; and that, in this way, what appears to be tangled and unregulated in the case of individuals will be recognized in the history of the whole species as a continually advancing, though slow, development of its original capacities and endowments. Thus, marriages, births, and deaths appear to be incapable of being reduced to any rule by which their numbers might be calculated beforehand, on account of the great influence which the free will of man exercises upon them; and yet the annual statistics of great countries prove that these events take place according to constant natural laws. In this respect they may be compared with the very inconstant changes of the weather, which cannot be determined beforehand in detail, but which yet, on the whole, do not fail to maintain the growth of plants, the flow of rivers and other natural processes, in a uniform uninterrupted course. Individual men, and even whole nations, little think, while they are pursuing their own purposes —each in his own way and often one in direct opposition to another—that they are advancing unconsciously under the guidance of a purpose of nature which is unknown to them, and that they are toiling for the realization of an end which, even if it were known to them, might be regarded as of little importance.

Men, viewed as a whole, are not guided in their efforts merely by instinct, like the lower animals; nor do they proceed in their actions, like the citizens of a purely rational world, according to a preconcerted plan. And so it appears as if no regular systematic history of mankind would be possible, as in the case, for instance, of bees and beavers. Nor can one help feeling a certain repugnance in looking at the conduct of men as it is exhibited on the great stage of the world. With glimpses of wisdom appearing in individuals here and there, it seems, on examining it externally as if the whole web of human history were woven out of folly and childish vanity and the frenzy of destruction, so that at the end one hardly knows what idea to form of our race, albeit so proud of its prerogatives. In such circumstances there is no resource for the philosopher but, while recognizing the fact that a rational conscious purpose cannot be supposed to determine mankind and the play of their actions as a whole, to try whether he cannot discover a universal purpose of nature in this paradoxical movement of human things, and whether in view of this purpose a history of creatures who proceed without a plan of their own may nevertheless be possible according to a determinate plan of nature. We will accordingly see whether we can succeed in finding a clue to such a history; and, in the event of doing so, we shall then leave it to nature to bring forth the man who will be fit to compose it. Thus she did bring forth a Kepler, who in an unexpected way, reduced the eccentric paths of the planets to definite laws; and then she brought forth a Newton, who explained those laws by a universal natural cause.

First proposition. All the capacities implanted in a creature by nature are destined to unfold themselves, completely and conformably to their end, in the course of time.

This proposition is established by observation, external as well as internal or anatomical, in the case of all animals. An organ which is not to be used, or an arrangement which does not attain its end, is a contradiction in the teleological science of nature. For, if we turn away from that fundamental principle, we have then before us a nature moving without a purpose, and no longer conformable to law; and the cheerless gloom of chance takes the place of the guiding light of reason.

Second proposition. In man, as the only rational creature on earth, those natural capacities which are directed toward the use of his reason could be completely developed only in the species and not in the individual.

Reason, in a creature, is a faculty of which it is characteristic to extend the laws and purposes involved in the use of all its powers far beyond the sphere of natural instinct, and it knows no limit in its efforts. Reason, however, does not itself work by instinct, but requires experiments, exercise, and instruction in order to advance gradually from one stage of insight to another. Hence each individual man would necessarily have to live an enormous length of time in order to learn by himself how to make a complete use of all his natural endowments. Otherwise, if nature should have given him but a short lease of life—as is actually the case—reason would then require the production of an almost inconceivable series of generations, the one handing down its enlightenment to the other, in order that her germs, as implanted in our species may be at last unfolded to that stage of development which is completely conformable to her inherent design. And the point of time at which this is to be reached must, at least in idea, form the goal and aim of man's endeavors, because his natural capacities would otherwise have to be regarded as, for the most part, purposeless and bestowed in vain. But such a view would abolish all our practical principles, and thereby also throw on nature the suspicion of practicing a childish play in the case of man alone, while her wisdom must otherwise be recognized as a fundamental principle in judging of all other arrangements.

Third proposition. Nature has willed that man shall produce wholly out of himself all that goes beyond the mechanical structure and arrangement of his animal existence, and that he shall participate in no other happiness or perfection than that which he has procured for himself, apart from instinct, by his own reason.

Nature, according to this view, does nothing that is superfluous, and is not prodigal in the use of means for her ends. As she gave man reason and freedom of will on the basis of reason, this was at once a clear indication of her purpose in respect of his endowments. With such equipment, he was not to be guided by instinct nor furnished and instructed by innate knowledge; much rather must he produce everything out of himself. The invention of his own covering and shelter from the elements and the means of providing for his external security and defense,—for which nature gave him neither the horns of the bull, nor the claws of the lion, nor the fangs of the dog,—as well as all the sources of delight which could make life agreeable, his very insight and prudence, and even the goodness of his will, all these were to be entirely his own work. Nature seems to have taken pleasure in exercising her utmost parsimony in this case and to have measured her animal equipments very sparingly. She seems to have fitted them exactly to the most necessitous requirements of the mere beginning of an existence, as if it had been her will that man, when he had at last struggled up from the greatest crudeness of life to the highest capability and to internal perfection in his habit of thought, and thereby also—so far as it is possible on earth—to happiness, should claim the merit of it as all his own and owe it only to himself. It thus looks as if nature had laid more upon his rational self-esteem than upon his mere well-being. For in this movement of human life a great host of toils and troubles wait upon man. It appears, however, that the purpose of nature was not so much that he should have an agreeable life, but that he should carry forward his own self-culture until he made himself worthy of life and well-being. In this connection it is always a subject of wonder that the older generations appear only to pursue their weary toil for the sake of those who come after them, preparing for the latter another stage on which they may carry higher the structure which nature has in view; and that it is to be the happy fate of only the latest generations to dwell in the building upon which the long series of their forefathers has labored, without so much as intending it and yet with no possibility of participating in the happiness which they were preparing. Yet, however mysterious this may be, it is as necessary as it is mysterious when we once accept the position that one species of animals was destined to possess reason, and that, forming a class of rational beings mortal in all the individuals but immortal in the species, it was yet to attain to a complete development of its capacities.

Fourth proposition. The means which nature employs to bring about the development of all the capacities implanted in men is their mutual antagonism in society, but only so far as this antagonism becomes at length the cause of an order among them that is regulated by law.

By this antagonism I mean the unsocial sociability of men; that is their tendency to enter into society, conjoined, however, with an accompanying resistance which continually threatens to dissolve this society. The disposition for this manifestly lies in human nature. Man has an inclination to socialize himself by associating with others, because in such a state he feels himself more than a natural man, in the development of his natural capacities. He has, moreover, a great tendency to individualize himself by isolation from others, because he likewise finds in himself the unsocial disposition of wishing to direct everything merely according to his own mind; and hence he expects resistance everywhere, just as he knows with regard to himself that he is inclined on his part to resist others. Now it is this resistance or mutual antagonism that awakens all the powers of man, that drives him to overcome all his propensity to indolence, and that impels him, through the desire of honor or power or wealth, to strive after rank among his fellow men—whom he can neither bear to interfere with himself, nor yet let alone. Then the first real steps are taken from the rudeness of barbarism to the culture of civilization, which particularly lies in the social worth of man. All his talents are now gradually developed, and with the progress of enlightenment a beginning is made in the institution of a mode of thinking which can transform the crude natural capacity for moral distinctions, in the course of time, into definite practical principles of action; and thus a pathologically constrained combination into a form of society is developed at last to a moral and rational whole. Without those qualities of an unsocial kind out of which this antagonism arises—which viewed by themselves are certainly not amiable but which every one must necessarily find in the movements of his own selfish propensities—men might have led an Arcadian shepherd life in complete harmony, contentment, and mutual love, but in that case all their talents would have forever remained hidden in their germ. As gentle as the sheep they tended, such men would hardly have won for their existence a higher worth than belonged to their domesticated cattle; they would not have filled up with their rational nature the void remaining in the creation, in respect of its final end. Thanks be then to nature for this unsociableness, for this envious jealousy and vanity, for this unsatiable desire of possession or even of power. Without them all the excellent capacities implanted in mankind by nature would slumber eternally undeveloped. Man wishes concord; but nature knows better what is good for his species, and she will have discord. He wishes to live comfortably and pleasantly; but nature wills that, turning from idleness and inactive contentment, he shall throw himself into toil and suffering even in order to find out remedies against them, and to extricate his life prudently from them again. The natural impulses that urge man in this direction, the sources of that unsociableness and general antagonism from which so many evils arise, do yet at the same time impel him to new exertion of his powers, and consequently to further development of his natural capacities. Hence they clearly manifest the arrangement of a wise Creator, and do not at all, as is often supposed, betray the hand of a malevolent spirit that has deteriorated His glorious creation, or spoiled it from envy.

Fifth proposition. The greatest practical problem for the human race, to the solution of which it is compelled by nature, is the establishment of a civil society, universally administering right according to law.

It is only in a society which possesses the greatest liberty, and which consequently involves a thorough antagonism of its members—with, however, the most exact determination and guarantee of the limits of this liberty in order that it may coexist with the liberty of others—that the highest purpose of nature, which is the development of all her capacities, can be attained in the case of mankind. Now nature also wills that the human race shall attain through itself to this, as to all the other ends for which it was destined. Hence a society in which liberty under external laws may be found combined in the greatest possible degree with irresistible power, or a perfectly just civil constitution, is the highest natural problem prescribed to the human species. And this is so because nature can only by means of the solution and fulfillment of this problem realize her other purposes with our race. A certain necessity compels man, who is otherwise so greatly prepossessed in favor of unlimited freedom, to enter into this state of coercion and restraint. Indeed, it is the greatest necessity of all that does this; for it is created by men themselves whose inclinations make it impossible for them to exist long beside each other in wild, lawless freedom. But in such a complete growth as the civil union these very inclinations afterward produce the best effects. It is with them as with the trees in a forest; for just because every one strives to deprive the other of air and sun they compel each other to seek them both above, and thus they grow beautiful and straight; whereas those that in freedom and apart from one another shoot out their branches at will grow stunted and crooked and awry. All the culture and art that adorn humanity and the fairest social order are fruits of that unsociableness which is necessitated of itself to discipline itself and which thus constrains man, by compulsive art, to develop completely the germs of his nature.

Sixth proposition. This problem is likewise the most difficult of its kind, and it is the latest to be solved by the human race.

The difficulty which the mere idea of this problem brings into view is that man is an animal, and if he lives among others of his kind he has need of a master. For he certainly misuses his freedom in relation to his fellow men; and although as a rational creature he desires a law which may set bounds to the freedom of all, yet his own selfish animal inclinations lead him, wherever he can, to except himself from it. He, therefore, requires a master to break his self-will and compel him to obey a will that is universally valid, and in relation to which every one may be free. Where, then, does he obtain this master? Nowhere but in the human race. But this master is an animal too, and also requires a master. Begin, then, as he may, it is not easy to see how he can procure a supreme authority over public justice that would be essentially just, whether such an authority may be sought in a single person or in a society of many selected persons. The highest authority has to be just in itself, and yet to be a man. This problem is, therefore, the most difficult of its kind; and, indeed, its perfect solution is impossible. Out of such crooked material as man is made of, nothing can be hammered quite straight. So it is only an approximation to this idea that is imposed upon us by nature.* It further follows that this problem is the last to be practically worked out, because it requires correct conceptions of the nature of a possible constitution, great experience founded on the practice of ages, and above all a good will prepared for the reception of the solution. But these three conditions could not easily be found together; and if they are found it can only be very

---

* The part that has to be played by man is, therefore, a very artificial one. We do not know how it may be with the inhabitants of other planets or what are the conditions of their nature; but, if we execute well the commission of nature, we may certainly flatter ourselves to the extent of claiming a not insignificant rank among our neighbors in the universe. It may perhaps be the case that in those other planets every individual completely attains his destination in this life. With us it is otherwise; only the species can hope for this.

late in time, and after many attempts to solve the problem have been made in vain.

Seventh proposition. The problem of the establishment of a perfect civil constitution is dependent on the problem of the regulation of the external relations between the states conformably to law; and without the solution of this latter problem it cannot be solved.

What avails it to labor at the arrangement of a commonwealth as a civil constitution regulated by law among individual men? The same unsociableness which forced men to it becomes again the cause of each commonwealth's assuming the attitude of uncontrolled freedom in its external relations, that is, as one State in relation to other States; and consequently any one State must expect from any other the same sort of evils as oppressed individual men and compelled them to enter into a civil union regulated by law. Nature has accordingly again used the unsociableness of men, and even of great societies and political bodies, her creatures of this kind, as a means to work out through their mutual antagonism a condition of rest and security. She works through wars, through the strain of never-relaxed preparation for them, and through the necessity which every State is at last compelled to feel within itself, even in the midst of peace, to begin some imperfect efforts to carry out her purpose. And, at last, after many devastations, overthrows and even complete internal exhaustion of their powers, the nations are driven forward to the goal which reason might easily have impressed upon them, even without so much sad experience. This is none other than the advance out of the lawless state of savages and the entering into a federation of nations. It is thus brought about that every State, including even the smallest, may rely for its safety and its rights not on its own power or its own judgment of right, but only on this great international federation (*foedus amphictionum*), on its combined power and on the decision of the common will according to laws. However visionary this idea may appear to be—and it has been ridiculed in the way in which it has been presented by an Abbe de St. Pierre or Rousseau (perhaps because they believed its realization to be so near)—it is nevertheless the inevitable issue of the necessity in which men involve one another.

IDEA OF A UNIVERSAL HISTORY

For this necessity must compel the nations to the very resolution —however hard it may appear—to which the savage in his uncivilized state was so unwillingly compelled when he had to surrender his brutal liberty and seek rest and security in a constitution regulated by law.

All wars are, accordingly, so many attempts—not, indeed, in the intention of men, but yet according to the purpose of nature —to bring about new relations between the nations; and by destruction, or at least dismemberment, of them all to form new political corporations. These new organizations, again, are not capable of being preserved either in themselves or beside one another, and they must therefore pass in through similar new revolutions, till at last, partly by the best possible arrangement of the civil constitution within, and partly by common convention and legislation without, a condition will be attained, which, in the likeness of a civil commonwealth and after the manner of an automaton, will be able to preserve itself.

Three views may be put forward as to the way in which this condition is to be attained. In the first place, it may be held that from an Epicurean concourse of causes in action it is to be expected that the States, like little particles of matter, will try by their fortuitous conjunctions all sorts of formations, which will be again destroyed by new collisions, till at last some one constitution will by chance succeed in preserving itself in its proper form, —a lucky accident which will hardly ever come about! In the second place, it may rather be maintained that nature here pursues a regular march in carrying our species up from the lower stage of animality to the highest stage of humanity, and that this is done by a compulsive art that is inherent in man, whereby his natural capacities and endowments are developed in perfect regularity through an apparently wild disorder. Or, in the third place, it may even be asserted that out of all these actions and reactions of men as a whole nothing at all—or at least nothing rational—will ever be produced; that it will be in the future as it has ever been in the past, and that no one will ever be able to say whether the discord which is so natural to our species may not be preparing for us, even in this civilized state of society, a hell of evils at the end; nay, that it is not perhaps advancing even now to annihilate again by barbaric devastation this actual state of society and all the progress hitherto made in civilization,—a fate against which there is no guarantee under a government of blind chance, identical as it is with lawless freedom in action, unless a connecting wisdom is covertly assumed to underlie the system of nature.

Now, which of these views is to be adopted depends almost entirely on the question whether it is rational to recognize harmony and design in the parts of the constitution of nature, and to deny them of the whole. We have glanced at what has been done by the seemingly purposeless state of savages; how it checked for a time all the natural capacities of our species, but at last by the very evils in which it involved mankind it compelled them to pass from this state, and to enter into a civil constitution, in which all the germs of humanity could be unfolded. And, in like manner, the barbarian freedom of the States, when once they were founded, proceeded in the same way of progress. By the expenditure of all the resources of the commonwealth in military preparations against each other, by the devastations occasioned by war, and still more by the necessity of holding themselves continually in readiness for it, the full development of the capacities of mankind is undoubtedly retarded in their progress; but, on the other hand, the very evils which thus arise, compel men to find out means against them. A law of equilibrium is thus discovered for the regulation of the really wholesome antagonism of contiguous States as it springs up out of their freedom; and a united power, giving emphasis to this law, is constituted, whereby there is introduced a universal condition of public security among the nations. And that the powers of mankind may not fall asleep, this condition is not entirely free from danger; but it is at the same time not without a principle which operates, so as to equalize the mutual action and reaction of these powers, that they may not destroy each other. Before the last step of bringing in a universal union of the States is taken—and accordingly when human nature is only halfway in its progress—it has to endure the hardest evils of all, under the deceptive semblance of outward prosperity; and Rousseau was not so far wrong when he preferred the state of the savages, if the last stage which our race has yet to surmount be left out of view. We are cultivated in a high degree by science and art. We are civilized, even to excess, in the way of all sorts of social forms of politeness and elegance. But there is still much to be done before we can be regarded as moralized. The idea of morality certainly belongs to real culture; but an application of this idea which extends no farther than the likeness of morality in the sense of honor and external propriety merely constitutes civilization. So long, however, as States lavish all their resources upon vain and violent schemes of aggrandizement, so long as they continually impede the slow movements of the endeavor to cultivate the newer habits of thought and character on the part of the citizens, and even withdraw from them all the means of furthering it, nothing in the way of moral progress can be expected. A long internal process of improvement is thus required in every commonwealth as a condition for the higher culture of its citizens. But all apparent good that is not grafted upon a morally good disposition is nothing but mere illusion and glittering misery. In this condition the human race will remain until it shall have worked itself, in the way that has been indicated, out of the existing chaos of its political relations.

Eighth proposition. The history of the human race, viewed as a whole, may be regarded as the realization of a hidden plan of nature to bring about a political constitution, internally, and, for this purpose, also externally perfect, as the only state in which all the capacities implanted by her in mankind can be fully developed.

This proposition is a corollary from the preceding proposition. We see by it that philosophy may also have its millennial view, but in this case the chiliasm is of such a nature that the very idea of it—although only in a far-off way—may help to further its realization; and such a prospect is, therefore, anything but visionary. The real question is whether experience discloses anything of such a movement in the purpose of nature. I can only say it does a little, for the movement in this orbit appears to require such a long time till it goes full round that the form of its path and the relation of its parts to the whole can hardly be determined out of the small portion which the human race has yet passed through in this relation. The determination of this problem is just as difficult and uncertain as it is to calculate from all previous astronomical observations what course our sun, with the whole host of his attendant train, is pursuing in the great system of the fixed stars, although on the ground of the total arrangement of the structure of the universe and the little that has been observed of it, we may infer, confidently enough, the reality of such a movement. Human nature, however, is so constituted that it cannot be indifferent even in regard to the most distant epoch that may affect our race, if only it can be expected with certainty. And such indifference is the less possible in the case before us when it appears that we might by our own rational arrangements hasten the coming of this joyous period for our descendants. Hence the faintest traces of the approach of this period will be very important to ourselves. Now the States are already in the present day involved in such close relations with each other that none of them can pause or slacken in its internal civilization without losing power and influence in relation to the rest; and hence the maintenance, if not the progress, of this end of nature is, in a manner, secured even by the ambitious designs of the States themselves. Further, civil liberty cannot now be easily assailed without inflicting such damage as will be felt in all trades and industries, and especially in commerce; and this would entail a diminution of the powers of the State in external relations. This liberty, moreover, gradually advances further. But if the citizen is hindered in seeking his prosperity in any way suitable to himself that is consistent with the liberty of others, the activity of business is checked generally; and thereby the powers of the whole State are again weakened. Hence the restrictions on personal liberty even in religion come to be conceded. And thus it is that, notwithstanding the intrusion of many a delusion and caprice, the spirit of enlightenment gradually arises as a great good which the human race must derive even from the selfish purposes of aggrandizement on the part of its rulers, if they understand what is for their own advantage. This enlightenment however, and along with it a certain sympathetic interest which the enlightened man cannot avoid taking in the good which he perfectly understands, must by and by pass up to the throne and exert an influence even upon the principles of government. Thus although our rulers at present have no money to spend on public educational institutions, or in general on all that concerns the highest good of the world—because all their resources are already placed to the account of the next war—yet they will certainly find it to be to their own advantage at least not to hinder the people in their own efforts in this direction, however weak and slow these may be. Finally, war itself comes to be regarded as a very hazardous and objectionable undertaking, not only from its being so artificial in itself and so uncertain as regards its issue on both sides, but also from the afterpains which the State feels in the ever-increasing burdens it entails in the form of national debt—a modern infliction—which it becomes almost impossible to extinguish. And to this is to be added the influence which every political disturbance of any State of our continent—linked as it is so closely to others by the connections of trade—exerts upon all the States and which becomes so observable that they are forced by their common danger, although without lawful authority, to offer themselves as arbiters in the troubles of any such State. In doing so, they are beginning to arrange for a great future political body, such as the world has never yet seen. Although this political body may as yet exist only in a rough outline, nevertheless a feeling begins, as it were, to stir in all its members, each of which has a common interest in the maintenance of the whole. And this may well inspire the hope that, after many political revolutions and transformations, the highest purpose of nature will be at last realized in the establishment of a universal cosmopolitical institution, in the bosom of which all the original capacities and endowments of the human species will be unfolded and developed.

Ninth proposition. A philosophical attempt to work out the universal history of the world according to the plan of nature in its aiming at a perfect civil union must be regarded as possible, and as even capable of helping forward the purpose of nature.

It seems, at first sight, a strange and even an absurd proposal to suggest the composition of a history according to the idea of how the course of the world must proceed, if it is to be conformable to certain rational laws. It may well appear that only a romance could be produced from such a point of view. However, if it be assumed that nature, even in the play of human freedom, does not proceed without plan and design, the idea may well be regarded as practicable; and, although we are too shortsighted to see through the secret mechanism of her constitution, yet the idea may be serviceable as a clue to enable us to penetrate the otherwise planless aggregate of human actions as a whole, and to represent them as constituting a system. For the idea may so far be easily verified. Thus, suppose we start from the history of Greece, as that by which all the older or contemporaneous history has been preserved, or at least accredited to us.* Then, if we study its influence upon the formation and malformation of the political institutions of the Roman people, which swallowed up the Greek states, and if we further follow the influence of the Roman Empire upon the Barbarians who destroyed it in turn, and continue this investigation down to our own day, conjoining with it episodically the political history of other peoples according as the knowledge of them has gradually reached us through these more enlightened nations, we shall discover a regular movement of progress through the political institutions of our continent, which is probably destined to give laws to all other parts of the world. Applying the same method of study everywhere, both to the internal civil constitutions and laws of the States and to their external relations to each other, we see how in both relations the good they contained served for a certain period to elevate and glorify particular nations, and with themselves their arts and sciences,—until the defects attaching to their institutions came in time to cause their overthrow. And yet their very ruin leaves always a germ of growing enlightenment behind, which, being further developed by every revolution, acts as a preparation for a subsequent higher stage of progress and improvement. Thus, as I believe, we can discover a clue which may serve for more than the explanation of the confused play of human things, or for the art of political prophecy in reference to

---

* It is only a learned public which has had an uninterrupted existence from its beginning up to our time that can authenticate ancient history. Beyond it, all is *terra incognita;* and the history of the peoples who lived out of its range can only be begun from the date at which they entered within it. In the case of the Jewish people this happened in the time of the Ptolemies through the Greek translation of the Bible, without which little faith would have been given to their isolated accounts of themselves. From that data taken as a beginning, when it has been determined, their records may then be traced upward. And so it is with all other peoples. The first page of Thucydides, says Hume, is the beginning of all true history.

future changes in States,—a use which has been already made of the history of mankind, even though it was regarded as the incoherent effect of an unregulated freedom! Much more than all this is attained by the idea of human history viewed as founded upon the assumption of a universal plan in nature. For this idea gives us a new ground of hope, as it opens up to us a consoling view of the future, in which the human species is represented in the far distance as having at last worked itself up to a condition in which all the germs implanted in it by nature may be fully developed, and its destination here on earth fulfilled. Such a justification of nature—or rather, let us say, of Providence—is no insignificant motive for choosing a particular point of view in contemplating the course of the world. For what avails it to magnify the glory and wisdom of the creation in the irrational domain of nature, and to recommend it to devout contemplation, if that part of the great display of the supreme wisdom which presents the end of it all in the history of the human race is to be viewed as only furnishing perpetual objections to that glory and wisdom? The spectacle of history if thus viewed would compel us to turn away our eyes from it against our will; and the despair of ever finding a perfect rational purpose in its movement would reduce us to hope for it, if at all, only in another world.

This idea of a universal history is no doubt to a certain extent of an a priori character, but it would be a misunderstanding of my object were it imagined that I have any wish to supplant the empirical cultivation of history, or the narration of the actual facts of experience. It is only a thought of what a philosophical mind—which, as such, must be thoroughly versed in history —might be induced to attempt from another standpoint. Besides, the praiseworthy circumstantiality with which our history is now written may well lead one to raise the question as to how our remote posterity will be able to cope with the burden of history as it will be transmitted to them after a few centuries. They will surely estimate the history of the oldest times, of which the documentary records may have been long lost, only from the point of view of what will interest them; and no doubt this will be what the nations and governments have achieved, or failed to achieve, in the universal world-wide relation. We should give thought to this relation; and at the same time to draw the attention of ambitious rulers and their servants to the only means by which they can leave an honorable memorial of themselves to latest times. And this may also form a minor motive for attempting to produce such a philosophical history.

BIBLIOGRAPHY

Kant's essay "The Idea of a Universal History" as translated by W. Hastie was published in 1914 in the volume, *Eternal Peace and Other International Essays*. A different translation along with other essays by Kant on the philosophy of history can be found in the paperback, *Kant on History*, edited by Lewis White Beck and published by Bobbs-Merrill in 1963.

ARMSTRONG, A. C. "Kant's Philosophy of Peace and War," *Journal of Philosophy*, 1931.

AXINN, SIDNEY. *A Study of Kant's Philosophy of History*. Ann Arbor: 1955.

AXINN, SIDNEY. "Kant, Logic, and the Concept of Mankind," *Ethics*, 1958.

BARTH, KARL. *Protestant Thought from Rousseau to Ritschl*. New York: 1959.

BECKER, CARL L. *The Heavenly City of the Eighteenth Century Philosophers*. New Haven: 1932.

BOURKE, JOHN. "Kant's Doctrine of 'Perpetual Peace,'" *Philosophy*, 1942.

COPLESTON, F. C. *History of Philosophy*, Vol. VI. Westminster, Md.: 1960.

FACKENHEIM, EMIL. "Kant and Radical Evil," *University of Toronto Quarterly*, 1954.

FACKENHEIM, EMIL. "Kant's Concept of History," *Kant-Studien*, 1957.

FLINT, ROBERT. *The Philosophy of History in France and Germany*, Book II. London: 1874.

HANCOCK, ROGER. "Ethics and History in Kant and Mill," *Ethics*, 1957.

KRIEGER, L. "Kant and the Crisis in Natural Law," *Journal of the History of Ideas*, 1965.

BIBLIOGRAPHY

MAZLISH, B. *The Riddle of History*. New York: 1966.

WALSH, W. H. *An Introduction to the Philosophy of History*. London: 1951.

WILKINS, B. T. "Teleology in Kant's Philosophy of History," *History and Theory*, 1962.

4 Johann Gottfried Herder (1744–1803)

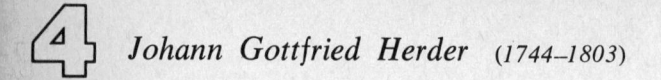

The first part of Herder's *Ideas Toward a Philosophy of the History of Man* was published in the same year (1784) as Kant's short essay, "Idea of a Universal History." While Herder had studied under Kant at Königsberg University, he and Kant came to represent different eras in the history of ideas. Kant's philosophy of history is typical of the Enlightenment; Herder's work is an early expression of Romanticism and is essentially a reaction to the Enlightenment approach to history. Some of the major differences between these two approaches to history are:

1. The Enlightenment, beginning with a firm belief in the inevitability of human progress, regarded all history as the record

of man's development from barbarism and superstition to enlightenment and rationalism. Herder countered by teaching that while it is possible to detect some progress in history, it is not progress toward the Enlightenment view of a final perfect state as the goal of history. Herder insisted that whatever development there may be in history, it is largely unconscious and irrational. The striving evident in history is irrational in the sense that mankind in different places and at different times develops in its own way without unnatural limitations. Since God does not interfere in human history, history is a natural phenomenon.

2. The Enlightenment tended to treat past history with a contempt befitting that which is believed to be barbaric and unenlightened. According to Herder, however, the historian should not condemn or judge the past; he should treat it with sympathy and not with disdain. As much as possible, the historian should enter into the life of each culture and try to understand it from within. Whereas the Enlightenment tended to pigeonhole the richness of human experience, Herder urged historians to judge each civilization by its own standards and not by the historian's. Each culture is unique and should not be compared to others.

3. The Enlightenment assumed that human nature is uniform and unchanging. In Herder's view, each age and culture has its own nature. Mankind has assumed many forms. In fact, Herder's major premise is that everything that can happen, does happen in accordance with whatever limitations space and time may impose. A favorite analogy during the Enlightenment was that of a machine. Herder replaced this with another analogy—that of a plant. Each culture grows like a plant—unevenly and spontaneously—depending on the soil in which it is planted. The growth of each culture is simply a result of the right people being in the right place at the right time. Cultures have developed, each in its own way, without being fixed by universal laws.

4. Because of the Enlightenment presupposition about the fixity of human nature, it tended to ignore the influence of man's environment upon his history. Herder argued, on the contrary, that whatever happens to man is determined by conditions in his environment. The large variety of civilizations can be attributed to the fact that every possible manifestation of the human spirit will be realized.

5. The Enlightenment approached history already equipped with certain presuppositions which it then sought to confirm in the data. Herder objected to this procedure of forcing the data of history into preconceived patterns. He insisted on an examination of the past free from bias.

Herder planned that his book should contain five parts consisting of five books each. However, only the first four parts (twenty books) were ever published. In the first two parts (Books I–X) he discusses man's physical environment—the stage on which human history has been enacted. He argues that an understanding of the universe and of man's place within it is a necessary prerequisite to understanding history. Books XI through XX are more interesting for the student of the philosophy of history. Interwoven with discussions of the history of a number of nations are significant comments that throw light on Herder's view of speculative history. Two of the more important concepts that appear are those of Humanity and *das Volk*.

Herder tells us repeatedly that the goal of history is Humanity. Unfortunately, he never clarifies this concept. As one of Herder's interpreter's explains,

> Toward what does history drive? Herder is not clear; history is like a play (he was a great admirer of Shakespeare) whose outcome the actors do not know, but whose author they can trust to tie the threads of the plot together. The goal is in man's full development of all his potentialities. [N.B. Not just the development of man's *rational* capacities as in Kant, but of *all* his capacities—Ed.] Man is a partly natural and partly supernatural being, who strives to fulfill the purpose for which God put him on earth. This purpose Herder calls "Humanity," which is in fact the central concept of the book, but which is never really defined; to define it might have been to put limits to its spontaneity and growth. Humanity is, paradoxically, the divinity in man, the summit of what he was divinely intended to achieve. It is Herder's substitute for the Idea of Progress, which is not in itself a particularly rational idea, but had been used too much by the rationalists to make him really at home with it. Its highest expression is Christianity, not in its dogmatic forms . . . but as an ideal.[1]

[1] Pardon E. Tillinghast, *Approaches to History* (Englewood Cliffs, New Jersey: Prentice-Hall, 1963), p. 151 f.

Herder constantly emphasizes the primary reality of the group. History is not the record of particular men but of the evolving social units to which men belong. Herder anticipates Hegel and Marx when he says that the individual apart from his social unit is a mere abstraction.[2] The group is the means of individual development and the most important group is the nation (*das Volk*). The individual can receive his full justification only as a member of some Volk.

Given Herder's rejection of rationalism, it might be too much to expect complete consistency in his writing. He does not disappoint this expectation. The significance of his work is to be found not in a polished and finished system but in flashes of insight that will lead later thinkers to move still further down the paths he blazed.

JOHANN GOTTFRIED HERDER
OUTLINES OF A PHILOSOPHY OF THE HISTORY OF MAN [*]

At an early age, when the dawn of science appeared to my sight in all that beauty, which is greatly diminished at the noon of life, the thought frequently occurred to me, whether, as everything in the world has its philosophy and science, there must not also be a philosophy and science of what concerns us most nearly, of the history of mankind at large. Every thing enforced this upon my mind; metaphysics and morals, physics and natural history, and lastly religion above all the rest. Shall he, who has ordered everything in nature, said I to myself, by number, weight, and measure; who has so regulated according to these the essence of things, their forms and relations, their course and subsistence, that only one wisdom, goodness, and power prevail from the system of the universe to the grain of sand, from the power that supports worlds and suns to the texture of a spider's web; who has so wonderfully and divinely weighed everything in our body, and in the faculties of our mind, that, when we attempt

---

[2] Herder also echoes Plato. See Karl Popper's *The Open Society and Its Enemies* (London: 1945).

[*] Translated from the German *Ideen zur Philosophie der Geschichte der Menschheit* by T. Churchill (London: 1800).

to reflect on the *only-wise* ever so remotely, we lose ourselves in an abyss of his purposes; shall that God depart from His wisdom and goodness in the general destination and disposition of our species, and act in these without a plan? Or can He have intended to keep us in ignorance of this, while He has displayed to us so much of His eternal purposes in the inferior part of the creation, in which we are much less concerned? . . .

Everywhere the great analogies of nature have led me to religious truths, which, though I find it difficult, I must suppress, since I would not prematurely anticipate, but faithfully follow step by step that light, which everywhere beams upon me from the hidden presence of the Creator in His works. It will be so much the greater satisfaction both to my reader and to myself, if, as we proceed on our way, this obscurely dawning light rise upon us at length with the splendor of an unclouded sun.

Let no one be misled, therefore, by my occasionally employing the term nature, personified. Nature is no real entity; but *God in all his works;* this sacred name, however, which no creature, that comes under the cognizance of our senses, ought to pronounce without the profoundest reverence, I was desirous at least not to abuse by employing it too frequently, since I could not introduce it with sufficient solemnity on all occasions. Let him, to whose mind the term nature has been degraded, and rendered unmeaning, by many writers of the present day, conceive instead of it that *almighty power, goodness, and wisdom,* and mentally name that invisible being, for whom no language upon Earth can find an expression.

It is the same when I speak of the *organic powers of the creation:* I do not imagine, that they will be considered as *occult qualities,* since their operations are apparent to us, and I know not how to give them a more precise and determinate name. . . .

The unity and diversity of mankind. No two leaves of any one tree in nature are to be found perfectly alike; and still less do two human faces, or human frames, resemble each other. Of what endless variety is our artful structure susceptible. . . . As the human intellect, however, seeks unity in every kind of variety, and the divine mind, its prototype, has stamped the most innumerable multiplicity upon the Earth with unity, we may venture from the vast realm of change to revert to the simplest proposition: *all mankind are only one and the same species.* . . .

Man is dependent on others for the development of his faculties. Man is an artificial machine, endued with a genetic disposition, it is true, and plenitude of life; but the machine does not work itself, and the ablest of mankind must learn how to work it. Reason is an aggregate of the experiences and observations of the mind, the sum of the education of man, which the pupil ultimately finishes in himself, as an extraneous artist, after certain extraneous models.

In this lies the principle of the history of mankind, without which no such history could exist. Did man receive everything from himself and develop everything independently of external circumstances, we might have a history of an individual indeed, but not of the species. But as our specific character lies in this, that, born almost without instinct, we are formed to manhood only by the practice of a whole life, and both the perfectibility and corruptibility of our species depend on it, the history of mankind is necessarily a whole, that is a chain of socialness and plastic tradition, from the first link to the last. There is an education, therefore, of the human species since everyone becomes a man only by means of education, and the whole species lives solely in this chain of individuals. . . . The philosophy of history, therefore . . . is, to speak properly, the true history of mankind. . . .

The principal law of history. What is the principal law that we have observed in all the great occurrences of history? In my opinion it is this: *that everywhere on our Earth whatever could be has been, according to the situation and wants of the place, the circumstances and occasions of the times, and the native or generated character of the people.* Admit active human powers in a determinate relation to the age and to their place on the Earth and all the vicissitudes in the history of man will ensue. Here kingdoms and states crystallize into shape: there they dissolve and assume other forms. Here from a wandering horde rises a Babylon; there from the straitened inhabitants of a coast springs up a Tyre; here, in Africa, an Egypt is formed; there, in the deserts of Arabia, a Jewish state; and all these in one part of the

World, all in the neighborhood of each other. Time, place, and national character alone, in short the general cooperation of active powers in their most determinate individuality govern all the events that happen among mankind as well as all the occurrences in nature. Let us place this predominant law of the creation in a suitable light.

1. *Active human powers are the springs of human history:* and as man originates from and in one race, his figure, education, and mode of thinking are thus genetic. Hence that striking national character which, deeply imprinted on the most ancient people, is unequivocally displayed in all their operations on the Earth. As a mineral water derives its component parts, its operative powers, and its taste from the soil through which it flows, so the ancient character of nations arose from the family features, the climate, the way of life and education, the early actions and employments, that were peculiar to them. The manners of the fathers took deep root and became the internal prototype of the race. . . . Now Nature has given the whole Earth to mankind, her children; and allowed everything that place, time, and power would permit to spring up thereon. Everything that can exist, exists; everything that is possible to be produced will be produced, if not today, yet tomorrow. Nature's year is long; the blossoms of her plants are as various as the plants themselves and the elements by which they are nourished. In Hindustan, Egypt, and China, in Canaan, Greece, Rome, and Carthage, took place what would have occurred no where else and at no other period. The law of necessity and convenience, composed of power, time and place, everywhere produces different fruits.

2. If the complexion of a kingdom thus depends principally on *the time and place in which it arose, the parts that composed it, and the external circumstances by which it was surrounded,* we perceive the chief part of its fate springs also from these. A monarchy framed by wandering tribes, whose political system is a continuation of their former mode of life, will scarcely be of long duration: it ravages and subjugates till at last itself is destroyed; the capture of the metropolis, or frequently the death of a king alone, is sufficient to drop the curtain on the predatory scene. . . . It is not so with states which, springing up from a root, rest on themselves; they may be subdued, but the nation

remains. Thus it is with China. We well know how much labor it cost its conquerors to introduce there a simple custom, the mongol mode of cutting the hair. Thus it is with the brahmins and Jews, whose ceremonial systems will eternally separate them from all the nations upon Earth. Thus Egypt long withstood any intermixture with other nations; and how difficult was it to extirpate the Phoenicians merely because they were a people rooted in this spot. . . .

3. Finally, from the whole region over which we have wandered, we perceive *how transitory all human structures are, nay how oppressive the best institutions become in the course of a few generations*. The plant blossoms and fades; your fathers have died and moldered into dust; your temple is fallen; your tabernacle, the tables of your law, are no more; language itself, that bond of mankind, becomes antiquated; and shall a political constitution, shall a system of government or religion that can be erected solely on these, endure forever? If so, the wings of Time must be enchained and the revolving Globe hang fixed, an idle ball of ice over the abyss. . . . Tradition in itself is an excellent institution of Nature, indispensable to the human race. But when it fetters the thinking faculty both in politics and education, and prevents all progress of the intellect and all the improvement that new times and circumstances demand, it is the true narcotic of the mind, as well to nations and sects, as to individuals. . . .

General reflections on the history of Greece. As the botanist cannot obtain a complete knowledge of a plant unless he follow it from the seed through its germination, blossoming, and decay; such is the Grecian history to us. It is only to be regretted that, according to the usual course, it is yet far from having been studied like that of Rome. At present it is my place to indicate, from what has been said, some points of view in this important fragment of general history which most immediately present themselves to the eye of observation; and here I must repeat the first grand principle:

Whatever can take place among mankind, within the sphere of given circumstances of times, places and nation, actually does take place. Of this Greece affords the amplest and most beautiful proofs.

In natural philosophy we never reckon upon miracles; we observe laws which we perceive everywhere equally effectual, undeviating, and regular. And shall man, with his powers, changes, and passions, burst these chains of nature? Had Greece been peopled with Chinese, our Greece would never have existed; had our Greeks been fixed where Darius led the enslaved Eretrians, they would have formed no Athens, they would have produced no Sparta. Behold Greece now. The ancient Greeks are no more to be seen; nay frequently their country no longer appears. . . . But as the modern Greeks have become what they are only by the course of time through a given series of causes and effects, so did the ancient; and not less every other nation upon Earth. The whole history of mankind is a pure natural history of human powers, actions, and propensities modified by time and place. . . .

This philosophy will first and most eminently guard us from attributing the facts that appear in history to the particular hidden purposes of a scheme of things unknown to us, or the magical influence of invisible powers which we would not venture to name in connection with natural phenomena. Fate reveals its purposes through the events that occur and as they occur. Accordingly, the investigator of history develops these purposes merely from what is before him and what displays itself in its whole extent. Why did the enlightened Greeks appear in the world? Because Greeks existed, and existed under such circumstances that they could not be otherwise than enlightened. Why did Alexander invade India? Because he was Alexander, the son of Philip; and from the dispositions his father had made, the deeds of his nation, his age and character, his reading of Homer, etc., he knew nothing better that he could undertake. But if we attribute his bold resolution to the secret purposes of some superior power, and his heroic achievements to his peculiar fortune, we run the hazard, on the one hand, of exalting his most atrocious actions into designs of the deity; and, on the other, of detracting from his personal courage and military skill, while we deprive the whole occurrence of its natural form. . . . History is the science of what is, not of what possibly may be according to the hidden designs of fate.

Secondly, *What is true of one people holds equally true with regard to the connection of several together; they are joined as time and place unites them; they act upon one another as the combination of active powers directs.*

The Greeks have been acted upon by the Asiatics, and the Asiatics reacted upon by the Greeks. They have been conquered by Romans, Goths, Christians, and Turks; and Romans, Goths, and Christians have derived from them various means of improvement. How are these things consistent? Through place, time, and the natural operations of active powers. The Phoenicians imparted to them the use of letters; but they had not invented letters for them. They imparted them by sending a colony into Greece. So it was with the Hellenes and Egyptians; so with the Greeks that migrated to Bactra; so with all the gifts of the muse which we have received from their hands. Homer sung, but not for us; yet as his works have reached us and are in our possession, we could not avoid being instructed by him. Had any event in the course of time deprived us of these, as we have been deprived of many other excellent works, who would accuse some secret purpose of fate when the natural cause of the loss was apparent? Let a man take a view of the writings that are lost and those that remain, of the works of art that are destroyed and those that are preserved, with the accounts that are given of their destruction and preservation, and venture to point out the rule which fate has followed in transmitting to us these and depriving us of those. . . . Thus the whole of the cultivation of our minds has depended precisely upon the most trivial and precarious circumstances. . . .

General reflections on the history and fate of Rome. In the physical world all things that act together, and upon each other, whether generating, supporting, or destroying, must be considered as one whole: the same is true in the natural world of history.

It is a pleasing exercise of the mind, to inquire, on this occasion or that, what Rome would have been under different circumstances: as, if it had been founded on a different spot; if at an early period it had been transported to Veii; if the Capitol had been taken by Brennus; if Italy had been attacked by Alexander; if the city had been conquered by Hannibal; or if his counsel had been followed by Antiochus. In like manner we may inquire, how Caesar would have reigned in the place of Augustus; how

Germanicus, in the place of Tiberius; what would have been the state of the World, without the powerful spread of Christianity; etc. These inquiries would lead us to such an accurate concatenation of circumstances, that at length we should learn to consider Rome, after the manner of the oriental sage, as a living creature, capable under such circumstances alone of rising from the banks of the Tiber, as from the sea; gradually acquiring strength to contend with all nations, by sea and land, subdue, and crush them; and lastly finding within itself the limits of its glory, and the origin of its corruption, as it actually did find them. Thus contemplated, everything arbitrary and irrational vanishes from history. In it, as in every production of nature, all, or nothing, is fortuitous; all, or nothing, is arbitrary. Every phenomenon in history is a natural production, and for man perhaps of all most worthy of contemplation; as in it so much depends on men, and he may find the most useful kernel, though included perhaps in a bitter shell, even in what lies without the sphere of his own powers, in the overbearing weight of times and circumstances; in the oppression of a Greece, a Carthage, or Numantia; in the murder of a Sertorius, a Spartacus, or a Viriatus; in the ruin of the younger Pompey, Drusus, Germanicus, or Britannicus. This is the only philosophical method of contemplating history, and it has been even unconsciously practiced by all thinking minds. Nothing has tended more to obstruct this impartial view, than the attempt to consider even the bloody history of Rome as subservient to some secret limited design of Providence: as, for instance, that Rome was raised to such a height principally for the production of orators and poets, for extending the Roman law and Latin language to the limits of its empire, and smoothing the way for the introduction of Christianity. . . .

Natural history has reaped no advantage from the philosophy of final causes, the sectaries of which have been inclined, to satisfy themselves with probable conjecture, instead of patient inquiry: how much less the history of mankind, with its endlessly complicated machinery of causes mutually acting upon each other!

We must also disapprove the opinion that, the Romans came on the stage in the succession of ages, to form a more perfect link in the chain of cultivation than the Greeks, as in a picture designed by man. . . . Nothing remains, therefore, but to consider the Roman nation, and the Latin languages, as bridges placed by Providence, for the conveyance of some of the treasures of antiquity to us. Yet for this purpose the bridges were the worst that could have been contrived, for of most of these treasures we were robbed by their very erection. The Romans were destroyers, and in their turn destroyed: but destroyers are not preservers of the World. They irritated all nations, till at length they became their prey; and Providence performed no miracle in their behalf. Let us, therefore, contemplate this, like any other natural phenomenon, the causes and effects of which we would investigate freely, without any preconceived hypothesis. The Romans were precisely what they were capable of becoming: everything perishable belonging to them perished, and what was susceptible of permanence remained. Ages roll on; and with them the offspring of ages, multiform man. Every thing that could blossom upon Earth has blossomed; each in its due season, and its proper sphere: it has withered away, and will blossom again, when its time arrives. The work of Providence pursues its eternal course according to grand universal laws. . . .

Humanity is the end of human nature. Thus everything in history is transient: the inscription on her temple is, evanescence and decay. We tread on the ashes of our forefathers and stalk over the entombed ruins of human institutions and kingdoms. Egypt, Persia, Greece, Rome, flit before us like shadows: like ghosts they rise from their graves and appear to us in the field of history.

When any political body has outlived its maturity, who would not wish it a quiet dissolution? Who does not shudder, when, in the circle of living active powers, he stumbles over the graves of ancient institutions, which rob the living of light and narrow their habitations? And when the present race has cleared away these catacombs, how soon will its institutions have a similar appearance to another, and be in like manner leveled with the earth!

The cause of this transitoriness of all terrestrial things lies in their essence, in the place they inhabit, and in the general laws to which our nature is subject. Man's body is a fragile, ever-renovating shell which at length can renew itself no longer: but his mind operates upon Earth only in and with the body. We fancy ourselves independent; yet we depend on all nature: implicated in a chain of incessantly fluctuating things, we must follow the laws of its permutation, which are nothing more than to be born, exist, and die. A slender thread connects the human race, which is every moment breaking, to be tied anew. The sage, whom time has made wise, sinks into the grave; that his successor may likewise begin his course as a child, perhaps madly destroy the work of his father, and leave to his son the same vain toil in which he too consumes his days. Thus year runs into year: thus generations and empires are linked together. The sun sets, that night may succeed, and mankind rejoices at the beams of a new morn.

Now were any advancement observable in all this, it would be something: but where is it to be found in history? In it we everywhere perceive destruction without being able to discern that what rises anew is better than what was destroyed. Nations flourish and decay: but in a faded nation no new flower, not to say a more beautiful one, ever blooms. Cultivation proceeds; yet becomes not more perfect by progress: in new places new capacities are developed; the ancient of the ancient places irrevocably pass away. Were the Romans more wise or more happy than the Greeks? Are we more so than either?

The nature of man remains ever the same: in the ten thousandth year of the World he will be born with passions, as he was born with passions in the two thousandth, and ran through his course of follies to a late, imperfect, useless wisdom. We wander in a labyrinth, in which our lives occupy but a span; so that it is to us nearly a matter of indifference, whether there be any entrance or outlet to the intricate path.

Melancholy fate of the human race! With all their exertions chained to an Ixion's wheel, to Sisyphus' stone, and condemned to the prospect of a Tantalus. We must will; and we must die, without having seen the fruit of our labors ripen, or learned a single result of human endeavors from the whole course of history. If a people stand alone, its characters wear away under the hand of Time: if it come into collision with others, it is thrown into the crucible where its impression is equally effaced. Thus we hew out blocks of ice; thus we write on the waves of the sea: the wave glides by, the ice melts; our palaces and our thoughts are both no more.

To what purpose then the unblessed labor to which God has condemned man as a daily task during his short life? To what purpose the burden under which every one toils on his way to the grave; while no one is asked, whether he will take it up or not, whether he will be born on this spot, at this period, and in this circle or no? Nay, as most of the evils among mankind arise from themselves, from their defective constitutions and governments, from the arrogance of oppressors, and from the almost inevitable weakness both of the governors and the governed; what fate was it that subjected man to the yoke of his fellows, to the mad or foolish will of his brother? Let a man sum up the periods of the happiness and unhappiness of nations, their good and bad rulers, nay the wisdom and folly, the predominance of reason and passion in the best: how vast will be the negative number! Look at the despots of Asia, of Africa, nay of almost the whole Earth: behold those monsters on the throne of Rome under whom a World groaned for centuries: note the troubles and wars, the oppressions and tumults that took place and mark the event. A Brutus falls and an Anthony triumphs; a Germanicus dies and a Tiberius, a Caligula, a Nero, reign; Aristides is banished; Confucius is a wanderer upon the Earth; Socrates, Phocion, Seneca are put to death. Everywhere it must be confessed, is discoverable the proposition: "What is, is; what can be, will be; what is susceptible of dissolution, dissolves:" a melancholy concession, however, which universally proclaims, that rude Violence, and his sister, malignant Cunning, are everywhere victorious upon Earth. . . .

Yet, if there be a god in nature, there is in history too: for man is also a part of the creation, and in his wildest extravagances and passions must obey laws, not less beautiful and excellent than those, by which all the celestial bodies move. Now as I am persuaded, that man is capable of knowing, and destined to attain the knowledge of everything that he ought to know: I step freely and confidently from the tumultuous scenes through which we have been wandering to inspect the beautiful and sublime laws of nature by which they have been governed.

The end of whatever is not merely a dead instrument must be

implicated in itself. Were we created to strive with eternally vain endeavors after a point of perfection external to ourselves, and which we could never reach, as the magnet turns to the north; we might not only pity ourselves as blind machines, but the Being likewise that had condemned us to such a state of tantalism in forming us for the purpose of such a malignant and diabolical spectacle. . . . But happily we are taught no such doctrine by the nature of things. If we consider mankind as we know it, and according to the laws intrinsic to it, we perceive nothing in man superior to humanity; for even if we think of angels or of gods, we conceive them as ideal, superior men. . . . In all states, in all societies, man has had nothing in view and could aim at nothing else but humanity, whatever may have been the idea he formed of it. For it, the arrangements of sex, and the different periods of life were made by nature; that our childhood might be of long continuance, and we might learn a kind of humanity by means of education. For it, all the different modes of life throughout the wide World have been established, all the forms of society introduced. . . . Thus whatever good appears in history to have been accomplished, humanity was the gainer; whatever foolish, vicious or execrable was perpetrated ran counter to humanity: so that in all his earthly institutions man can conceive no other end than what lies in himself, that is, in the weak or strong, base or noble nature that God gave him. . . .

This law of nature is not more simple than it is worthy of God, consistent and fertile in its consequences to mankind. Were man intended to be what he is and to become what he was capable of becoming, he must preserve a spontaneity of nature and be encompassed by a sphere of free actions disturbed by no preternatural miracle. . . .

The fundamental principle of this divine law of nature reconciles us wonderfully not only with the appearance of our species all over the Globe, but likewise with its variations through the different periods of time. Everywhere man is what he was capable of rendering himself, what he had the will and the power to become. . . .

Religion is the highest humanity of mankind. Let no one be surprised that I thus estimate it. If the understanding be the noblest endowment of man, it is the business of the understanding to trace the connection between cause and effect and to divine it where it is not apparent. . . . Eternal force of all life, all being and all form, Thou hast not foreborn to manifest Thyself to Thy creatures. The prone brute obscurely feels Thy power and goodness while he exercises his faculties and appetites suitably to his organization: to him man is the visible divinity of the Earth. But Thou hast exalted man so that, even without his knowing or intending it, he inquires after the causes of things, divines their connection and thus discovers Thee, Thou great bond of all things, Being of beings! Thy inmost nature he knows not; for he sees not the essence of any one power: and when he would figure Thee, he has erred and must err; for Thou art without figure though the first and sole cause of all forms. Still this false glimmering of Thee is light; and the illusive altar he has erected to Thee is an unerring monument, not only of Thy being, but of the power of man to know and worship Thee. Thus religion, considered merely as an exercise of the understanding, is the highest humanity, the noblest blossom of the human mind.

But it is more than this: it is an exercise of the human heart, and the purest direction of its capacities and powers. If man be created free and subject to no earthly law but what he imposes on himself, he must soon become the most savage of all creatures, if he does not quickly perceive the law of God in the works of Nature and strive as a child to imitate the perfections of his father. . . . True religion therefore is a filial service of God, an imitation of the most high and beautiful represented in the human form, with the extreme of inward satisfaction, active goodness and love of mankind. . . .

BIBLIOGRAPHY

Herder's *Ideen zur Philosophie der Geschichte der Menschheit* in 4 volumes was first published between 1784 and 1791. This work was translated by T. O. Churchill under the title *Outlines of a Philosophy of the History of Man* and published in London in 1800. A second edition came out in 1803.

BARNARD, F. M. *Between Enlightenment and Political Romanticism.* Oxford: 1964.

BARNARD, F. M. *Herder's Social and Political Thought.* Oxford: 1965.

BARNARD, F. M. "Herder's Treatment of Causation and Continuity," *Journal of the History of Ideas,* 1963.

CLARK, R. T. *Herder: His Life and Thought.* Berkeley: 1955.

COPLESTON, F. C. *History of Philosophy,* Vol. VI. Westminster, Md.: 1960.

ERGANG, R. R. *Herder and the Foundations of German Nationalism.* New York: 1963.

GILLIES, A. *Herder.* Oxford: 1945.

GILSON, E. and LANGAN, T. *Modern Philosophy: Descartes to Kant.* New York: 1963.

LOVEJOY, A. O. "Herder and the Enlightenment Theory of History," *Essays in the History of Ideas,* New York: 1960.

MCEACHRAN, FRANK. *The Life and Philosophy of Johann Gottfried Herder.* Oxford: 1939.

NEVINSON, H. A. *A Sketch of Herder and His Times.* London: 1884.

ROUCHE, M. *La Philosophie de l'histoire de Herder.* Paris: 1940.

SIMPSON, G. R. Herder's Conception of *"das Volk."* Chicago: 1921.

WELLS, G. A. *Herder and After: A Study in the Development of Sociology.* The Hague: 1959.

WELLS, G. A. "Herder's Determinism," *Journal of the History of Ideas,* 1958.

WELLS, G. A. "Herder's Two Philosophies of History," *Journal of the History of Ideas,* 1960.

5 G. W. F. Hegel   (1770–1831)

With Hegel, we come to perhaps the most important figure in the philosophy of history. R. G. Collingwood could say that in Hegel's writings, "History for the first time steps out full-grown on the stage of philosophical thought." [1] In the judgment of another, philosophy and history meet in Hegel. Hegel "was the outstanding philosopher of history, as well as historian of philosophy. But more than that, he was the one philosopher who decisively changed history." [2]

---

[1] R. G. Collingwood, *The Idea of History* (New York: Oxford University Press, 1946), p. 113.
[2] R. S. Hartman in the introduction to his translation of Hegel's Intro-

Hegel's *Lectures on the Philosophy of History* were delivered late in his life and were edited and published posthumously. Hegel conceives the task of the philosopher of history to be the discovery of the rationality of history. Is there any meaning and purpose in the historical process as a whole? Is history more than just a series of disconnected events? Hegel believed that only one assumption was necessary in his approach to history—"that Reason is the Sovereign of the world; that the history of the world, therefore, presents us with a rational process." While he admitted that this was an assumption in the philosophy of history, he believed that he had already proven this thesis in his other writings.

What we find in history, according to Hegel, is a record of how the human spirit (expressed in freedom) has developed or evolved out of nature. God or the World Spirit (*Weltgeist*) is manifested in time as human spirit. The essential nature of spirit is freedom; God seeks to produce this freedom in history. True freedom can exist only in a rational state; it is a voluntary, self-conscious obedience to law by people who are aware of their part in their culture. These people are not forced to obey the law. Obedience is a natural outgrowth of their being loyal citizens. Genuine freedom is never selfish or individualistic; individualistic freedom always produces anarchy.

Hegel is an uncompromising holist and statist. The individual counts for naught in his view. "All the worth which the human being possesses—all spiritual reality, he possesses only through the State." Only in the state is man's essence present to him objectively; only in a rational state does he become fully conscious. Truth is the synthesis of man's subjective will (his own thinking) and the universal Will (which is objectified in the laws and organization of the State). "The State," Hegel writes, "is the Divine Idea as it exists on Earth."

If the ultimate goal of history is the attainment of human free-

---

duction to his *Lectures,* published under the title, *Reason in History* (New York: Liberal Arts Press, 1953), p. ix. Hartman is referring, of course, to Hegel's impact on history through his influence on Communism and Fascism. The history of this influence is traced in Sidney Hook's *From Hegel to Marx* (New York: 1935) and H. Marcuse's *Reason and Revolution* (New York: 1941).

dom within the limits of a rational state, what is the means by which this goal is reached? Hegel's reply, somewhat reminiscent of Kant's "unsocial sociability" and similar concepts in Herder and Vico, is the passions of men. Freedom develops through the external phenomena which we see in history. Spirit uses and works through the totality of blind drives, passions, and interests of men. Spirit progresses as men are moved by their desires. Thus, the passions of men are the main spring of history. These passions, however despicable, and the acts which may follow should never be considered wrong since they are necessary means to an end.

Hegel, again sounding like Kant, admits that history presents us with discouraging scenes of murder, mayhem, vice, and greed which seem to vitiate his claim that history is a teleological process. Even though history is "the slaughter bench at which the happiness of peoples, the wisdom of states, and the virtues of individuals have been victimized," all this carnage is part of the Spirit's process of self-realization. Hegel calls this "the cunning of reason." In the depressing record of tragedy, heartbreak, and stupidity is to be found the very means by which Freedom develops. Individual men—their dreams, hopes, ambitions, and happiness—are grist to its mill. Only the Universal, the State, is real. The individual and the particular must perish. But through their destruction, the Universal is realized.

Whenever the World Spirit must initiate new and difficult turns in human history, it makes use of certain individuals whom Hegel calls "Heroes." These world-historical men are those who seem to grasp a higher universal, make it their own purpose and realize it in accordance with the Spirit's higher law. They seem to be, and even think themselves, that they are merely following their own desires. They have no consciousness of the Spirit itself. But in reality, their own particular purposes contain substantially the will of the World Spirit. While these "heroes" are not aware of the Spirit as such, while they think they are only working for their own satisfaction, they nonetheless have their finger on the pulse of the time. They know what things are needed; they are the leaders of their age. But they can never be happy for they are always in breathless pursuit of what they take to be their aim. In Hegel's words, "Their whole life was labor and trouble, their whole nature was naught else but their Master Passion. When their object is attained, they fall off like empty hulls from the kernel." Alexander died young, Caesar was murdered, Napoleon was exiled to Saint Helena. The world-historical individual is not considerate. He drives relentlessly toward his one purpose, often crushing down as he would helpless flowers, many innocent individuals in his path.

The development of Freedom in human history can be seen in several stages. Hegel first drew attention to the nations of the East such as China and India. He spoke of them as "the immersion of Spirit in natural life." The State appeared first in them as an immediate, natural unity—as a despotism. Because the form of government was an absolute monarchy, Freedom was merely potential. Because the orientals did not know that man, the universal, is free, they were not free. Even the ruler, the despot, was not free since true Freedom can exist only under law. The "freedom" of the despot was merely caprice.

As time passed, individuals became more conscious of their potentialities and began to organize their relationships in accordance with reason. The scene shifted from the Orient to the Mediterranean; the principal units of history became the nations of Greece and Rome. In place of a despotism, the form of government was now democratic or aristocratic. No longer was just one man free; there was now some measure of individual freedom. The important innovation among the Greeks was the introduction of the notion of law. Social order thus was transformed into the dialectical tension between law and citizen, between universal and particular. But the Greeks only knew that some men were free, not that man, the universal, was free. Since only some were subject to law in Greece, the essential rights of all men, insofar as they were men, were not yet recognized. Therefore, Freedom for the Greeks was "accidental."

In Hegel's own Christian Germany, he believed, the state rose out of the particular forms of freedom existing in the past into universal freedom. In the constitutional governments of his day, all men were free. There was "one lord and no serf" because men willingly submerged themselves in the universal idea.

Without attempting to enter into a full-fledged critique of

Hegel, at least one major difficulty seems to stand out. Given Hegel's belief that history is a rational process moving inevitably toward a particular goal, does it not follow for him that everything that happens is justified by the mere fact that it happens? Despite all of Hegel's talk about blood and gore in history, it does seem as if he dismisses all too casually the problem of evil.

At any rate, Hegel's philosophy of history is an obvious continuation of the work begun by St. Augustine and carried on by Vico, Herder, Kant, and others. But Hegel's work also sets the stage for the next speculative approach to history that we shall notice—that of Marx and Engels.

G. W. F. HEGEL
THE PHILOSOPHY OF HISTORY *

The history of the world is nothing but the development of the Idea of Freedom. But Objective Freedom—the laws of *real* freedom—demand the subjugation of the mere contingent Will —for this is in its nature formal. If the Objective is in itself rational, human insight and conviction must correspond with the Reason which it embodies, and then we have the other essential element—Subjective Freedom—also realized.[1] We have confined ourselves to the consideration of that progress of the Idea [which has led to this consummation], and have been obliged to forego the pleasure of giving a detailed picture of the prosperity, the periods of glory that have distinguished the career of peoples, the beauty and grandeur of the character of individuals, and the interest attaching to their fate in weal or woe. Philosophy concerns itself only with the glory of the Idea mirroring itself in the history of the world. Philosophy escapes from the weary strife of passions that agitate the surface of society into the calm region of

---

* The following selections are taken from J. Sibree's translation of the second German edition of Hegel's *Philosophy of History* (1840). The passages come from Hegel's conclusion to the entire work, from his Introduction, and from his section entitled "Classification of Historical Data."

[1] That is, the will of the individual goes along with the requirements of reasonable laws.—Tr.

contemplation; that which interests it is the recognition of the process of development which the Idea has passed through in realizing itself—i.e., the Idea of Freedom, whose reality is the consciousness of freedom and nothing short of it.

That the history of the world, with all the changing scenes which its annals present, is this process of development and the realization of Spirit—this is the true *Theodicaea,* the justification of God in history. Only *this* insight can reconcile Spirit with the history of the world—viz., that what has happened, and is happening every day, is not only not "without God," but is essentially His work. . . .

The presupposition of the philosophy of history. The only thought which philosophy brings with it to the contemplation of history, is the simple conception of *Reason;* that Reason is the Sovereign of the world; that the history of the world, therefore, presents us with a rational process. This conviction and intuition is a hypothesis in the domain of history as such. In that of philosophy it is no hypothesis. It is there proved by speculative cognition, that Reason—and this term may here suffice us, without investigating the relation sustained by the Universe to the Divine Being—is *Substance,* as well as *Infinite Power;* its own *Infinite Material* underlying all the natural and spiritual life which it originates, as also the *Infinite Form*—that which sets this Material in motion. On the one hand, Reason is the *substance* of the Universe; viz., that by which and in which all reality has its being and subsistence. On the other hand, it is the *Infinite Energy* of the Universe; since Reason is not so powerless as to be incapable of producing anything but a mere ideal, a mere intention—having its place outside reality, nobody knows where; something separate and abstract, in the heads of certain human beings.
. . . That this "Idea" or "Reason" is the *True,* the *Eternal,* the absolutely powerful *essence;* that it reveals itself in the world, and that in that world nothing else is revealed but this and its honor and glory—is the thesis which, as we have said, has been proved in philosophy, and is here regarded as demonstrated. . . .

The world is not abandoned to chance and external contingent causes, but . . . a *Providence* controls it. . . . *Divine* Providence is Wisdom, endowed with an infinite Power, which realizes its aim, viz., the absolute rational design of the world. Reason is Thought conditioning itself with perfect freedom. . . . To explain history is to depict the passions of mankind, the genius, the active powers, that play their part on the great stage; and the providentially determined process which these exhibit constitutes what is generally called the "plan" of Providence. . . .

What is the ultimate design of the world? . . . It must be observed at the outset, that the phenomenon we investigate—Universal History—belongs to the realm of *Spirit*. The term *"World,"* includes both physical and psychical Nature. Physical Nature also plays its part in the World's History, and attention will have to be paid to the fundamental natural relations thus involved. But Spirit, and the course of its development, is our substantial object. Our task does not require us to contemplate Nature as a Rational System in itself—though in its own proper domain it proves itself such—but simply in its relation to *Spirit*. . . .

We have therefore to mention here:

1) The abstract characteristics of the nature of Spirit.

2) What means Spirit uses in order to realize its Idea.

3) Lastly, we must consider the shape which the perfect embodiment of Spirit assumes—the State.

1) The nature of Spirit may be understood by a glance at its direct opposite—*Matter*. As the essence of Matter is gravity, so, on the other hand, we may affirm that the substance, the essence of Spirit is Freedom. All will readily assent to the doctrine that Spirit, among other properties, is also endowed with Freedom; but philosophy teaches that all the qualities of Spirit exist only through Freedom; that all are but means for attaining Freedom; that all seek and produce this and this alone. It is a result of speculative philosophy, that Freedom is the sole truth of Spirit. . . . Spirit is *self-contained existence*. Now this is Freedom exactly. For if I am dependent, my being is referred to something else which I am not; I cannot exist independently of something external. I am free, on the contrary, when my existence depends upon myself. This self-contained existence of Spirit is none other than self-consciousness—consciousness of one's own being. Two things must be distinguished in consciousness; first, the fact *that I know;* secondly, *what I know*. In *self* consciousness these

are merged in one; for Spirit *knows itself*. It involves an appreciation of its own nature, as also an energy enabling it to realize itself; to make itself *actually* that which it is *potentially*. According to this abstract definition it may be said of Universal History, that it is the exhibition of Spirit in the process of working out the knowledge of that which it is potentially. . . . The Orientals have not attained the knowledge that Spirit—Man *as such*—is free; and because they do not know this, they are not free. They only know that *one is free*. But on this very account, the freedom of that one is only caprice; ferocity—brutal recklessness of passion, or a mildness and tameness of the desires, which is itself only an accident of Nature—mere caprice like the former. That *one* is therefore only a Despot; not a *free man*. The consciousness of Freedom first arose among the Greeks, and therefore they were free; but they, and the Romans likewise, knew only that *some* are free—not man as such. Even Plato and Aristotle did not know this. The Greeks, therefore, had slaves; and their whole life and the maintenance of their splendid liberty, was implicated with the institution of slavery: a fact, moreover, which made that liberty on the one hand only an accidental, transient, and limited growth; on the other hand, constituted it a rigorous thralldom of our common nature—of the Human. The German nations, under the influence of Christianity, were the first to attain the consciousness, that man, as man, is free: that it is the *freedom* of Spirit which constitutes its essence. . . . The history of the world is none other than the progress of the consciousness of freedom; a progress whose development according to the necessity of its nature it is our business to investigate. . . .

2) The question of the *means* by which Freedom develops itself to a world, conducts us to the phenomenon of history itself. Although Freedom is, primarily, an undeveloped idea, the means it uses are external and phenomenal; presenting themselves in History to our sensuous vision. The first glance at history convinces us that the actions of men proceed from their needs, their passions, their characters and talents; and impresses us with the belief that such needs, passions, and interests are the sole springs of action—the efficient agents in this scene of activity. Among these may, perhaps, be found aims of a liberal or universal kind

—benevolence it may be, or noble patriotism; but such virtues and general views are but insignificant as compared with the world and its doings. We may perhaps see the Ideal of Reason actualized in those who adopt such aims, and within the sphere of their influence; but they bear only a trifling proportion to the mass of the human race; and the extent of that influence is limited accordingly. Passions, private aims, and the satisfaction of selfish desires, are, on the other hand, most effective springs of action. Their power lies in the fact that they respect none of the limitations which justice and morality would impose on them; and that these natural impulses have a more direct influence over man than the artificial and tedious discipline that tends to order and self-restraint, law and morality. When we look at this display of passions, and the consequences of their violence; the Unreason which is associated not only with them, but even (rather we might say *especially*) with *good* designs and righteous aims; when we see the evil, the vice, the ruin that has befallen the most flourishing kingdoms which the mind of man ever created; we can scarce avoid being filled with sorrow at this universal taint of corruption; and, since this decay is not the work of mere Nature, but of the human will—a moral embitterment—a revolt of the Good Spirit (if it have a place within us) may well be the result of our reflections. . . . But even regarding history as the slaughter bench at which the happiness of peoples, the wisdom of states, and the virtue of individuals have been victimized—the question involuntarily arises—to what principle, to what final aim these enormous sacrifices have been offered. . . . We assert then that nothing has been accomplished without interest on the part of the actors; and—if interest be called passion, . . . we may affirm absolutely that *nothing great in the world has been accomplished without passion*. . . .

In the process of the world's history itself—as still incomplete—the abstract final aim of history is not yet made the distinct object of desire and interest. While these limited sentiments are still unconscious of the purpose they are fulfilling, the universal principle is implicit in them, and is realizing itself through them. . . . An additional result is commonly produced by human actions beyond that which they aim at and obtain—that which they immediately recognize and desire. They gratify their own interest; but something further is thereby accomplished, latent in the actions in question, though not present to their consciousness, and not included in their design. . . .

World-historical individuals. Caesar, in danger of losing a position, not perhaps at that time of superiority, yet at least of equality with the others who were at the head of the State, and of succumbing to those who were just on the point of becoming his enemies—belongs essentially to this category. These enemies —who were at the same time pursuing *their* personal aims— had the form of the constitution, and the power conferred by an appearance of justice, on their side. Caesar was contending for the maintenance of his position, honor, and safety; and, since the power of his opponents included the sovereignty over the provinces of the Roman Empire, his victory secured for him the conquest of that entire Empire; and he thus became (though leaving the form of the constitution) the Autocrat of the State. That which secured for him the execution of a design, which in the first instance was of negative import—the Autocracy of Rome —was, however, at the same time an independently necessary feature in the history of Rome and of the world. It was not then his private gain merely, but an unconscious impulse that occasioned the accomplishment of that for which the time was ripe. Such are all great historical men—whose own particular aims involve those large issues which are the will of the World Spirit. They may be called Heroes, inasmuch as they have derived their purposes and their vocation, not from the calm, regular course of things, sanctioned by the existing order; but from a concealed fount—one which has not attained to phenomenal, present existence—from that inner Spirit, still hidden beneath the surface, which, impinging on the outer world as on a shell, burst it in pieces, because it is another kernel than that which belonged to the shell in question. They are men, therefore, who appear to draw the impulse of their life from themselves; and whose deeds have produced a condition of things and a complex of historical relations which appear to be only *their* interest, and *their* work.

Such individuals had no consciousness of the general Idea they were unfolding, while prosecuting those aims of theirs; on the contrary, they were practical, political men. But at the same time they were thinking men, who had an insight into the requirements of the time—*what was ripe for development*. This was the very Truth for their age, for their world; the species next in order, so to speak, and which was already formed in the womb of time. It was theirs to know this nascent principle; the necessary, directly sequent step in progress, which their world was to take; to make this their aim, and to expend their energy in promoting it. World-historical men—the Heroes of an epoch—must, therefore, be recognized as its clear-sighted ones; *their* deeds, *their* words are the best of that time. Great men have formed purposes to satisfy themselves, not others. Whatever prudent designs and counsels they might have learned from others, would be the more limited and inconsistent features in their career; for it was they who best understood affairs; from whom *others* learned, and approved, or at least acquiesced in —their policy. For that Spirit which had taken this fresh step in history is the inmost soul of all individuals; but in a state of unconsciousness which the great men in question aroused. Their fellows, therefore, follow these soul-leaders; for they feel the irresistible power of their own inner Spirit thus embodied. If we go on to cast a look at the fate of these world historical persons, whose vocation it was to be the agents of the World Spirit, we shall find it to have been no happy one. They attained no calm enjoyment; their whole life was labor and trouble; their whole nature was naught else but their Master Passion. When their object is attained they fall off like empty hulls from the kernel. They die early, like Alexander; they are murdered, like Caesar; transported to St. Helena, like Napoleon. This fearful consolation—that historical men have not enjoyed what is called happiness, and of which only private life (and this may be passed under very various external circumstances) is capable—this consolation those may draw from history, who stand in need of it; and it is craved by Envy—vexed at what is great and transcendent—striving, therefore, to depreciate it, and to find some flaw in it. Thus in modern times it has been demonstrated *ad nauseam* that princes are generally unhappy on their thrones; in consideration of which the possession of a throne is tolerated, and men acquiesce in the fact that not themselves but the personages in question are its occupants. The Free Man, we may observe, is not envious, but gladly recognizes what is great and exalted, and rejoices that it exists.

It is in the light of those common elements which constitute the interest and therefore the passions of individuals, that these historical men are to be regarded. They are *great* men, because they willed and accomplished something great; not a mere fancy, a mere intention, but that which met the case and fell in with the needs of the age. . . . A World-historical individual is not so unwise as to indulge a variety of wishes to divide his regards. He is devoted to the One Aim, regardless of all else. It is even possible that such men may treat other great, even sacred interests, inconsiderately; conduct which is indeed obnoxious to moral reprehension. But so mighty a form must trample down many an innocent flower—crush to pieces many an object in its path.

The special interest of passion is thus inseparable from the active development of a general principle: for it is from the special and determinate and from its negation that the Universal results. Particularity contends with its like, and some loss is involved in the issue. *It* is not the general idea that is implicated in opposition and combat, and that is exposed to danger. It remains in the background, untouched and uninjured. This may be called the *cunning of reason*—that it sets the passions to work for itself, while that which develops its existence through such impulsion pays the penalty, and suffers loss. For it is *phenomenal* being that is so treated, and of this, part is of no value, part is positive and real. The particular is for the most part of too trifling value as compared with the general: individuals are sacrificed and abandoned. The Idea pays the penalty of determinate existence and of corruptibility, not from itself, but from the passions of individuals. . . .

(3) The third point to be analyzed is, therefore—what is the object to be realized by these means; i.e., what is the form it assumes in the realm of reality. We have spoken of *means;* but in the carrying out of a subjective, limited aim, we have also to take into consideration the element of a *material,* either already present or which has to be procured. Thus the question would arise: What is the material in which the Ideal of Reason is wrought out? The primary answer would be—Personality

itself—human desires—Subjectivity generally. In human knowledge and volition, as its material element, Reason attains positive existence. . . . As a subjective will, occupied with limited passions, it is dependent, and can gratify its desires only within the limits of this dependence. But the subjective will has also a substantial life—a reality—in which it moves in the region of *essential* being, and has the essential itself as the object of its existence. This essential being is the union of the *subjective* with the *rational* Will: it is the moral Whole, the *State,* which is that form of reality in which the individual has and enjoys his freedom; but on the condition of his recognizing, believing in and willing that which is common to the Whole. And this must not be understood as if the subjective will of the social unit attained its gratification and enjoyment through that common Will; as if this were a means provided for its benefit; as if the individual, in his relations to other individuals, thus limited his freedom, in order that this universal limitation —the mutual constraint of all—might secure a small space of liberty for each. Rather, we affirm, are Law, Morality, Government, and they alone, the positive reality and completion of Freedom. Freedom of a low and limited order is mere caprice, which finds its exercise in the sphere of particular and limited desires.

Subjective volition—Passion—is that which sets men in activity, that which effects "practical" realization. The Idea is the inner spring of action; the State is the actually existing, realized moral life. For it is the Unity of the universal, essential Will, with that of the individual; and this is "Morality." . . . The laws of morality are not accidental, but are the essentially Rational. It is the very object of the State that what is essential in the practical activity of men, and in their dispositions, should be duly recognized; that it should have a manifest existence, and maintain its position. It is the absolute interest of Reason that this moral Whole should exist: and herein lies the justification and merit of heroes who have founded states—however rude these may have been. In the history of the World, only those peoples can come under our notice which form a state. . . . In the history of the World, the *Individuals* we have to do with are *Peoples;* Totalities that are States. . . . For it must be understood that [the State] is the realization of Freedom, i.e., of the absolute final aim, and that it exists for its own sake. It must further be understood that all the worth which the human being possesses—all spiritual reality, he possesses only through the State. For his spiritual reality consists in this, that his own essence—Reason—is objectively present to him, that it possesses objective immediate existence for him. Thus only is he fully conscious; thus only is he a partaker of Morality—of a just and moral social and political life. For Truth is the Unity of the universal and subjective Will; and the Universal is to be found in the State, in its laws, its universal and rational arrangements. The State is the Divine Idea as it exists on earth. We have in it, therefore, the object of History in a more definite shape than before; that in which Freedom obtains objectivity, and lives in the enjoyment of this objectivity. For Law is the objectivity of Spirit; volition in its true form. Only that will which obeys law, is free; for it obeys itself—it is independent and so free. When the State or our country constitutes a community of existence; when the subjective will of man submits to laws—the contradiction between Liberty and Necessity vanishes. The Rational has necessary existence, as being the reality and substance of things, and we are free in recognizing it as law, and following it as the substance of our own being. The objective and the subjective will are then reconciled, and present one identical homogeneous whole. For the Morality (*Sittlichkeit*) of the State is not of that ethical (*moralische*) reflective kind, in which one's own conviction bears sway; this latter is rather the peculiarity of the modern time, while the true antique morality is based on the principle of abiding by one's duty [to the state at large]. . . .

Summing up what has been said of the State, we find that we have been led to call its vital principle, as actuating the individuals who compose it—Morality. The State, its laws, its arrangements, constitute the rights of its members; its natural features, its mountains, air, and waters, are *their* country, their fatherland, their outward material property; the history of this State, *their* deeds; what their ancestors have produced belongs to them and lives in their memory. All is their possession, just as they are possessed by it; for it constitutes their existence, their being.

Their imagination is occupied with the ideas thus presented, while the adoption of these laws, and of a fatherland so conditioned is the expression of their will. It is this matured totality which thus constitutes *one* Being, the spirit of *one* People. To it the individual members belong; each unit is the Son of his Nation, and at the same time—in as far as the State to which he belongs is undergoing development—the Son of his Age. None remains behind it, still less advances beyond it. This spiritual Being (the Spirit of his Time) is his; he is a representative of it; it is that in which he originated, and in which he lives. Among the Athenians the word Athens had a double import; suggesting primarily, a complex of political institutions, but no less, in the second place, that Goddess who represented the Spirit of the People and its unity. . . .

The remark next in order is, that each particular National genius is to be treated as only One Individual in the process of Universal History. For that history is the exhibition of the divine, absolute development of Spirit in its highest forms—that gradation by which it attains its truth and consciousness of itself. The forms which these grades of progress assume are the characteristic "National Spirits" of History; the peculiar tenor of their moral life, of their government, their art, religion, and science. To realize these grades is the boundless impulse of the World Spirit—the goal of its irresistible urging; for this division into organic members, and the full development of each, is its Idea. Universal History is exclusively occupied with showing how Spirit comes to a recognition and adoption of the Truth: the dawn of knowledge appears; it begins to discover salient principles, and at last it arrives at full consciousness. . . .

In the geographical survey, the course of the World's History has been marked out in its general features. The *Sun*—the Light—rises in the East. Light is a simply self-involved existence; but though possessing thus in itself universality, it exists at the same time as an individuality in the Sun. Imagination has often pictured to itself the emotions of a blind man suddenly becoming possessed of sight, beholding the bright glimmering of the dawn, the growing light, and the flaming glory of the ascending Sun. The boundless forgetfulness of his individuality in this pure splendor, is his first feeling—utter astonishment. But when the Sun is risen, this astonishment is diminished; objects around are perceived, and from them the individual proceeds to the contemplation of his own inner being, and thereby the advance is made to the perception of the relation between the two. Then inactive contemplation is quitted for activity; by the close of day man has erected a building constructed from his own inner Sun; and when in the evening he contemplates this, he esteems it more highly than the original external Sun. For now he stands in a *conscious relation* to his Spirit, and therefore a *free* relation. If we hold this image fast in mind, we shall find it symbolizing the course of History, the great Day's work of spirit.

The History of the World travels from East to West, for Europe is absolutely the end of History, Asia the beginning. The History of the World has an East (the term East in itself is entirely relative); for although the Earth forms a sphere, History performs no circle round it, but has on the contrary a determinate East, viz., Asia. Here rises the outward physical Sun, and in the West it sinks down: here consentaneously rises the Sun of self-consciousness, which diffuses a nobler brilliance. The History of the World is the discipline of the uncontrolled natural will, bringing it into obedience to a Universal principle and conferring subjective freedom. The East knew and to the present day knows only that *One* is Free; the Greek and Roman world, that *some* are free; the German world knows that *All* are free. The first political form therefore which we observe in History is *Despotism,* the second *Democracy* and *Aristocracy,* the third *Monarchy*.

To understand this division we must remark that as the State is the universal spiritual life, to which individuals by birth sustain a relation of confidence and habit, and in which they have their existence and reality—the first question is, whether their actual life is an unreflecting use and habit combining them in this unity, or whether its constituent individuals are reflective and personal beings having a properly subjective and independent existence. In view of this, *substantial* (objective) freedom must be distinguished from *subjective* freedom. Substantial freedom is the abstract undeveloped Reason implicit in volition, proceeding to develop itself in the State. But in this phase of Reason there is still wanting personal insight and will, that is, subjective freedom; which is realized only in the Individual, and which constitutes the reflection of the Individual in his own conscience. Where there is merely substantial freedom, commands and laws are regarded as something fixed and abstract, to which the subject holds himself in absolute servitude. These laws need not concur with the desire of the individual, and the subjects are consequently like children, who obey their parents without will or insight of their own. But as subjective freedom arises, and man descends from the contemplation of external reality into his own soul, the contrast suggested by reflection arises, involving the Negation of Reality. The drawing back from the actual world forms ipso facto an antithesis, of which one side is the absolute Being—the Divine—the other the human subject as an individual. In that immediate, unreflected consciousness which characterizes the East, these two are not yet distinguished. The substantial world is distinct from the individual, but the antithesis has not yet created a schism between [absolute and subjective] Spirit.

The first phase—that with which we have to begin—is the East. Unreflected consciousness—substantial, objective, spiritual existence—forms the basis; to which the subjective will first sustains a relation in the form of faith, confidence, obedience. In the political life of the East we find a realized rational freedom, developing itself without advancing to *subjective* freedom. It is the childhood of History. Substantial forms constitute the gorgeous edifices of Oriental *Empires,* in which we find all rational ordinances and arrangements, but in such a way that individuals remain as mere accidents. These revolve round the sovereign, who, as patriarch—not as despot in the sense of the *Roman* Imperial Constitution—stands at the head. For he has to enforce the moral and substantial; he has to uphold those essential ordinances which are already established; so that what among us belongs entirely to subjective freedom here proceeds from the entire and general body of the State.

The glory of the Oriental conception is the One Individual as that substantial being to which all belongs, so that no other individual has a separate existence, or mirrors himself in his subjective freedom. All the riches of imagination and Nature are appropriated to that dominant existence in which subjective freedom is essentially merged; the latter looks for its dignity *not* in itself, but in that absolute object. All the elements of a complete State—even subjectivity—may be found there, but not yet harmonized with the grand substantial being. For outside the One Power—before which nothing can maintain an independent existence—there is only revolting caprice, which, beyond the limits of the central power, roves at will without purpose or result. Accordingly we find the wild hordes breaking out from the Upland—falling upon the countries in question, and laying them waste, or settling down in them, and giving up their wild life; but in all cases resultlessly lost in the central substance. This phase of Substantiality, since it has not taken up its antithesis into itself and overcome it, directly divides itself into two elements. On the one side we see duration, stability—Empires belonging to mere space, as it were (as distinguished from Time)—unhistorical History;—as, for example, in China, the State based on the Family relation;—a paternal Government, which holds together the constitution by its provident care, its admonitions, retributive or rather disciplinary inflictions;—a prosaic Empire, because the antithesis of Form, viz., Infinity, Ideality, has not yet asserted itself. On the other side, the Form of Time stands contrasted with this spatial stability. The States in question, without undergoing any change in themselves, or in the principle of their existence, are constantly changing their position toward each other. They are in ceaseless conflict, which brings on rapid destruction. The opposing principle of individuality enters into these conflicting relations; but it is itself as yet only unconscious, merely natural Universality—Light, which is not yet the light of the personal soul. This History, too (i.e., of the struggles before mentioned), is, for the most part, really *unhistorical*, for it is only the repetition of the same majestic ruin. The new element, which in the shape of bravery, prowess, magnanimity, occupies the place of the previous despotic pomp, goes through the same circle of decline and subsidence. This subsidence is therefore not really such, for through all this restless change no advance is made. History passes at this point—and only outwardly, i.e., without connection with the previous phase—to Central Asia. Continuing the comparison with the ages of the individual man, this would be the boyhood of History, no longer manifesting the repose and trustingness of the child, but boisterous and turbulent. The Greek world may then be compared with the period of adolescence, for here we have individualities forming themselves. This is the *second* main principle in human History. Morality is, as in Asia, a principle; but it is morality impressed on individuality, and consequently denoting the free volition of Individuals. Here, then, is the Union of the Moral with the subjective Will, or the Kingdom of *Beautiful Freedom,* for the Idea is united with a plastic form. It is not yet regarded abstractedly, but immediately bound up with the Real, as in a beautiful work of Art; the Sensuous bears the stamp and expression of the Spiritual. This Kingdom is consequently true Harmony; the world of the most charming, but perishable or quickly passing bloom: it is the natural, unreflecting observance of what is *becoming* —not yet true *Morality.* The individual will of the Subjects adopts unreflectingly the conduct and habit prescribed by Justice and the Laws. The Individual is therefore in unconscious unity with the Idea—the social weal. That which in the East is divided into two extremes—the substantial as such, and the individuality absorbed in it—meets here. But these distinct principles are only *immediately* in unity, and consequently involve the highest degree of contradiction; for this aesthetic Morality has not yet passed through the struggle of subjective freedom, in its second birth, its *palingenesis;* it is not yet purified to the standard of the free subjectivity that is the essence of true Morality.

The third phase is the realm of abstract Universality (in which the Social aim absorbs all individual aims): it is the *Roman State,* the severe labors of the *Manhood* of History. For true manhood acts neither in accordance with the caprice of a despot, nor in obedience to a graceful caprice of its own; but works for a general aim, one in which the individual perishes and realizes his own private object only in that general aim.

The State begins to have an abstract existence, and to develop itself for a definite object, in accomplishing which its members have indeed a share, but not a complete and concrete one [calling their whole being into play]. Free *individuals* are sacrificed to the severe demands of the *National* objects, to which they must surrender themselves in this service of abstract generalization. The Roman State is not a repetition of such a State of Individuals as the Athenian Polis was. The geniality and joy of soul that existed there have given place to harsh and rigorous toil. The interest of History is detached from individuals, but these gain for themselves abstract, formal Universality. The Universal subjugates the individuals; they have to merge their own interests in it; but in return the abstraction which they themselves embody—that is to say, their personality—is recognized: in their individual capacity they become persons with definite rights as such. In the same sense as individuals may be said to be incorporated in the abstract idea of Person, *National Individualities* (those of the Roman Provinces) have also to experience this fate: in this form of Universality their concrete forms are crushed, and incorporated with it as a homogeneous and indifferent mass. Rome becomes a Pantheon of all deities, and of all Spiritual existence, but these divinities and this Spirit do not retain their proper vitality. The development of the State in question proceeds in two directions. On the one hand, as based on reflection—abstract Universality—it has the express outspoken antithesis in itself: it therefore essentially involves in itself the struggle which that antithesis supposes; with the necessary issue, that individual caprice—the purely contingent and thoroughly worldly power of one despot—gets the better of that abstract universal principle. At the very outset we have the antithesis between the Aim of the State as the abstract universal principle on the one hand, and the abstract personality of the individual on the other hand. But when subsequently, in the historical development, individuality gains the ascendant, and the breaking up of the community into its component atoms can only be restrained by external compulsion, then the subjective might of *individual despotism* comes forward to play its part, as if summoned to fulfil this task. For the mere abstract compliance with Law implies on the part of the subject of law the supposition that he has not attained to self-organization and self-control; and this principle of obedience, instead of being hearty and voluntary, has for its motive and ruling power only the arbitrary and contingent disposition of the individual; so that the latter is led to seek consolation for the loss of his freedom in exercising and developing his private right. This is the purely *worldly* harmonization of the antithesis. But in the next place, the pain inflicted by Despotism begins to be felt, and Spirit, driven back into its utmost depths, leaves the godless world, seeks for a harmony in itself, and begins now an inner life—a complete concrete subjectivity, which possesses at the same time a substantiality that is not grounded in mere external existence. Within the soul therefore arises the *Spiritual* pacification of the struggle, in the fact that the individual personality, instead of following its own capricious choice, is purified and elevated into universality;—a subjectivity that of its own free will adopts principles tending to the good of all—reaches, in fact, a divine personality. To that worldly empire, this Spiritual one wears a predominant aspect of opposition, as the empire of a subjectivity that has attained to the knowledge of itself—itself in its essential nature—the Empire of Spirit in its full sense.

The *German* world appears at this point of development—the fourth phase of world history. . . . The German Spirit is the Spirit of the new world. Its aim is the realization of absolute Truth as the unlimited self-determination of freedom—*that* freedom which has its own absolute form itself as its purport.[2] The destiny of the German peoples is, to be the bearers of the Christian principle. The principle of Spiritual Freedom—of Reconciliation [of the Objective and Subjective], was introduced

---

[2] That is: The Supreme Law of the universe is recognized as identical with the dictates of conscience—becomes a "law of liberty." Morality —that authority which has the incontestable right to determine men's actions, which therefore is the only absolutely *free* and unlimited power —is no longer a compulsory enactment, but the free choice of human beings. The good man would make Law for himself if he found none made for him.—Tr.

into the still simple, unformed minds of those peoples; and the part assigned to them in the service of the World Spirit was that of not merely possessing the Idea of Freedom as the substratum of their religious conceptions, but of producing it in free and spontaneous developments from their subjective self-consciousness. . . .

[The German world] would answer in the comparison with the periods of human life to its *Old Age*. The Old Age of *Nature* is weakness; but that of *Spirit* is its perfect maturity and *strength*, in which it returns to unity with itself, but in its fully developed character as *Spirit*. . . . That principle of the German world which we are now discussing, attained concrete reality only in the history of the German Nations. The contrast of the Spiritual principle animating the *Ecclesiastical* State, with the rough and wild barbarism of the Secular State, is here likewise present. The secular *ought* to be in harmony with the spiritual principle, but we find nothing more than the *recognition* of that obligation. The secular power forsaken by the spirit, must in the first instance vanish in the presence of the ecclesiastical [as representative of Spirit]; but while this latter degrades itself to mere secularity, it loses its influence with the loss of its proper character and vocation. From this corruption of the ecclesiastical element—that is, of the Church—results the higher form of rational thought. Spirit, once more driven back upon itself, produces its work in an intellectual shape, and becomes capable of realizing the Ideal of Reason from the secular principle alone. Thus it happens, that in virtue of elements of universality, which have the principle of Spirit as their basis, the empire of Thought is established actually and concretely. The antithesis of Church and State vanishes. The spiritual becomes reconnected with the secular, and develops this latter as an independently organic existence. The State no longer occupies a position of real inferiority to the Church, and is no longer subordinate to it. The latter asserts no prerogative, and the spiritual is no longer an element foreign to the State. Freedom has found the means of realizing its Ideal—its true existence. This is the ultimate result which the process of history is intended to accomplish. . . .

BIBLIOGRAPHY

J. Sibree's translation of the third German edition of Hegel's *Vorlesungen über die Philosophie der Geschichte* was first published in 1858. It has since been reprinted many times both in hard covers and in paperback. R. S. Hartman's *Reason in History*, New York: Liberal Arts Press, 1953, is an edited translation of the introduction to Hegel's lectures on the philosophy of history. Also helpful are Hegel's *The Philosophy of Right* and *Hegel's Political Writings*, both translated by T. M. Knox and published by Oxford University Press.

CHRISTENSEN, D. E. "Nelson and Hegel on Philosophy of History," *Journal of the History of Ideas*, 1964.
DRAY, W. H. *Philosophy of History*. Englewood Cliffs, New Jersey: 1964.
DUPRE, LOUIS K. *The Philosophical Foundations of Marxism*. New York: 1966.
FINDLAY, J. N. *Hegel: A Re-Examination*. London: 1958.
FOSTER, M. B. *The Political Philosophies of Plato and Hegel*. Oxford: 1935.
HOOK, SIDNEY. *From Hegel to Marx*. New York: 1950.
HOOK, SIDNEY. *The Hero of History*. New York: 1943.
KAUFMANN, W. "The Hegel Myth and Its Methods," *From Shakespeare to Existentialism*, Boston: 1959.
LÖWITH, KARL. *Meaning in History*. Chicago: 1949.
MARCUSE, H. *Reason and Revolution*. New York: 1954.
MAZLISH, B. *The Riddle of History*. New York: 1966.
MORRIS, G. S. *Hegel's Philosophy of the State and of History*. Chicago: 1892.
MURE, G. R. G. *An Introduction to Hegel*. Oxford: 1940.
POPPER, KARL. *The Open Society and Its Enemies*, Vol. II. New York: 1963.
STACE, W. T. *The Philosophy of Hegel*. London: 1924.
TUCKER, R. C. "The Cunning of Reason in Hegel and Marx," *Review of Politics*, 1956.
WALSH, W. H. *An Introduction to the Philosophy of History*. London: 1951.
WALSH, W. H. "On the Philosophy of Hegel," *Philosophy*, 1942.

6 Karl Marx (1818–1883) *and* Friedrich Engels (1820–1895)

Karl Marx began his intellectual career as a disciple of Hegel. Sidney Hook explains,

> No two names are at once so suggestive of both agreement and opposition as are the names Hegel and Marx. . . . No one can plausibly call into question the historical influence of Hegel upon the formation of Marx's thought. That has been amply documented by Marx himself in published and unpublished writings.[1]

[1] Sidney Hook, *From Hegel to Marx* (Ann Arbor: University of Michigan Press, 1962), pp. 15, 16.

As Marx's views developed, his writings betrayed an increasing indebtedness to the thought of Ludwig Feuerbach, the German materialist, and to others like Saint Simon who influenced Marx's social and economic views.

Marx's view of history is alternately labeled Historical Materialism and Economic Determinism. The latter title refers to Marx's conviction that all aspects of man's life (political, aesthetic, religious, scientific, etc.) are determined by the ways in which man makes a living. The most important factor in explaining man's present or past history is an economic one. It seems clear, however, that the most accurate name for Marx's theory of history is Historical Materialism. It is doubtful that Marx ever meant to say that the *only* factor determining human life is economic. What he probably meant was that economic conditions are the *most important* influence on human history. Sidney Hook describes what Marx's materialism meant for his view of history:

> By a *materialistic* conception of history Marx means any theory which seeks to explain history by empirical laws whose predictions and descriptions are in principle verifiable by observation of the behavior of men, things, and the institutions which relate them. Denying the adequacy of physicalistic or racial or psychological theories, he asserted that, broadly speaking, the economic structure of society and its changes were the independent variables out of which all other cultural changes were a function. Or more simply put, the economic structure of society determines the life of any society in historic times.[2]

The selection from the Preface to Marx's *Contribution to the Critique of Political Economy* summarizes his materialist approach to history in five propositions.

Marx believed that history was his teacher. However, it is clear that he came to his study of history already presupposing the principle of the dialectic which he had borrowed from Hegel [3] and he came away from history with his theory of the

---

[2] Sidney Hook, *Marx and the Marxists: The Ambiguous Legacy* (Princeton: Van Nostrand, 1955), p. 19.

[3] "Dialectic" was Hegel's term for a process of change and development which he believed characterized all of reality. This change took place by

class struggle and the state. Marx proposed the dialectic within a system of materialism and political revolution. As Marx himself boasted, he had turned Hegelianism right-side up. While Hegel had made his dialectic the ground for a philosophy of idealism and a plea for political accommodation, Marx used the dialectic in a system of materialism as a weapon of social revolution.[4] Marx was not particularly impressed with the triad of thesis, antithesis, and synthesis that he found in the dialectic; he was more interested in the relation of opposition and conflict. In Marx's hand, the dialectic became a tool for the study of history. He wanted to explain the conflict and opposition he found in history and the dialectic gave him the clue he needed.

Like Hegel and Kant before him, Marx wrote that at first glance there appears to be no rhyme or reason to history. As we view the conflicts between members of society, the contradictions of social life, and the struggles between individuals, societies, and nations, all seems to be chaos. But, as Lenin read Marx, "Marxism provides a clue which enables us to discover the reign of law in this seeming labyrinth and chaos: the theory of the class struggle . . . The conflict of strivings arises from differences in the situation and modes of life of the classes into which society is divided."[5] As Marx and Engels point out in the selection from *The Communist Manifesto*, history records the oppression of one class by another: "The whole history of mankind has been a history of class struggles, contests between exploiting and exploited, ruling and oppressed classes. . . . The history of all hitherto existing society is the history of class struggle." History tells the story of the continuing struggle between "The Haves" and "The Have-Nots." The exploitation of the Have-Nots by the Haves has taken different forms at different times but it has always been the result of the economic situ-

---

means of strife, conflict, and contradiction. For example, one event or truth (a thesis) is negated by a contrary event or truth (antithesis). Out of this conflict arises a higher truth (synthesis) which preserves something of each prior truth but raises it to a higher level.

[4] The Marxist opposition to Hegelianism and idealism is spelled out in the selection from Engel's *Socialism: Utopian and Scientific*.

[5] V. I. Lenin, *Teachings of Karl Marx* (New York: International Publishers, 1930), p. 17.

ation of the time. In ancient history, the class struggle took the form of slavery. The Haves were the slaveowners, the Have-Nots were the slaves. The exploitation centered around private property, in this case, the slave himself. During the middle ages, the struggle assumed the form of feudalism. At stake was ownership of the land; the Haves were the landowners and the Have-Nots were the serfs. Finally in Marx's own day, the class struggle had assumed the form of capitalism. Now Bourgeoisie (the owner of the means of production) confronted Proletarian (the wage laborer) in what Marx was convinced would be a fight to the death. The Bourgeois exploitation of the Proletariat under capitalism had produced many social evils which Marx and many others justly criticized. However, unlike some of the other critics of social injustice in his day, Marx felt that if the evils of the class struggle were to be overcome, there must first be a change in the control of the instruments of production. Private property must be abolished, and other changes just as drastic must be introduced.

If private property is the basis of oppression and conflict in human history, the obvious way to end this oppression is to eliminate its cause. However, this cannot be done easily. No significant change in this regard can be brought about without the overthrow of the state, and this, of course, means revolution. Marx held that the state is essentially evil since it is one result of the class conflict. The state is an instrument used by the bourgeoisie in its exploitation and oppression of the proletariat. When the class struggle ends in the triumphant proletarian overthrow of the bourgeoisie, society will become classless and the need for the state will vanish causing the state to "wither away." Accordingly, Marx declares that the first task of the proletarian revolution is the capture and destruction of the bourgeois state.

Marx's doctrine of the revolution is one of the more ambiguous and confused aspects of his system. Later Marxists were to dispute at great length and with great fervor over the question, must the revolution be violent? Some later Marxists like the British Fabians and the German Social Democrats argued that the revolution could be brought about by peaceful means. This disagreement even existed in Russia where Lenin and the Bolsheviks accused the Mensheviks of obliterating, distorting, and omitting the revolutionary side of Marx's teachings.

Marx blundered when he came to predict the time of the revolution. As late as 1859, he believed that "No social order ever disappears before all the productive forces, for which there is room in it, have been developed; and new higher relations of production never appear before the material conditions of their existence have matured in the womb of the old society." [6] What Marx meant seems obvious. A proletarian revolution cannot occur without a proletariat. But before there can be a proletariat, capitalism must exist. However, in many nations of Marx's day (Russia, for example), feudalism still existed. Therefore, Marx seemed to be arguing that in those countries where industrialization was proceeding unevenly or slowly, the proletariat would have to assist the development of capitalism before they could dare begin their own revolution. A bourgeois revolution destroying any remnants of feudalism would have to occur before the proletarian revolution. This created problems among later Marxists. As E. H. Carr points out,

> [This] was the view seriously propounded by Russian Marxists, Bolsheviks and Mensheviks alike, down to 1905—perhaps even down to 1917. Meanwhile, however, in the Spring of 1905, Lenin's practical mind worked out a new scheme under which the proletariat was to seize power in conjunction with the peasantry, creating a "democratic dictatorship" of workers and peasants; and this became the official doctrine of the October Revolution.[7]

Near the end of his life, Marx did admit that the full development of capitalism might not be necessary in such a predominantly peasant country like Russia. While this was an interesting concession to expediency, it was hardly consistent with the pattern he had claimed to find in history.

The purpose of the proletarian revolution was to begin the equalization of wealth and put an end to the injustices found in capitalism. But even a successful proletarian revolution would

---

[6] Preface to *A Contribution to the Critique of Political Economy*. See the selection from this writing which follows.

[7] E. H. Carr, *Studies in Revolution* (London: Macmillan, 1950), pp. 24, 25.

not automatically usher in the classless society. Marx believed that capitalism was too well entrenched. After the revolution, at least two more steps would have to be taken toward the goal of a communist society: the dictatorship of the proletariat and the withering away of the state.

The first of these steps was what Marx called "the dictatorship of the proletariat." During this time, the state would be controlled by the proletariat and would be used as a means of coercion and oppression in destroying any remnants of capitalism. Marx regarded the dictatorship of the proletariat as a transition period between capitalism and the classless society. However, neither he nor Engels had much to say about it or about the exact conditions under which this proletarian state would finally be abolished. Engels did write that when the time was ripe, the state would "wither away." After Lenin had gained control of the Russian revolution in October, 1917, he made a number of tactical errors that brought the Russian economy to the brink of ruin. He quickly recognized that Russia was not yet ready for the classless society so he jumped on Marx's phrase, "the dictatorship of the proletariat," and used it to justify the tight controls he imposed upon Russia. While Marx had thought of the dictatorship of the proletariat as a kind of worker's democracy, Lenin turned it into a dictatorship of the small, exclusivist communist party over the proletariat. Of course, as time passed, even the party in Russia came under the control of the smaller central committee and for years, under Stalin, Russia was governed by the rule of a dictator over even the party.

To summarize, Marx's picture of history seems to combine elements of both the cyclical and linear views of history. The cyclical element is seen in the repetition of the life and death struggle between the Haves and the Have-Nots. The linear aspect is seen in the inevitable movement of history toward the final revolution which will prepare the world for the classless society.

The following selections give the substance of Marx's and Engels' view of history. They are followed by a brief selection in which the eminent authority on Marxist thought, Sidney Hook, evaluates the Marxist philosophy of history.

KARL MARX
HISTORICAL MATERIALISM [*]

The first work undertaken for the solution of the question that troubled me, was a critical revision of Hegel's *Philosophy of Law;* the introduction to that work appeared in the "Deutsch-Französische Jahrbücher," published in Paris in 1844. I was led by my studies to the conclusion that legal relations as well as forms of state could neither be understood by themselves, nor explained by the so-called general progress of the human mind, but that they are rooted in the material conditions of life, which are summed up by Hegel after the fashion of the English and French of the eighteenth century under the name "civic society"; the anatomy of that civic society is to be sought in political economy. The study of the latter which I had taken up in Paris, I continued at Brussels whither I emigrated on account of an order of expulsion issued by Mr. Guizot. The general conclusion at which I arrived and which, once reached, continued to serve as the leading thread in my studies, may be briefly summed up as follows: In the social production which men carry on they enter into definite relations that are indispensable and independent of their will; these relations of production correspond to a definite stage of development of their material powers of production. The sum total of these relations of production constitutes the economic structure of society—the real foundation, on which rise legal and political superstructures and to which correspond definite forms of social consciousness. The mode of production in material life determines the general character of the social, political, and spiritual processes of life. It is not the consciousness of men that determines their existence, but, on the contrary, their social existence determines their consciousness. At a certain stage of their development, the material forces of production in society come in conflict with the existing relations of produc-

---

[*] Taken from the Preface to Karl Marx's *A Contribution to the Critique of Political Economy,* trans. N. I. Stone (Chicago: Charles H. Kerr and Co., 1904).

tion, or—what is but a legal expression for the same thing—with the property relations within which they had been at work before. From forms of development of the forces of production these relations turn into their fetters. Then comes the period of social revolution. With the change of the economic foundation the entire immense superstructure is more or less rapidly transformed. In considering such transformations the distinction should always be made between the material transformation of the economic conditions of production which can be determined with the precision of natural science, and the legal, political, religious, aesthetic or philosophic—in short ideological forms in which men become conscious of this conflict and fight it out. Just as our opinion of an individual is not based on what he thinks of himself, so can we not judge of such a period of transformation by its own consciousness; on the contrary, this consciousness must rather be explained from the contradictions of material life, from the existing conflict between the social forces of production and the relations of production. No social order ever disappears before all the productive forces, for which there is room in it, have been developed; and new higher relations of production never appear before the material conditions of their existence have matured in the womb of the old society. Therefore, mankind always takes up only such problems as it can solve; since, looking at the matter more closely, we will always find the problem itself arises only when the material conditions necessary for its solution already exist or are at least in the process of formation. In broad outlines we can designate the Asiatic, the ancient, the feudal, and the modern bourgeois methods of production as so many epochs in the progress of the economic formation of society. The bourgeois relations of production are the last antagonistic form of the social process of production—antagonistic not in the sense of individual antagonism, but of one arising from conditions surrounding the life of individuals in society; at the same time the productive forces developing in the womb of bourgeois society create the material conditions for the solution of that antagonism. This social formation constitutes, therefore, the closing chapter of the prehistoric stage of human society.

MARX AND ENGELS
THE COMMUNIST MANIFESTO *

A specter is haunting Europe—the specter of Communism. All the Powers of old Europe have entered into a holy alliance to exorcise this specter: Pope and Czar, Metternich and Guizot, French Radicals and German police spies.

Where is the party in opposition that has not been decried as Communistic by its opponents in power? Where the Opposition that has not hurled back the branding reproach of Communism, against the more advanced opposition parties, as well as against its reactionary adversaries?

Two things result from this fact.

I. Communism is already acknowledged by all European Powers to be itself a Power.

II. It is high time that Communists should openly, in the face of the whole world, publish their views, their aims, their tendencies, and meet this nursery tale of the Specter of Communism with a Manifesto of the party itself. . . .

I. *Bourgeois and proletarians.* The history of all hitherto existing society is the history of class struggles.

Freeman and slave, patrician and plebeian, lord and serf, guild master and journeyman, in a word, oppressor and oppressed, stood in constant opposition to one another, carried on an uninterrupted, now hidden, now open fight, a fight that each time ended, either in a revolutionary reconstitution of society at large, or in the common ruin of the contending classes.

In the earlier epochs of history, we find almost everywhere a complicated arrangement of society into various orders, a manifold gradation of social rank. In ancient Rome we have patricians, knights, plebeians, slaves; in the Middle Ages, feudal lords,

---

* From the *Manifesto of the Communist Party* by Karl Marx and Friedrich Engels, authorized English translation, ed. Engels (Chicago: Charles H. Kerr and Co., 1888).

vassals, guild masters, journeymen, apprentices, serfs; in almost all of these classes, again, subordinate gradations.

The modern bourgeois society that has sprouted from the ruins of feudal society has not done away with class antagonisms. It has but established new classes, new conditions of oppression, new forms of struggle in place of the old ones.

Our epoch, the epoch of the bourgeoisie, possesses, however, this distinctive feature: it has simplified the class antagonisms. Society as a whole is more and more splitting up into two great hostile camps, into two great classes directly facing each other: Bourgeoisie and Proletariat. . . .

The bourgeoisie, historically, has played a most revolutionary part.

The bourgeoisie, wherever it has got the upper hand, has put an end to all feudal, patriarchal, idyllic relations. It has pitilessly torn asunder the motley feudal ties that bound man to his "natural superiors," and has left remaining no other nexus between man and man than naked self-interest, than callous "cash payment." It has drowned the most heavenly ecstasies of religious fervor, of chivalrous enthusiasm, of philistine sentimentalism, in the icy water of egotistical calculation. It has resolved personal worth into exchange value, and in place of the numberless indefeasible chartered freedoms, has set up that single, unconscionable freedom—Free Trade. In one word, for exploitation, veiled by religious and political illusions, it has substituted naked, shameless, direct, brutal exploitation.

The bourgeoisie has stripped of its halo every occupation hitherto honored and looked up to with reverent awe. It has converted the physician, the lawyer, the priest, the poet, the man of science, into its paid wage laborers.

The bourgeoisie has torn away from the family its sentimental veil, and has reduced the family relation to a mere money relation.

The bourgeoisie . . . has been the first to show what man's activity can bring about. It has accomplished wonders far surpassing Egyptian pyramids, Roman aqueducts, and Gothic cathedrals; it has conducted expeditions that put in the shade all former Exoduses of nations and Crusades.

The bourgeoisie cannot exist without constantly revolutionizing the instruments of production, and thereby the relations of productions, and with them the whole relations of society. . . .

The need of a constantly expanding market for its products chases the bourgeoisie over the whole surface of the globe. It must nestle everywhere, settle everywhere, establish connections everywhere. . . .

The bourgeoisie, during its rule of scarce one hundred years, has created more massive and more colossal productive forces than have all preceding generations together. Subjection of Nature's forces to man, machinery, application of chemistry to industry and agriculture, steam navigation, railways, electric telegraphs, clearing of whole continents for cultivation, canalization of rivers, whole populations conjured out of the ground—what earlier century had even a presentiment that such productive forces slumbered in the lap of social labor?

We see then: the means of production and of exchange, on whose foundation the bourgeoisie built itself up, were generated in feudal society. At a certain stage in the development of these means of production and of exchange, the conditions under which feudal society produced and exchanged, the feudal organization of agriculture and manufacturing industry, in one word, the feudal relations of property became no longer compatible with the already developed productive forces; they became so many fetters. They had to be burst asunder; they were burst asunder.

Into their place stepped free competition, accompanied by a social and political sway of the bourgeois class.

A similar movement is going on before our own eyes. Modern bourgeois society with its relations of production, of exchange and of property, a society that has conjured up such gigantic means of production and of exchange, is like the sorcerer, who is no longer able to control the powers of the nether world whom he has called up by his spells. For many a decade past the history of industry and commerce is but the history of the revolt of modern productive forces against modern conditions of production, against the property relations that are the conditions for the existence of the bourgeoisie and of its rule. It is enough to mention the commercial crises that by their periodical return put on its trial, each time more threateningly, the existence of the entire bourgeois society. In these crises a great part not only of the existing products, but also of the previously created productive forces, are periodically destroyed. In these crises there breaks out an epidemic that, in all earlier epochs, would have seemed an absurdity—the epidemic of overproduction. Society suddenly finds itself put back into a state of momentary barbarism; it appears as if a famine, a universal war of devastation, had cut off the supply of every means of subsistence; industry and commerce seem to be destroyed; and why? Because there is too much civilization, too much means of subsistence, too much industry, too much commerce. The productive forces at the disposal of society no longer tend to further the development of the conditions of bourgeois property; on the contrary, they have become too powerful for these conditions, by which they are fettered, and so soon as they overcome these fetters, they bring disorder into the whole of bourgeois society, endanger the existence of bourgeois property. The conditions of bourgeois society are too narrow to comprise the wealth created by them. And how does the bourgeoisie get over these crises? On the one hand by enforced destruction of a mass of productive forces; on the other, by the conquest of new markets, and by the more thorough exploitation of the old ones. That is to say, by paving the way for more extensive and more destructive crises, and by diminishing the means whereby crises are prevented.

The weapons with which the bourgeoisie felled feudalism to the ground are now turned against the bourgeoisie itself.

But not only has the bourgeoisie forged the weapons that bring death to itself; it has also called into existence the men who are to wield those weapons, the modern working class—the proletarians. . . .

The proletariat goes through various stages of development. With its birth begins its struggle with the bourgeoisie. At first the contest is carried on by individual laborers, then by the workpeople of a factory, then the operatives of one trade, in one locality, against the individual bourgeois who exploits them. . . .

But with the development of industry the proletariat not only increases in number; it becomes concentrated in greater masses, its strength grows, and it feels that strength more. The various interests and conditions of life within the ranks of the proletariat are more and more equalized, in proportion as machinery obliterates all distinctions of labor, and nearly everywhere reduces wages to the same low level. . . . The workers begin to form combinations (Trades' Unions) against the bourgeois; they club together in order to keep up the rate of wages; they found permanent associations in order to make provision beforehand for these occasional revolts. Here and there the contest breaks out into riots.

Now and then the workers are victorious, but only for a time. The real fruit of their battle lies, not in the immediate result, but in the ever expanding union of the workers. . . .

Finally, in time even the class struggle nears the decisive hour, the process of dissolution going on within the ruling class, in fact within the whole range of old society, assumes such a violent, glaring character, that a small section of the ruling class cuts itself adrift, and joins the revolutionary class, the class that holds the future in its hands. Just as, therefore, at an earlier period, a section of the nobility went over to the bourgeoisie, so now a portion of the bourgeoisie goes over to the proletariat, and in particular, a portion of the bourgeois ideologists, who have raised themselves to the level of comprehending theoretically the historical movement as a whole. . . .

All the preceding classes that got the upper hand sought to fortify their already acquired status by subjecting society at large to their conditions of appropriation. The proletarians cannot become masters of the productive forces of society, except by abolishing their own previous mode of appropriation, and thereby also every other previous mode of appropriation. They have nothing of their own to secure and to fortify; their mission is to destroy all previous securities for, and insurances of, individual property.

All previous historical movements were movements of minorities, or in the interest of minorities. The proletarian movement is the self-conscious, independent movement of the immense majority, in the interest of the immense majority. The proletariat, the lowest stratum of our present society, cannot stir, cannot raise itself up, without the whole superincumbent strata of official society being sprung into the air. In depicting the most general phases of the development of the proletariat, we traced the more or less veiled civil war, raging within existing society, up to the point where that war breaks out into open revolution, and where the violent overthrow of the bourgeoisie lays the foundation for the sway of the proletariat.

Hitherto, every form of society has been based as we have already seen, on the antagonism of oppressing and oppressed classes. But in order to oppress a class, certain conditions must be assured to it under which it can, at least, continue its slavish existence. The serf, in the period of serfdom, raised himself to membership in the commune, just as the petty bourgeois, under the yoke of feudal absolutism, managed to develop into a bourgeois. The modern laborer, on the contrary, instead of rising with the progress of industry, sinks deeper and deeper below the conditions of existence of his own class. He becomes a pauper, and pauperism develops more rapidly than population and wealth. And here it becomes evident, that the bourgeoisie is unfit any longer to be the ruling class in society, and to impose its conditions of existence upon society as an overriding law. It is unfit to rule because it is incompetent to assure an existence to its slave within his slavery, because it cannot help letting him sink into such a state, that it has to feed him, instead of being fed by him. Society can no longer live under this bourgeoisie, in other words, its existence is no longer compatible with society.

The essential condition for the existence, and for the sway of the bourgeois class, is the formation and augmentation of capital; the condition for capital is wage labor. Wage labor rests exclusively on competition between the laborers. The advance of industry, whose involuntary promoter is the bourgeoisie, replaces the isolation of the laborers, due to competition, by their revolutionary combination, due to association. The development of Modern Industry, therefore, cuts from under its feet the very foundation on which the bourgeoisie produces and appropriates products. What the bourgeoisie, therefore, produces, above all, are its own gravediggers. Its fall and the victory of the proletariat are equally inevitable.

ENGELS
IDEALISM AND MATERIALISM *

This new German philosophy culminated in the Hegelian system. In this system—and herein is its great merit—for the first time the whole world, natural, historical, intellectual, is represented as a process, i.e., as in constant motion, change, transformation, development; and the attempt is made to trace out the internal connection that makes a continuous whole of all this movement and development. From this point of view the history of mankind no longer appeared as a wild whirl of senseless deeds of violence, all equally condemnable by the judgment of mature philosophic reason and best forgotten as quickly as possible, but as the process of evolution of man himself. It was now the task of the intellect to follow the gradual march of this process through all its devious ways, and to trace out the inner law running through all its apparently accidental phenomena.

That the Hegelian system did not solve the problem it propounded is here immaterial. Its epoch-making merit was that it propounded the problem. This problem is one that no single individual will ever be able to solve. Although Hegel was—with Saint-Simon—the most encyclopedic mind of his time, yet he was limited, first, by the necessarily limited extent of his own knowledge and, second, by the limited extent and depth of the knowledge and conceptions of his age. To these limits a third must be added. Hegel was an idealist. To him the thoughts within his brain were not the more or less abstract pictures of actual things and processes, but, pictures of the "Idea," existing somewhere from eternity before the world was. This way of thinking turned everything upside down, and completely reversed the actual connection of things in the world. Correctly and ingeniously as many individual groups of facts were grasped by Hegel, yet, for the reasons just given, there is much that is

---

* From Friedrich Engels, *Socialism: Utopian and Scientific*, trans. Edward Aveling (Chicago: Charles H. Kerr and Co., 1908).

IDEALISM AND MATERIALISM

botched, artificial, labored, in a word, wrong in point of detail. The Hegelian system, in itself, was a colossal miscarriage—but it was also the last of its kind. It was suffering, in fact, from an internal and incurable contradiction. On the one hand, its essential proposition was the conception that human history is a process of evolution, which, by its very nature, cannot find its intellectual final term in the discovery of any so-called absolute truth. But on the other hand, it laid claim to being the very essence of this absolute truth. A system of natural and historical knowledge, embracing everything, and final for all time, is a contradiction of the fundamental law of dialectic reasoning. This law, indeed, by no means excludes, but, on the contrary, includes the idea that the systematic knowledge of the external universe can make giant strides from age to age.

The perception of the fundamental contradiction in German idealism led necessarily back to materialism, but, nota bene, not to the simply metaphysical, exclusively mechanical materialism of the eighteenth century. Old materialism looked upon all previous history as a crude heap of irrationality and violence; modern materialism sees in it the process of evolution of humanity, aims at discovering the laws thereof. With the French of the eighteenth century, and even with Hegel, the prevailing conception was one of Nature as a whole, moving in narrow circles, and forever immutable, with its eternal celestial bodies, as Newton taught, and unalterable organic species, as Linnaeus taught. Modern materialism embraces the more recent discoveries of natural science, according to which Nature also has its history in time, the celestial bodies, like the organic species that, under favorable conditions, people them, being born and perishing. And even if Nature, as a whole, must still be said to move in recurrent cycles, these cycles assume infinitely larger dimensions. In both aspects, modern materialism is essentially dialectic, and no longer requires the assistance of that sort of philosophy which, queenlike, pretended to rule the remaining mob of sciences. As soon as each special science makes clear its position in the great totality of things and our knowledge of things, a special science dealing with this totality is superfluous or unnecessary. That which still survives of all earlier philosophy is the science of thought and its laws—formal logic and dialectics. Everything else is subsumed in the positive science of Nature and history.

While, however, the revolution in the conception of Nature could only be made in proportion to the corresponding positive materials furnished by research, already much earlier certain historical facts had occurred which led to a decisive change in the conception of history. In 1831, the first working-class rising took place in Lyons; between 1838 and 1842, the first national working-class movement, that of the English Chartists, reached its height. The class struggle between proletariat and bourgeoisie came to the fore in the history of the most advanced countries in Europe, in proportion to the development, on the one hand, of modern industry, and on the other, of the newly acquired political supremacy of the bourgeoisie. Facts more and more forcefully gave the lie to the teachings of bourgeois economy as to the identity of the interests of capital and labor, as to the universal harmony and universal prosperity that would be the consequence of unbridled competition. All these things could no longer be ignored, any more than the French and English socialism, which, though very imperfect, was their theoretical expression. But the old idealist conception of history, which was not yet dislodged, knew nothing of class struggles based upon economic interests, knew nothing of economic interests; production and all economic relations appeared in it only as incidental, subordinate elements in the "history of civilization."

The new facts made imperative a new examination of all past history. Then it was seen that *all* past history, with the exception of its primitive stages, was the history of class struggles; that these warring classes of society are always the products of the modes of production and of exchange—in a word, of the *economic* conditions of their time; that the economic structure of society always furnishes the real basis, starting from which we can alone work out the ultimate explanation of the whole superstructure of juridical and political institutions as well as of the religious, philosophical, and other ideas of a given historical period. Hegel had freed history from metaphysics—he had made it dialectic; but his conception of history was essentially idealistic. But now idealism was driven from its last refuge, the philosophy of history; now a materialistic treatment of history was propounded, and a method found of explaining man's "knowing" by his "being," instead of, as heretofore, his "being" by his "knowing."

From that time forward socialism was no longer an accidental discovery of this or that ingenious brain, but the necessary outcome of the struggle between two historically developed classes —the proletariat and the bourgeoisie. Its task was no longer to manufacture a system of society as perfect as possible, but to examine the historico-economic succession of events from which these classes and their antagonism had of necessity sprung, and to discover in the economic conditions thus created the means of ending the conflict. But the socialism of earlier days was as incompatible with this materialistic conception as the conception of Nature of the French materialists was with dialectics and modern natural science. The socialism of earlier days certainly criticized the existing capitalistic mode of production and its consequences. But it could not explain them, and, therefore, could not master them. It could only simply reject them as bad. The more strongly this earlier socialism denounced the exploitation of the working class, inevitable under capitalism, the less able was it clearly to show in what this exploitation consisted and how it arose. But for this it was necessary—(1) to present the capitalistic method of production in its historical connection and its inevitableness during a particular historical period, and therefore, also, to present its inevitable downfall; and (2) to lay bare its essential character, which was still a secret. This was done by the discovery of *surplus value*. It was shown that the appropriation of unpaid labor is the basis of the capitalist mode of production and of the exploitation of the worker that occurs under it; that even if the capitalist buys the labor power of his laborer at its full value as a commodity on the market, he yet extracts more value from it than he paid for; and that in the ultimate analysis this surplus value forms those sums of value from which are heaped up the constantly increasing masses of capital in the hands of the possessing classes. The genesis of capitalist production and the production of capital were both explained.

These two great discoveries, the materialistic conception of history and the revelation of the secret of capitalistic production through surplus value, we owe to Marx. With these discoveries socialism became a science. The next thing was to work out all its details and relations.

The materialist conception of history starts from the proposition that the production of the means to support human life and, next to production, the exchange of things produced, is the basis of all social structure; that in every society that has appeared in history, the manner in which wealth is distributed and society divided into classes or orders is dependent upon what is produced, how it is produced, and how the products are exchanged. From this point of view the final causes of all social changes and political revolutions are to be sought, not in man's brain, not in man's better insight into eternal truth and justice, but in changes in the modes of production and exchange. They are to be sought not in the *philosophy*, but in the *economics* of each particular epoch. The growing perception that existing social institutions are unreasonable and unjust, that reason has become unreason and right wrong, is only proof that in the modes of production and exchange changes have silently taken place with which the social order, adapted to earlier economic conditions, is no longer in keeping. From this it also follows that the means of getting rid of the incongruities that have been brought to light must also be present, in a more or less developed condition, within the changed modes of production themselves. These means are not to be invented by deduction from fundamental principles, but are to be discovered in the stubborn facts of the existing system of production. . . .

While the capitalist mode of production more and more completely transforms the great majority of the population into proletarians, it creates the power which, under penalty of its own destruction, is forced to accomplish this revolution. While it forces on more and more the transformation of the vast means of production, already socialized, into state property, it shows itself the way to accomplish this revolution. *The proletariat seizes political power and turns the means of production into state property*.

But, in doing this, it abolishes itself as proletariat, abolishes all class distinctions and class antagonisms, abolishes also the state as state. Society thus far, based upon class antagonisms, had need of the state; that is, of an organization of the particular class which was pro tempore the exploiting class, an organization for the purpose of preventing any interference with the existing conditions of production, and, therefore, especially, for the purpose of forcibly keeping the exploited classes in the condition of oppression corresponding with the given mode of production (slavery, serfdom, wage labor). The state was the official representative of society as a whole, the gathering of it into a visible embodiment. But it was this only in so far as it was the state of that class which itself represented, for the time being, society as a whole: in ancient times, the state of slaveowning citizens; in the Middle Ages, the feudal lords; in our own time, the bourgeoisie. When at last it becomes the real representative of the whole of society, it renders itself unnecessary. As soon as there is no longer any social class to be held in subjection; as soon as class rule, and the individual struggle for existence based upon our present anarchy in production, with the collisions and excesses arising from these, are removed, nothing more remains to be repressed, and a special repressive force, a state, is no longer necessary. The first act by virtue of which the state really constitutes itself the representative of the whole of society—of society—this is, at the same time, its last independent act as a state. State interference in social relations becomes, in one domain after another, superfluous, and then dies out by itself; the government of persons is replaced by the administration of things and by the conduct of the processes of production. The state is not "abolished." *It dies out.* This gives the measure of the value of the phrase "*a free state*," both as to its justifiable use at times by agitators and as to its ultimate scientific insufficiency; and also of the demands of the so-called anarchists for the abolition of the state out of hand.

Since the historical appearance of the capitalist mode of production, the appropriation by society of all the means of production has often been dreamed of, more or less vaguely, by individuals, as well as by sects, as the ideal of the future. But it could become possible, could become a historical necessity, only when the actual conditions for its realization were there. Like every other social advance, it becomes practicable, not by men understanding that the existence of classes is in contradiction to justice, equality, etc., not by the mere willingness to abolish these classes, but by virtue of certain new economic conditions. The separation of society into an exploiting and an exploited class, a ruling and an oppressed class, was the necessary consequence of the deficient and restricted development of production in former times. So long as the total social labor only yields a product which but slightly exceeds that barely necessary for existence of all; so long, therefore, as labor engages all or almost all the time of the great majority of the members of society—so long, of necessity, is this society divided into classes. Side by side with the great majority, exclusively bond slaves to labor, arises a class freed from direct productive labor, which looks after the general affairs of society: the direction of labor, state business, law, science, art, etc. It is, therefore, the law of division of labor that lies at the basis of the division into classes. But this does not prevent the division into classes from being carried out by means of violence and robbery, trickery and fraud. It does not prevent the ruling class, once having the upper hand, from consolidating its power at the expense of the working class, from turning its social leadership into an intensified exploitation of the masses.

But if, upon this showing, division into classes has a certain historical justification, it has this only for a given period, only under given social conditions. It was based upon the insufficiency of production. It will be swept away by the complete development of modern productive forces. And, in fact, the abolition of classes in society presupposes a degree of historical evolution at which the existence, not simply of this or that particular ruling class, but of any ruling class at all, and, therefore, the existence of class distinction itself has become an obsolete anachronism. It presupposes, therefore, the development of production carried out to a degree at which appropriation of the means of production and of the products, and, with this, of political domination, of the monopoly of culture, and of intellectual leadership by a particular class of society, has become not only superfluous but economically, politically and intellectually, a hindrance to development.

This point is now reached. Their political and intellectual bankruptcy is scarcely any longer a secret to the bourgeoisie themselves. Their economic bankruptcy recurs regularly every ten years. In every crisis, society is suffocated beneath the weight of its own productive forces and products, which it cannot use, and stands helpless, face to face with the absurd contradiction that the producers have nothing to consume, because consumers are wanting. The expansive force of the means of production bursts the bonds that the capitalist mode of production had imposed upon them. Their deliverance from these bonds is the one precondition for an unbroken, constantly accelerated development of the productive forces, and therewith for a practically unlimited increase of production itself. Nor is this all. The socialized appropriation of the means of production does away, not only with the present artificial restrictions upon production, but also with the positive waste and devastation of productive forces and products that are at the present time the inevitable concomitants of production and that reach their height in the crises. Further, it sets free for the community at large a mass of means of production and of products by doing away with the senseless extravagance of the ruling classes of today and their political representatives. The possibility of securing for every member of society, by means of socialized production, an existence not only sufficient materially, and becoming day by day more fully so, but existence guaranteeing to all the free development and exercise of their physical and mental faculties—this possibility is now for the first time here, but *it is here*.

With the seizing of the means of production by society, production of commodities and, simultaneously, the mastery of the product over the producer are abolished. Anarchy in social production is replaced by systematic, definite organization. The struggle for individual existence disappears. Then for the first time man, in a certain sense, is finally marked off from the rest of the animal kingdom and emerges from mere animal conditions of existence into really human ones. The whole sphere of the conditions of life which surround man, and which have hitherto ruled man, now comes under the dominion and control of man, who for the first time becomes the real, conscious lord of Nature, because he has now become master of his own social organization. The laws of his own social action, hitherto standing face to face with man as laws of Nature foreign to and dominating him, will then be used with full understanding and thereby mastered by him. Man's own social organization, hitherto confronting him as a necessity imposed by Nature and history, now becomes the result of his own free action. The extraneous objective forces that have hitherto governed history pass under the control of man himself. Only from that time will man himself, more and more consciously, make his own history—only from that time will the social causes set in motion by him have, in the main and in a constantly growing measure, the results intended by him. It is the ascent of man from the kingdom of necessity to the kingdom of freedom. . . .

DISCUSSION
SIDNEY HOOK:
AN EVALUATION OF MARX'S VIEW OF HISTORY *

Rigorous examination is one thing Marx's ideas will not stand because they were not rigorously formulated. To do justice to his intent they must often be reinterpreted and qualified. They constitute a mixture of the true, the vague, and the false.

At the outset it should be apparent to any sensitive reader that Marx writes primarily as a critic of capitalism, as a man fired with a passionate ideal to eliminate the social inequalities, the poverty, and injustices of his time. Much of what he said makes sense and good sense considered as a description of the capitalist society of his time and as a prediction of the probable historical development of any capitalist system *on the assumption* that nothing outside that system, especially political influences, interferes with its development. Marx's fundamental errors arise from an uncritical extrapolation of what he observed in capitalist societies to all class societies, and from a disregard of the enormous influence which political, national, and moral forces have exerted on the development of capitalism as an economic system.

Historical Materialism. Modern historiography, even when it is not avowedly Marxist, reflects the profound impact of Marx's

* Reprinted from *Marx and the Marxists* by Sidney Hook, pp. 35–40, 41–42, 44–45, by permission of D. Van Nostrand Company, Inc. Copyright 1955 by D. Van Nostrand Company, Inc., Princeton, N.J.

ideas albeit in a diluted form. Marx's ideas have enriched historical writing, made it more realistic and down to earth, and set interesting problems for investigation. Even so Christian an historian as Professor Butterfield pays tribute to the wholesome effect of Marx's approach on historical scholarship. As a rough approximation, Marx's theory of history plausibly accounts at most for the *general* character of nineteenth-century industrial society up to the First World War, for the urbanization of culture, its commercialization, many of the consequences of science upon society, the major political struggles of the period, and the imperialistic expansion of Europe to a commanding world influence.

No matter how charitably interpreted, however, it does not explain the transition from feudalism to capitalism. Feudal societies have existed in many periods and regions of the world. But only in Europe, in a tiny corner of the world, did capitalism arise. It spread elsewhere not by virtue of any immanent law of the development of the social relations of feudalism but by conquest or adaptation (e.g., Japan). There is even less evidence that the transition from slave to feudal societies was universal and that where it occurred it fitted into Marx's scheme. His claims about primitive society, derived mainly from Lewis H. Morgan, have been conclusively refuted by the findings of modern anthropology.

Even for the period of capitalism the theory of historical materialism in most of its customary formulations is inadequate. It seeks to explain all major political and cultural changes in terms of development in the mode of economic production. Such a sweeping claim cannot be established except on a statistical basis after piecemeal investigations of major political and cultural phenomena have been undertaken. It ignores the fact that the economic basis of society at any given time is often compatible with more than one political form, and that therefore the degree of democracy present or absent in any particular country may be explained by other than factors attributable to its mode of production.

The very metaphors of the theory are misleading and can be turned against it. The mode of production is regarded as the "foundation" of society. But a foundation does not completely determine whether any stories will be built on it, the number of stories, their style, function, and use. Nor do foundations develop. They are purposefully built and sometimes purposefully destroyed; on occasions they may be replaced without affecting the superstructure. At most, just as existing foundations may *limit* the possibilities of further construction, so the mode of production may limit the cultural and political possibilities. Its existence may make certain alternatives relatively impossible, but it cannot prevent human beings from *attempting* the historically impossible. The cause of ensuing disaster would then be attributable to the decision to attempt the impossible as much as to the obstacles which doomed the attempt.

Historical materialism in its orthodox form systematically confuses ultimate and proximate causes and forgets that science is not concerned with ultimate causes. It admits, when pressed, that there is a reciprocal influence among various factors, and between economic cause and cultural and political effects. But this is minimized as incidental, and in the most "a priori" fashion the mode of production is declared to be *always* the decisive influence "in the last analysis." Yet independent developments in science which originally had not the slightest relevant connection with the mode of economic production, like the theory of relativity which led to the liberation of nuclear energy, may have a far greater influence on the politics of our era, indeed on the mode of economic production itself, than any immanent law of the latter.

Historical materialism tends to see heroes of thought and action merely as carriers or "expressions" of social forces, ultimately economic, but it cannot account for the fact that an event-making person like Lenin had far greater causal influence on the Bolshevist October Revolution of 1917 in Russia than the state of the forces of production or the degree of development of the relations of production. The existence of states like Ireland and Israel illustrates another type of historical phenomenon which the theory neither predicted nor could plausibly explain in its own terms even *after* the event.

As a monistic theory in quest of total solutions, historical materialism is not intelligible and serves only as an excuse to avoid thought about troublesome questions. As a pluralistic theory which gives greatest weight to the mode of economic production, it is a useful *heuristic* principle with which to approach specific problems. We should applaud Engels' remark in this connection that the proof of the pudding is in the eating. But enough puddings have been eaten to warrant considerable skepticism of the large claims made for it. That the mode of economic production had more to do in determining the major political events from 1750 to 1914 in Europe than any other single factor may be true, although it still remains to be conclusively established. But it is noteworthy that neither Marx nor Engls nor any leading protagonist of historical materialism predicted the rise of Fascism in any of its varieties. Nor is it easy to fit Fascism and other forms of totalitarianism, which are neither socialist nor capitalist, into Marx's analysis.

Without denying in the least the continuing influence of the mode of economic production, it does not seem to have had as great an importance since the rise of totalitarianism as it did previously. Political decisions like the Treaty of Versailles, the New Deal, the long years of appeasement of Hitler, the failure to support the original democratic regime in Spain, the war against Hitler, the appeasement of Stalin, the demobilization of the American army in Europe, UNRRA and the Marshall Plan, the U. S. involvement in Korea, the rearmament of the West to counter Communist aggression, have had a more powerful influence on economic development than the mode of economic production on political affairs.

Historical development. If it is true, that, as Marx claimed, "no social order ever perishes before all the productive forces for which there is room in it have developed," then it is difficult to see why any social system not destroyed by war or natural disaster, should perish. An indefinite number of possibilities for expansion exist. Slavery would not have disappeared until it had at least become universal. Capitalism might keep on going by opening new frontiers of need requiring new industries for their gratification. Theoretically, human ingenuity under any system can build contrivance upon contrivance to develop productive forces. Historically, there is no evidence whatsoever that in October, 1917, when the Communists took power in Russia, capitalism had run its course. Marx never made a convincing case for his assertion that capitalism *must* be followed by socialism rather than *other* forms of society. There are various alternatives which he ignored, like one which continues private ownership of means of production with extensive social control of its operation or a mixed economy with private and public sectors of production. Both of these alternatives are equally removed from his conceptions of capitalism and socialism and closer to present-day realities in various countries.

Class struggles. Although not distinctive to Marx, the concepts of social classes and class struggles are used in his writings in a brilliant way to illumine some crucial periods in modern history. Since Marx's time these concepts have become part of the intellectual tool kit of all empirical historians. It is one thing, however, to recognize the role of classes in political and social life. It is quite another to assume that economic classes, no matter how economic classes are defined, always have an overriding significance in relation to other class divisions—religious, national, or racial. It was clearly to the interests of the working classes in all countries to oppose the First World War. Their chief political parties had pledged themselves to do so before the war broke out. But they rallied to the support of their respective governments with no less patriotic enthusiasm than other classes.

The term "class" in Marx is used in various senses, not all strictly derivative from each other. Sometimes its defining feature is the role a group plays in production, sometimes it is their common mode of life, including culture and traditions, sometimes the source of their income or the level of their income, sometimes their vocation or, in the case of the unemployed, their lack of any. If, as the *Communist Manifesto* declares, "all history is the history of class struggles," it certainly is not true that all class struggles have been economic in any of the above senses. Nor is it true that all history is the history *only* of class struggles; it is just as much, if not more, a history of class cooperation. Antagonisms often remain latent when classes join forces either in meeting a common danger or uniting in a common effort for their mutual benefit. The frequency and intensity with which Marxists have denounced "class collaboration" is eloquent testimony of how pervasive such cooperation is even in areas where one might expect open clash of interests. It proves that "the law of class struggle" is either not a law, since it has so many exceptions, or is of very limited validity.

Here, as elsewhere in Marx, it is not so much the concept of class struggle which is illegitimate but its uncritical extension and the tendency, especially among Marx's followers, to interpret cultural, religious, and intellectual conflicts, as well as scientific development, as corollaries of a struggle for a greater share of social wealth and power. No doubt the latter is often an attendant feature of these conflicts, sometimes a genuinely relevant causal factor. But in relation to vast areas of culture, especially the arts and sciences, and to some extremely significant events, like some of the Crusades or the rise of many nationalist movements or the war against Hitlerism, they are altogether negligible or contributory only to a minor degree. . . .

Marx vastly underestimated the regenerative power of capitalism to overcome its own periodic crises, the diversification of forms it has taken, the economic influence of organized trade-union action, the pressure labor could exert through the extension of political democracy on the distribution of wealth and on social security, the rise in the effective purchasing power of wages, the improvement of health and standards of living. Although appreciative of the transforming effects of applied science, he underestimated its importance for the multiplication of new industries. He sensed the significance of the separation of ownership from management in modern capitalism but failed to take into account its consequences—increasing social regulation of industry and greater social mobility. He barely conceived of the possibility that industry could be made an appendage of the state independently of the interests of the owners of the instruments of production and that by a succession of controls on prices, wages, and profits, as well as by currency regulation, deficit financing, taxation, and public banking, the state could profoundly affect the channels of reinvestment, and this not only in times of war.

Marx believed that an "ideal" system of capitalism, i.e., one which developed in relative isolation of the effects of political intervention on the part of the state or of the organized working class itself, could not at one and the same time guarantee sufficient profits to be a spur to necessary reinvestment, provide full employment for all able and willing to work, and guarantee an adequate standard of living above the subsistence level for the masses. He never really proved this even for an "ideal" system. But there never was, nor in all likelihood will there be, an ideal system of capitalism or indeed of any system.

In existing capitalisms at any definite time, profit may not be guaranteed for all capitalists but only for a certain number. But this number may be sufficient to keep production up to a level where most workers are employed while those who are temporarily unemployed receive social benefits. Marx was indisputably right in anticipating periodic economic dislocations where the market still operates in an unplanned economy. It remains an open question, however, whether even in a planned economy some economic dislocations, as well as unemployment hidden by a swollen and inefficient labor force, may not occur.

Today, at any rate, the British, American, and Western-European economies show features almost as profoundly different from those Marx predicted as inescapably involved in the development of capitalism as are the characteristic features of Soviet economy from those Marx expected to follow upon the disappearance of capitalism. . . .

The socialist society. Because Marx was primarily interested in the critique of capitalism, he gave very little thought to the structure of the socialist system he assumed must succeed it. He was so aroused by the evils of the status quo that he never inquired whether the evils of the post status quo might not even be worse, particularly if the means used were not checked by their consequences on the professed ends which guided them. He never seriously examined the possibility that the workers might be just as much, or even more, exploited under a system of collective ownership where they faced one big boss, panoplied in the armed powers of the state, as under a system of private or mixed ownership in which there were many bosses often at odds with each other. He assumed without argument that democratic political institutions would necessarily thrive when capitalism had been overthrown and that free enterprise in the life of mind would flourish when free enterprise in economy had been completely abolished. He overlooked the demonstrable truth that under socialism the degree of political democracy which prevails is of far greater importance than the degree of economic collectivism. For without democracy, a collectivized economy becomes at best a tool of benevolent despots and bureaucrats, and at worst, the most terrible instrument of oppression in the history of mankind. Recent historical events have brought home even to followers of Marx that by itself socialization or a change in the legal relations of property does not necessarily affect differences in power, status, or privilege.

The two clearest illustrations of Utopianism in Marx are his belief that the state will wither away under Communism and that its rule of distribution will be based only on need. Even if absolute and total collectivism existed under democratic political forms, differences would undoubtedly arise as to how the production of wealth would be distributed among different social or vocational groups. These may be peacefully arbitrated or not. If there is to be no forced labor, the right to strike must be respected. In any event, for these and other reasons, a complex society must always have at command some agencies of coercion to prevent conflicts from getting out of hand, and, in emergencies, to safeguard the public interest.

In a world where it is technically impossible to produce more than enough of everything *at the same time,* the proposal to distribute goods and services in accordance with need alone is unworkable. Needs are indefinite, subjective, and potentially unlimited. Wherever there exists scarcity in quantity at any moment of time there must be an order of priority in distribution based on merit or chance or some other selective principle. It may be technologically feasible so to arrange things that everyone's *basic* needs for food, clothing, and shelter can be gratified irrespective of their capacity to work or even their willingness to work. But this leaves luxuries, everything over and above the basic needs, to be distributed.

And even the concept of "basic needs" is a historical variable. What Marx had in mind was a system of society whose ties of organization approximated the bonds which united a loving family in which the varied needs of individual members are gratified in a spirit of fraternity rather than in accordance with rules of justice. But the whole of society can never become one family, not all families are free of conflict, and even in loving families love is not always enough. . . .

BIBLIOGRAPHY

The most important Marxist writings are available in several translations and editions. Three helpful and inexpensive collections are: *Marx and the Marxists*, ed. Sidney Hook, New York: Van Nostrand, 1955; *Essential Works of Marxism*, ed. A. P. Mendel, New York: Bantam Books, 1961; and Karl Marx, *Capital and Other Writings*, New York: Modern Library, 1932.

ACTON, H. B. "The Materialist Conception of History," *Proceedings of the Aristotelian Society*, 1951.
BERLIN, ISAIAH. *Karl Marx*. New York: 1963.
BOBER, M. M. *Karl Marx's Interpretation of History*. Cambridge, Mass.: 1948.
CORNFORTH, M. *Historical Materialism*. London: 1953.
DAWSON, C. "Karl Marx and the Outline of History," *The Dynamics of World History*, New York: 1956.
DUPRE, LOUIS. *The Philosophical Foundations of Marxism*. New York: 1966.
HOOK, S. *From Hegel to Marx*. New York: 1935.
HOOK, S. (ed.). *Marx and the Marxists*. New York: 1955.
HOOK, S. *Towards the Understanding of Karl Marx*. London: 1935.
KAUTSKY, K. *Ethics and the Materialistic Conception of History*. Chicago: 1918.
KLINE, G. L. "A Philosophical Critique of Soviet Marxism," *Review of Metaphysics*, 1955.
LICHTHEIM, G. *Marxism: An Historical and Critical Study*. New York: 1961.
LÖWITH, KARL. *Meaning in History*. Chicago: 1949.
MARCUSE, H. *Reason and Revolution*, 2nd ed. London: 1955.
MAYO, H. B. "Marxism as a Philosophy of History," *Canadian Historical Review*, 1953.
MAZLISH, B. *The Riddle of History*. New York: 1966.
PLAMENATZ, J. *Man and Society*, Vol. II. London: 1963.

PLEKHANOV, G. V. *The Materialist Conception of History.* New York: 1940.

POPPER, KARL R. *The Open Society and Its Enemies,* Vol. II. London: 1945.

TREVOR-ROPER, H. R. "Karl Marx and the Study of History," *Men and Events,* New York: 1957.

TUCKER, R. C. *Philosophy and Myth in Karl Marx.* Cambridge, England: 1961.

7 *Oswald Spengler* (1880–1936)

Oswald Spengler's *Decline of the West* was published in Germany in 1918. The pessimistic conclusions of his book were so in tune with the mood of the day that he and his book quickly gained a wide hearing. However, the early influence of the book could hardly be attributed to the content or style of the book which was repetitious, obscure, and unsystematic.

Spengler set forth principles derived, he claimed, from history itself. These principles drew attention to basic similarities in the history of the major cultures of the world and also made it possible, Spengler believed, for him to predict generally the course of future history. Spengler's prediction so far as Western culture

DECLINE OF THE WEST

was concerned was one of doom; even now, he maintained, we can see the beginning of the end.

According to Spengler, the basic units of history are cultures. Each culture is self-contained; there is no interdependence between them. The purpose of the philosophy of history is to set forth a "comparative morphology of cultures." Spengler tried to apply the biologist's concept of living forms to the basic cultures in history. He believed that each culture went through a cycle similar to that of living organisms. Each of the eight fully developed cultures [1] has suffered through the same cycle of growth and decay. Cultures are born, grow strong, weaken, and die. Some live longer, some have been stronger, but all have ossified and fallen into a period of decadence and dissolution marked by commercialization and vulgarization.

Spengler contrasted what he called the Ptolemaic systems of history with his own Copernican approach. Ptolemaic systems of history all assume that history should be interpreted from the standpoint of the historian's own perspective in Western culture. According to this view, "the great Cultures are made to follow orbits round us as the presumed center of all world happenings." Such histories, Spengler argued, suffer from being based upon too limited or incorrect a point of reference. They ignore the whole process of history outside the sphere of Western influence. In opposition to this, Spengler's own "Copernican" approach to history admits no sort of privileged position to the Classical or Western Culture as over against the cultures of India, Babylon, China, Egypt, the Arabs, or Mexico. There is not just one history whose supposed linear development leads inexorably and progressively to our own "modern" day. There are many histories of many cultures, each with their own ideas, life, will, feeling—and their own death.

Each culture has its own basic world concept, i.e., a basic model or picture. The basic world concept for Greece and Rome, for example, was the atom; in our own age, it is infinity. This model symbolizes modern man's confidence that his horizons are unlimited.

---

[1] Egyptian, Chinese, Ancient Semitic, Indian, Apollinian (Greek or Roman), Magian (Hebrew and Arabian), Faustian (or Western), and Mexican.

Crucial to Spengler's analysis of Western Culture is his view that events in different cultures and different ages can be "contemporaneous" with each other. For example, Napoleon was morphologically contemporaneous with Alexander the Great, Hannibal was contemporaneous with World War I. In 1918, Spengler announced that the West was still awaiting its Julius Caesar.[2] Not only is this morphological principle helpful in predicting the future, it is an indispensable guide (providing one accepts it) for reconstructing the unknown past. Needless to say, few historians and philosophers have been satisfied with either of Spengler's uses of this principle.

Spengler's philosophy can be summed up in three words: Relativism, Pessimism, and Determinism. His relativism was a consequence of his views that history has no ultimate point of reference and that each culture is wholly self-contained. There are no abiding religious or moral ideas since all beliefs are relative to their respective culture. If this were true (and of course, given Spengler's relativism, even *his* position cannot be true), it would mean that members of one culture would be unable to make value judgments about the actions and beliefs of people in other cultures. Spengler even went so far as to say a member of one culture could never understand the beliefs and ideals of any other culture. He was apparently unaware that this argument vitiated his entire philosophy of history.

Spengler's work grows dim in the light of the internal inconsistencies of his system and the later achievements of Arnold Toynbee. While we may be forced to agree with Spengler that Western Culture is declining, we will have to assert this on grounds different from those he espoused.

OSWALD SPENGLER
THE DECLINE OF THE WEST *

In 1911, I proposed to myself to put together some broad considerations on the political phenomena of the day and their pos-

---

[2] Some critics have claimed that Spengler's position on this point helped prepare Germany for the advent of Hitler.

* The following selections are taken from Chapters I, III, and VI of

sible developments. At that time the World War appeared to me both as imminent and also as the inevitable outward manifestation of the historical crisis, and my endeavor was to comprehend it from an examination of the spirit of the preceding centuries —not years. In the course of this originally small task, the conviction forced itself on me that for an effective understanding of the epoch the area to be taken into the foundation plan must be very greatly enlarged, and that in an investigation of this sort, if the results were to be fundamentally conclusive and necessary results, it was impossible to restrict oneself to a single epoch and its political actualities, or to confine oneself to a pragmatical framework, or even to do without purely metaphysical and highly transcendental methods of treatment. It became evident that a political problem could not be comprehended by means of politics themselves and that, frequently, important factors at work in the depths could only be grasped through their artistic manifestations or even distantly seen in the form of scientific or purely philosophical ideas. Even the politico-social analysis of the last decades of the nineteenth century—a period of tense quiet between two immense and outstanding events: the one which, expressed in the Revolution and Napoleon, had fixed the picture of West-European actuality for a century and another of at least equal significance that was visibly and ever more rapidly approaching—was found in the last resort to be impossible without bringing in *all* the great problems of Being in all their aspects. For, in the historical as in the natural world picture, there is found nothing, however small, that does not embody in itself the entire sum of fundamental tendencies. And thus the original theme came to be immensely widened. A vast number of unexpected (and in the main entirely novel) questions and interrelations presented themselves. And finally it became perfectly clear that no single fragment of history could be thoroughly illuminated unless and until the secret of world history itself, to wit the story of higher mankind as an organism of regular structure, had been cleared up. And hitherto this has not been done, even in the least degree.

Oswald Spengler's *The Decline of the West,* Vol. I (New York: Alfred A. Knopf, Inc., 1928) by permission of Alfred A. Knopf, Inc. The translation is by Charles Francis Atkinson.

From this moment on, relations and connections—previously often suspected, sometimes touched on but never comprehended—presented themselves in ever-increasing volume. The forms of the arts linked themselves to the forms of war and state policy. Deep relations were revealed between political and mathematical aspects of the same Culture, between religious and technical conceptions, between mathematics, music, and sculpture, between economics and cognition forms. Clearly and unmistakably there appeared the fundamental dependence of the most modern physical and chemical theories on the mythological concepts of our Germanic ancestors, the style congruence of tragedy and power techniques and up-to-date finance, and the fact (bizarre at first but soon self-evident) that oil-painting perspective, printing, the credit system, long-range weapons, and contrapuntal music in one case, and the nude statue, the city-state, and coin currency (discovered by the Greeks) in another were identical expressions of one and the same spiritual principle. And, beyond and above all, there stood out the fact that these great *groups of morphological relations,* each one of which symbolically represents a particular sort of mankind in the whole picture of world history, are strictly symmetrical in structure. It is this perspective that first opens out for us the true style of history. Belonging itself as symbol and expression to one time and therefore inwardly possible and necessary only for present-day Western man, it can but be compared—distantly—to certain ideas of ultra-modern mathematics in the domain of the Theory of Groups. These were thoughts that had occupied me for many years, though dark and undefined until enabled by this method to emerge in tangible form.

Thereafter I saw the present—the approaching World War—in a quite other light. It was no longer a momentary constellation of casual facts due to national sentiments, personal influences, or economic tendencies endowed with an appearance of unity and necessity by some historian's scheme of political or social cause and effect, but the type of *a historical change of phase* occurring within a great historical organism of definable compass at the point preordained for it hundreds of years ago. The mark of the great crisis is its innumerable passionate questionings and probings. In our own case there were books and ideas by the thousand; but, scattered, disconnected, limited by the horizons of specialisms as they were, they incited, depressed, and confounded but could not free. Hence, though these questions are seen, their identity is missed. . . .

And thus in the end I came to see the solution clearly before me in immense outlines, possessed of full inward necessity, a solution derived from one single principle that though discoverable had never been discovered, that from my youth had haunted and attracted me, tormenting me with the sense that it was there and must be attacked and yet defying me to seize it. Thus, from an almost accidental occasion of beginning, there has arisen the present work, which is put forward as the provisional expression of a new world picture. The book is laden, as I know, with all the defects of a first attempt, incomplete, and certainly not free from inconsistencies. Nevertheless I am convinced that it contains the incontrovertible formulation of an idea which, once enunciated clearly, will (I repeat) be accepted without dispute.

If, then, the narrower theme is an analysis of the Decline of that West-European Culture which is now spread over the entire globe, yet the object in view is the development of a philosophy and of the operative method of comparative morphology in world history. . . .

Our theme, which originally comprised only the limited problem of present-day civilization, broadens itself into a new philosphy—*the* philosophy of the future, so far as the metaphysically-exhausted soil of the West can bear such, and in any case the only philosophy which is within the *possibilities* of the West-European mind in its next stages. It expands into the conception of a *morphology of world history,* of the world-as-history in contrast to the morphology of the world-as-nature that hitherto has been almost the only theme of philosophy. And it reviews once again the forms and movements of the world in their depths and final significance, but this time according to an entirely different ordering which groups them, not in an ensemble picture inclusive of everything known, but in a picture of *life,* and presents them not as things-become, but as things-becoming. . . .

What, then, *is* world history? Certainly, an ordered presentation of the past, an inner postulate, the expression of a capacity for feeling form. But a feeling for form, however definite, is not the same as form itself. No doubt we feel world history, experience it, and believe that it is to be read just as a map is read. But, even today, it is only forms of it that we know and not *the* form of it, which is the mirror image of *our own* inner life.

Everyone of course, if asked, would say that he saw the inward form of History quite clearly and definitely. The illusion subsists because no one has seriously reflected on it, still less conceived doubts as to his own knowledge, for no one has the slightest notion how wide a field for doubt there is. In fact, the *layout* of world history is an unproved and subjective notion that has been handed down from generation to generation (not only of laymen but of professional historians) and stands badly in need of a little of that scepticism which from Galileo onward has regulated and deepened our inborn ideas of nature.

Thanks to the subdivision of history into "Ancient," "Medieval," and "Modern"—an incredibly jejune and *meaningless* scheme, which has, however, entirely dominated our historical thinking—we have failed to perceive the true position in the general history of higher mankind, of the little part-world which has developed on West-European soil from the time of the German-Roman Empire, to judge of its relative importance and above all to estimate its direction. The Cultures that are to come will find it difficult to believe that the validity of such a scheme with its simple rectilinear progression and its meaningless proportions, becoming more and more preposterous with each century, incapable of bringing into itself the new fields of history as they successively come into the light of our knowledge, was, in spite of all, never wholeheartedly attacked. The criticisms that it has long been the fashion of historical researchers to level at the scheme mean nothing; they have only obliterated the one existing plan without substituting for it any other. To toy with phrases such as "the Greek Middle Ages" or "Germanic antiquity" does not in the least help us to form a clear and inwardly convincing picture in which China and Mexico, the empire of Axum and that of the Sassanids have their proper places. And the expedient of shifting the initial point of "modern history" from the Crusades to the Renaissance, or from the Renaissance to the beginning of the nineteenth century, only goes to show that the scheme per se is regarded as unshakably sound.

It is not only that the scheme circumscribes the area of history. What is worse, it rigs the stage. The ground of West Europe is treated as a steady pole, a unique patch chosen on the surface of the sphere for no better reason, it seems, than because we live on it—and great histories of millennial duration and mighty faraway Cultures are made to revolve around this pole in all modesty. It is a quaintly conceived system of sun and planets! We select a single bit of ground as the natural center of the historical system, and make it the central sun. From it all the events of history receive their real light, from it their importance is judged in *perspective*. But it is in our own West-European conceit alone that this phantom "world history," which a breath of scepticism would dissipate, is acted out. . . .

The most appropriate designation for this current West-European scheme of history, in which the great Cultures are made to follow orbits round *us* as the presumed center of all world happenings, is the *Ptolemaic system* of history. The system that is put forward in this work in place of it I regard as the *Copernican discovery* in the historical sphere, in that it admits no sort of privileged position to the Classical or the Western Culture as against the Cultures of India, Babylon, China, Egypt, the Arabs, Mexico—separate worlds of dynamic being which in point of mass count for just as much in the general picture of history as the Classical, while frequently surpassing it in point of spiritual greatness and soaring power. . . . In opposition to all these arbitrary and narrow schemes, derived from traditional or personal choice, into which history is forced, I put forward the natural, the "Copernican," form of the historical process which lies deep in the essence of that process and reveals itself only to an eye perfectly free from prepossessions. . . .

We know it to be true of every organism that the rhythm, form, and duration of its life, and all the expression details of that life as well, are determined by the *properties of its species*. No one, looking at the oak, with its millennial life, dare say that it is at this moment, now, about to start on its true and proper course. No one as he sees a caterpillar grow day by day expects that it will go on doing so for two or three years. In these cases we feel, with an unqualified certainty, a *limit,* and this sense of the limit is identical with our sense of the inward form. In the case of higher human history, on the contrary, we take our ideas as to the course of the future from an unbridled optimism that sets at naught all historical, i.e., *organic,* experience, and everyone therefore sets himself to discover in the accidental present terms that he can expand into some striking progression series, the existence of which rests not on scientific proof but on predilection. He works upon unlimited possibilities—never a natural end—and from the momentary top course of his bricks plans artlessly the continuation of his structure.

"Mankind," however, has no aim, no idea, no plan, any more than the family of butterflies or orchids. "Mankind" is a zoological expression, or an empty word.[1] But conjure away the phantom, break the magic circle, and at once there emerges an astonishing wealth of *actual* forms—the Living with all its immense fullness, depth and movement—hitherto veiled by a catchword, a dryasdust scheme, and a set of personal "ideals." I see, in place of that empty figment of *one* linear history which can only be kept up by shutting one's eyes to the overwhelming multitude of the facts, the drama of a *number* of mighty Cultures, each springing with primitive strength from the soil of a mother region to which it remains firmly bound throughout its whole life cycle; each stamping its material, its mankind, in *its own* image; each having *its own* idea, *its own* passions, *its own* life, will, and feeling, *its own* death. Here indeed are colors, lights, movements, that no intellectual eye has yet discovered. Here the Cultures, peoples, languages, truths, gods, landscapes bloom and age as the oaks and the stone pines, the blossoms, twigs and leaves—but there is no aging "Mankind." Each Culture has its own new possibilities of self-expression which arise, ripen, decay, and never return. There is not *one* sculpture, *one* painting, *one* mathematics, *one* physics, but many, each in its deepest essence different from the others, each limited in duration and self-contained, just as each species of plant has its peculiar blossom or fruit, its special type of growth and decline. These cultures, sublimated life essences, grow with the same superb aimlessness as the flowers of the field. They belong, like the plants and the

---

[1] "Mankind? It is an abstraction. There are, always have been, and always will be, men and only men." (Goethe to Luden)

animals, to the living Nature of Goethe, and not to the dead Nature of Newton. I see world history as a picture of endless formations and transformations, of the marvelous waxing and waning of organic forms. The professional historian, on the contrary, sees it as a sort of tapeworm industriously adding on to itself one epoch after another. . . .

In other aspects, mankind is habitually, and rightly, reckoned as one of the organisms of the earth's surface. Its physical structure, its natural functions, the whole phenomenal conception of it, all belong to a more comprehensive unity. Only in *this* aspect is it treated otherwise, despite that deeply felt relationship of plant destiny and human destiny which is an eternal theme of all lyrical poetry, and despite that similarity of human history to that of any other of the higher life groups which is the refrain of endless beast legends, sagas, and fables.

But only bring analogy to bear on this aspect as on the rest, letting the world of human Cultures intimately and unreservedly work upon the imagination instead of forcing it into a ready-made scheme. Let the words youth, growth, maturity, decay—hitherto, and today more than ever, used to express subjective valuations and entirely personal preferences in sociology, ethics, and aesthetics—be taken at last as objective descriptions of organic states. Set forth the Classical Culture as a self-contained phenomenon embodying and expressing the Classical soul, put it beside the Egyptian, the Indian, the Babylonian, the Chinese, and the Western, and determine for each of these higher individuals what is typical in their surgings and what is necessary in the riot of incident. And then at last will unfold itself the picture of world history that is natural to us, men of the West, and to us alone. . . .

Henceforth we shall designate the soul of the Classical Culture, which chose the sensuously present individual body as the ideal type of the extended, by the name (familiarized by Nietzsche) of the *Apollinian*. In opposition to it we have the *Faustian* soul, whose prime symbol is pure and limitless space, and whose "body" is the Western Culture that blossomed forth with the birth of the Romanesque style in the tenth century in the Northern plain between the Elbe and the Tagus. The nude statue is Apollinian, the art of the fugue Faustian. Apollinian are: mechanical statics, the sensuous cult of the Olympian gods, the politically individual city-states of Greece, the doom of Oedipus and the phallus symbol. Faustian are: Galilean dynamics, Catholic and Protestant dogmatics, the great dynasties of the Baroque with their cabinet diplomacy, the destiny of Lear and the Madonna-ideal from Dante's Beatrice to the last line of *Faust II*. The painting that defines the individual body by contours is Apollinian, that which forms space by means of light and shade is Faustian—this is the difference between the fresco of Polygnotus and the oil painting of Rembrandt. The Apollinian existence is that of the Greek who describes his ego as *soma* and who lacks all idea of an inner development and therefore all real history, inward and outward; the Faustian is an existence which *is led* with a deep consciousness and introspection of the ego, and a resolutely personal culture evidenced in memoirs, reflections, retrospects and prospects, and conscience. And in the time of Augustus, in the countries between Nile and Tigris, Black Sea and South Arabia, there appears—aloof but able to speak to us through forms borrowed, adopted, and inherited—the Magian soul of the Arabian Culture with its algebra, astrology, and alchemy, its mosaics and arabesques, its caliphates and mosques, and the sacraments and scriptures of the Persian, Jewish, Christian, "post-Classical," and Manichaean religions. . . .

Let it be realized, then:

That the secret of historical form does not lie on the surface, that it cannot be grasped by means of similarities of costume and setting, and that in the history of men as in that of animals and plants there occur phenomena showing deceptive similarity but inwardly without any connection—e.g., Charlemagne and Haroun-al-Raschid, Alexander and Caesar, the German wars upon Rome and the Mongol onslaughts upon West Europe—and other phenomena of extreme outward dissimilarity but of identical import—e.g., Trajan and Rameses II, the Bourbons and the Attic Demos, Mohammed and Pythagoras.

That the nineteenth and twentieth centuries, hitherto looked on as the highest point of an ascending straight line of world history, are in reality a stage of life which may be observed in every Culture that has ripened to its limit—a stage of life characterized not by Socialists, Impressionists, electric railways, torpedoes, and differential equations (for these are only body constituents of the time), but by a civilized spirituality which possesses not only these but also quite other creative possibilities.

That, as our own time represents a transitional phase which occurs with certainty under particular conditions, there are perfectly well-defined states (such as have occurred more than once in the history of the past) *later* than the present-day state of West Europe, and therefore:

That, the future of the West is not a limitless tending upwards and onwards for all time toward our present ideals, but a single phenomenon of history, strictly limited and defined as to form and duration, which covers a few centuries and can be viewed and, in essentials, calculated from available precedents. . . .

And now it is possible to discover the ultimate elements of the historical form world.

Countless shapes that emerge and vanish, pile up, and melt again, a thousand-hued glittering tumult, it seems, of perfectly willful chance—such is the picture of world history when first it deploys before our inner eye. But through this seeming anarchy, the keener glance can detect those pure forms which underlie all human becoming, penetrate their cloud mantle, and bring them unwillingly to unveil.

But of the whole picture of world becoming, of that cumulus of grand planes that the Faust-eye sees piled one beyond another —the becoming of the heavens, of the earth's crust, of life, of man—we shall deal here only with that very small morphological unit that we are accustomed to call "world history," that history which Goethe ended by despising, the history of higher mankind during 6000 years or so, without going into the deep problem of the meaning and substance, and what has hitherto lain buried deep under a mass of tangible "facts" and "dates" that has hardly yet been bored through, is the *phenomenon of the Great Cultures*. Only after these prime forms shall have been seen and felt and worked out in respect of their physiognomic meaning will it be possible to say that the essence and inner form of human History as opposed to the essence of Nature are understood—or rather, that we understand them. Only after this inlook and this outlook will a serious philosophy of history become feasible. Only then will it be possible to see each fact in the historical picture—each idea, art, war, personality, epoch—according to its symbolic content, and to regard history not as a mere sum of past things without intrinsic order or inner necessity, but as an organism of rigorous structure and significant articulation, an organism that does not suddenly dissolve into a formless and ambiguous future when it reaches the accidental present of the observer.

Cultures are organisms, and world history is their collective biography. Morphologically, the immense history of the Chinese or of the Classical Culture is the exact equivalent of the petty history of the individual man, or of the animal, or the tree, or the flower. For the Faustian vision, this is not a postulate but an experience; if we want to learn to recognize inward forms that constantly and everywhere repeat themselves, the comparative morphology of plants and animals has long ago given us the methods. In the destinies of the several Cultures that follow upon one another, is compressed the whole content of human history. And if we set free their shapes, till now hidden all too deep under the surface of a trite "history of human progress," and let them march past us in the spirit, it cannot but be that we shall succeed in distinguishing amidst all that is special or unessential, the primitive culture form, *the* Culture that underlies as ideal all the individual Cultures.

I distinguish the *idea* of a Culture, which is the sum total of its inner possibilities, from its sensible *phenomenon* or appearance upon the canvas of history as a fulfilled actuality. It is the relation of the soul to the living body, to its expression in the light-world perceptible to our eyes. This history of a Culture is the progressive actualizing of its possible, and the fulfillment is equivalent to the end. In this way, the Apollinian soul, which some of us can perhaps understand and share in, is related to its unfolding in the realm of actuality, to the "Classical" or "antique" as we call it, of which the tangible and understandable relics are investigated by the archaeologist, the philologist, the aesthete and the historian.

Culture is the prime phenomenon of all past and future world history. . . .

A Culture is born in the moment when a great soul awakens out of the protospirituality (*dem urseelenhaften Zustande*) of ever-childish humanity, and detaches itself, a form from the formless, a bounded and mortal thing from the boundless and enduring. It blooms on the soil of an exactly definable landscape, to which plant-wise it remains bound. It dies when this soul has actualized the full sum of its possibilities in the shape of peoples, languages, dogmas, arts, states, sciences, and reverts into the protosoul. But its living existence, that sequence of great epochs which define and display the stages of fulfillment, is an inner passionate struggle against the resistance of the material and the stifling of the idea within him. Every Culture stands in a deeply symbolical, almost in a mystical, relation to the Extended, the space, in which and through which it strives to actualize itself. The aim once attained—the idea, the entire content of inner possibilities, fulfilled and made externally actual—the Culture suddenly hardens, it mortifies, its blood congeals, its force breaks down, and it becomes *Civilization,* the thing which we feel and understand in the words Egypticism, Byzantinism, Mandarinism. As such they may, like a worn-out giant of the primeval forest, thrust their decaying branches toward the sky for hundreds or thousands of years, as we see in China, in India, in the Islamic world. It was thus that the Classical Civilization rose gigantic, in the Imperial age, with a false semblance of youth and strength and fullness, and robbed the young Arabian Culture of the East of light and air.

This—the inward and outward fulfillment, the finality, that awaits every living Culture—is the purport of all the historic "declines," amongst them that decline of the Classical which we know so well and fully, and another decline, entirely comparable to it in course and duration, which will occupy the first centuries of the coming millennium but is heralded already and sensible in and around us today—the decline of the West. Every Culture passes through the age phases of the individual man. Each has its childhood, youth, manhood, and old age. . . .

The notion of life duration as applied to a man, a butterfly, an oak, a blade of grass, comprises a specific time value, which is quite independent of all the accidents of the individual case. Ten years are a slice of life which is approximately equivalent for all men, and the metamorphosis of insects is associated with a number of days exactly known and predictable in individual cases.

For the Romans the notions of *pueritia, adolescentia, inventus, virilitas, senectus* possessed an almost mathematically precise meaning. Without doubt the biology of the future will—in opposition to Darwinism and to the exclusion in principle of causal fitness motives for the origins of species—take these *preordained* life durations as the starting point for a new enunciation of its problem. The duration of a generation—whatever may be its nature—is a fact of almost mystical significance.

Now, such relations are valid also, and to an extent never hitherto imagined, for all the higher Cultures. *Every Culture, every adolescence and maturing and decay of a Culture, every one of its intrinsically necessary stages and periods, has a definite duration, always the same, always recurring with the emphasis of a symbol.* In the present work we cannot attempt to open up this world of most mysterious connections, but the facts that will emerge again and again as we go on will tell us of themselves how much lies hidden here. What is the meaning of that striking fifty-year period, the rhythm of the political, intellectual, and artistic "becoming" of all Cultures? Of the three-hundred-year period of the Baroque, of the Ionic, of the great mathematics, of Attic sculpture, of mosaic painting, of counterpoint, of Galilean mechanics? What does the *ideal* life of one millennium for each Culture mean in comparison with the individual man's "three-score years and ten"? As the plant's being is brought to expression in form, dress, and carriage by leaves, blossoms, twigs, and fruit, so also is the being of a Culture manifested by its religious, intellectual, political, and economic formations. Just as, say, Goethe's individuality discourses of itself in such widely different forms as the *Faust,* the *Farbenlehre,* the *Reineke Fuchs, Tasso, Werther,* the journey and the Friederike love, the *Westöstliche Diwan* and the *Römische Elegien;* so the individuality of the Classical world displays itself in the Persian wars, the Attic drama, the city-state, the Dionysia and not less in the Tyrannis, the Ionic column, the geometry of Euclid, the Roman legion, and the gladiatorial contests and "panem et circenses" of the Imperial age.

In this sense, too, every individual being that has any sort of importance recapitulates, of intrinsic necessity, all the epochs of the Culture to which it belongs. In each one of us, at that decisive

DECLINE OF THE WEST

moment when he begins to know that he is an ego, the inner life wakens just where and just how that of the Culture wakened long ago. . . .

Biology employs the term *homology* of organs to signify morphological equivalence in contradistinction to the term *analogy* which relates to functional equivalence. This important, and in the sequel most fruitful, notion was conceived by Goethe . . . and put into strict scientific shape by Owen; this notion also we shall incorporate in our historical method.

It is known that for every part of the bone structure of the human head an exactly corresponding part is found in all vertebrated animals right down to the fish, and that the pectoral fins of fish and the feet, wings, and hands of terrestrial vertebrates are homologous organs, even though they have lost every trace of similarity. The lungs of terrestrial, and the swim bladders of aquatic animals are homologous, while lungs and gills on the other hand are analogous—that is, similar in point of use. And the trained and deepened morphological insight that is required to establish such distinctions is an utterly different thing from the present method of historical research, with its shallow comparisons of Christ and Buddha, Archimedes and Galileo, Caesar and Wallenstein, parcelled Germany and parcelled Greece. More and more clearly as we go on, we shall realize what immense views will offer themselves to the historical eye as soon as the rigorous morphological method has been understood and cultivated. To name but a few examples, *homologous* forms are: Classical sculpture and West European orchestration, the Fourth Dynasty pyramids and the Gothic cathedrals, Indian Buddhism and Roman Stoicism (Buddhism and Christianity are *not even analogous*); the periods of "the Contending States" in China, the Hyksos in Egypt and the Punic Wars; the age of Pericles and the age of the Ommayads; the epochs of the Rigveda, of Plotinus, and of Dante. The Dionysiac movement is homologous with the Renaissance, analogous to the Reformation. For us, "Wagner is the *résumé* of modernity," as Nietzsche rightly saw; and the equivalent that logically *must* exist in the Classical modernity we find in Pergamene art.

The application of the "homology" principle to historical phenomena brings with it an entirely new connotation for the word "contemporary." I designate as contemporary two historical facts that occur in exactly the same—relative—positions in their respective Cultures, and therefore possess exactly equivalent importance. It has already been shown how the development of the Classical and that of the Western mathematic proceeded in complete congruence, and we might have ventured to describe Pythagoras as the contemporary of Descartes, Archytas of Laplace, Archimedes of Gauss. The Ionic and the Baroque, again, ran their course *contemporaneously*. Polygnotus pairs in time with Rembrandt, Polycletus with Bach. The Reformation, Puritanism and, above all, the turn to Civilization appear simultaneously in all Cultures; in the Classical this last epoch bears the names of Philip and Alexander, in our West those of the Revolution and Napoleon. Contemporary, too, are the building of Alexandria, of Baghdad, and of Washington; Classical coinage and our double-entry bookkeeping; the first Tyrannis and the Fronde; Augustus and Shih-huang-ti; Hannibal and the World War.

I hope to show that without exception all great creations and forms in religion, art, politics, social life, economy, and science appear, fulfill themselves and die down *contemporaneously* in all the Cultures; that the inner structure of one corresponds strictly with that of all the others; that there is not a single phenomenon of deep physiognomic importance in the record of one for which we could not find a counterpart in the record of every other; and that this counterpart is to be found under a characteristic form and in a perfectly definite chronological position. At the same time, if we are to grasp such homologies of facts, we shall need to have a far deeper insight and a far more critical attitude toward the visible foreground of things than historians have hitherto been wont to display; who amongst them, for instance, would have allowed himself to dream that the counterpart of Protestantism was to be found in the Dionysiac movement, and that English Puritanism was for the West what Islam was for the Arabian world?

Seen from this angle, history offers possibilities far beyond the ambitions of all previous research, which has contented itself in the main with arranging the facts of the past so far as these were known (and that according to a one-line scheme)—the possibilities, namely, of

Overpassing the present as a research limit, and predetermining the spiritual form, duration, rhythm, meaning, and produce of the *still unaccomplished* stages of our western history; and

Reconstructing long-vanished and unknown epochs, even whole cultures of the past, by means of morphological connections, in much the same way as modern paleontology deduces far-reaching and trustworthy conclusions as to skeletal structure and species from a single unearthed skull fragment.

It is possible, given the physiognomic rhythm, to recover from scattered details of ornament, building, script, or from odd political, economic, and religious data, the organic characters of whole centuries of history, and from known elements on the scale of art expression, to find corresponding elements on the scale of political forms, or from that of mathematical forms to read that of economic. This is a truly Goethian method—rooted in fact in Goethe's conception of the *prime phenomenon*—which is already to a limited extent current in comparative zoology, but can be extended, to a degree hitherto undreamed of, over the whole field of history.

DISCUSSION
R. G. COLLINGWOOD:
SPENGLER'S THEORY OF HISTORICAL CYCLES *

Since Plato announced that the course of history returned upon itself in 72,000 years, since Polybius discerned a "circular movement" by which the history of states came back, over and over again, to the same point, the theory of historical cycles has been a commonplace of European thought. Familiar to the thinkers of the Renaissance, it was modified by Vico in the early eighteenth century and again by Hegel in the early nineteenth; and a complete history of the idea would show many curious transformations and cover a long period of time. Here no at-

* Reprinted from *Antiquity* (1927), with the permission of the editor.

tempt will be made to summarize this story; the subject of the present paper is the latest and, to ourselves, most striking exposition of the general theory, contained in Dr. Oswald Spengler's *Decline of the West*.[1]

Spengler's view of history presents it as a succession of cultures, each having a peculiar physiognomy of its own which it maintains and works out down to the smallest details, and each following a definite course of development through a sequence of phases that is identical for all. Every culture has its spring, its dawning phase, economically based on rural life and spiritually recognizable by a rich mythological imagination expressing in epic and legend the whole world view which, later, is to be developed in philosophical and scientific form. Then follows its summer, at once a revolt against the mythology and scholasticism of the spring and their continuation; a period in which a young and vigorous urban intelligence pushes religion into the background and brings to the fore a strictly scientific form of consciousness to its limit, while at the same time it sees the decay of religion and the impoverishment of inward life; rationalism, enlightenment, are its obvious marks. Last comes winter, the decay of culture and the reign of civilization, the materialistic life of the great cities, the cult of science only so far as science is useful, the withering of artistic and intellectual creativeness, the rise of academic and professional philosophy, the death of religion, and the drying up of all the springs of spiritual life. The four-fold distinction of phases is not a necessity; at times it is convenient to distinguish more or fewer than four; but however many are distinguished in one culture the same number is necessarily distinguishable in all others. Thus, the revolt against Gothic which we call the Renaissance is a morphologically necessary phase of our culture; it is called the exhaustion of the early or primitive phase of a culture and the rise of the conscious or urban phase in which the individual working for himself takes the place of the anonymous corporate effort of the springtime. And therefore the same thing must happen in all cultures; in Egypt it is the revolt against the "pyramid style," in Greece the close of

[1] *Untergang des Abendlandes* (1918). I quote from the admirable English translation (Allen and Unwin, 1926).

the archaic period, and so forth. Again, Napoleon in the western culture marks the exact point of transition from autumn to winter, from culture proper to civilization; the breakup of the state proper and the beginning of imperialism, the victory of the great city over the country, the triumph of money over politics. Hence Napoleon is exactly parallel (or, as Spengler calls it, "contemporary") with Alexander, who marks the transition from the Hellenic world to the Hellenistic; in no sense parallel with Caesar, who marks a phase *within* the "winter" period, and is "contemporary" with a phase in western history that still lies in the future. The point which we have now reached is the plutocracy disguised by demagogism, and called "democracy," which is represented by the second century B.C. in Rome.

Thus the cycle repeats itself in the smallest details, every phase reappearing in every cycle; yet what reappears is never the same phase—nothing can happen twice—but only something *homologous* with it, something which in the new cycle corresponds structurally with something in the old. Here comparative anatomy is the clue. A whale and an elephant lead radically different lives; everything about each is adapted to its own life; a whale is altogether whale and an elephant is elephantine through and through; but every organ and every bone in the one is homologous with an organ or a bone in the other. The task of morphology is to grasp at once the homology or correspondence of parts, and their differentiation by the fundamental difference between the two species. Merely to say "this bone in the elephant reminds me of that in the whale," is unscientific; and it is equally unscientific to say "a whale and an elephant are so different that nothing is gained by comparing them." Similarly it is unscientific merely to mention likenesses in history, a likeness between Alexander and Caesar, or between Buddha and Christ; and equally unscientific to say that the differences between cultures are so profound as to make likenesses impossible. The only scientific thing to do is to recognize at once the likeness and the difference, combining them into the notion of homology or structural identity. We then see that Alexander and Caesar cannot be homologous, for they fall in the same culture; one closes its autumn, the other helps, though not crucially, to consolidate its winter; and that Buddha and Christ are still less to be compared, because the latter marks the creative spring of the Arabian culture, the former, the congealing winter of the Indian.

This conception is set forth at enormous length in a formless and chaotic volume, heavy with erudition and illuminated by a brilliant play of analogical insight, and a still more brilliant power of discrimination. The unforgettable things in the book are the passages in which the author characterizes such fundamental differences as those between classical things and their modern analogues: in which he illustrates the thesis that "Classical culture possessed no memory, no organ of history in the highest sense," or that the ancients thought of space as the nonexistent—this he proves not simply by quoting philosophers but by analyzing sculpture and architecture—whereas western man regards infinite space as his true home and proper environment; which again is proved not from Kant but from a study of Gothic and oil painting. For the philosopher only makes explicit in his own peculiar way an idea which has necessarily been the common heritage of his entire culture; and nothing is more admirable than the way in which Spengler sees and expounds this important truth.

The strange thing is that he seems to think his ideas altogether new. Learned as he is, he is either very ignorant or very reticent concerning the history of his own science. He asserts over and over again that the morphology of historical cultures is a wholly new thing. He seems ready to admit, in a single cautious sentence, that with regard to political history the idea is old; but he denies that any one has applied it to "*all* branches of a culture." That may be; all is a large word; but if he really knew of the cyclical doctrines of Plato, Polybius, Machiavelli, and above all Vico, which last both anticipates his own in all essentials and goes far beyond it in historical profundity; if he even knew of Professor Petrie's recent and fascinating exposition of the same doctrine, he cannot be acquitted of *suppressio veri*. He cannot claim to have omitted them for lack of space; his book consists largely of repetitions, and of its 250,000 words it would have been easy to devote 250 to naming his predecessors in the field. The fact that he has not done so, makes it incumbent on a critic like the present writer to confess that not only has the main thesis of Spengler's book been familiar to him all his life, but that the

SPENGLER'S THEORY OF HISTORICAL CYCLES

reading of it has not given him a single genuinely new idea; for all the applications of the thesis are mechanical exercises which, so far as the present writer is acquainted with the ground, he has long ago carried out for himself. This one may say without claiming to possess a quarter of Spengler's erudition.

This erudition, gigantic as it is, shows one gap. Spengler is at his worst in discussing philosophy. He shows what must be called a complete misunderstanding of Plato when he mistakes a deliberately "mythical" literary form for a "mystical" type of thought (what philosopher was ever less "mystical" than Plato?); he consistently attributes to the Stoics the fundamental conception of the Epicureans, and incidentally misunderstands its meaning; and he commits the appalling blunder of asserting that for Descartes the soul is in space—a statement which falsifies the whole modern conception of the relation between space and thought and goes far to explain his long rambling polemics against what he takes to be the philosophy of Kant.

This is not a matter of mere ignorance concerning one department of human history. He is not at all ill-informed on the history of philosophy, he is ill at ease in philosophy itself; and this means that whenever he tries to handle a fundamental problem he does so clumsily and without firmness or penetration. Brilliant on the surface, glittering in its details with a specious cleverness and apparent profundity, his "philosophy of history" is at bottom lacking in orientation, unsound on fundamentals, ill thought-out, and in consequence committed to a method which falsifies even its detail when a crucial case arises. These are serious charges; they are only made because Spengler's is a serious book which deserves to be taken seriously; and the first step toward proving them must be to quote falsified details. They are numerous; here are a few.

"The Greek and Roman alike sacrificed to the gods of the place in which he happened to stay or reside; all other deities were outside his range of vision." (p. 83) This *must* be true, because it follows from the fundamentally spaceless and timeless character of the classical mind, its insistence on the here and now as the only reality. But it is *not* true. Even Odysseus prays to his own Athene as he struggles for life in the stormy sea; and the Roman carries to the ends of the empire the Juppiter Optimus Maximus of the Capitol. The first half of Spengler's sentence is true; the second is false. This means that he has represented as the whole of the classical mind what was in reality only a part. The tendency to worship the gods of the land was very real; but it was only one tendency, and it was constantly balanced and checked by a countertendency to carry with one the cult of one's own place. *Caelum non animum mutant, qui trans mare currunt.*

Similarly, he asserts more than once that the classical mind was essentially polytheistic, and opposes to it "Magian monotheism" (p. 404), that is, alleges that monotheism is characteristic of the Arabian culture that filled the first millennium of our era. But this is, once more, inaccurate. All the Greek philosophers, until the decadence, were monotheists; and Spengler knows that philosophy is only a reasoned statement of ideas common to the culture. The monotheism of the philosophers can only indicate a profound strain of monotheism in the whole Greco-Roman world. And indeed Spengler himself would recognize that strain (for its existence is notorious enough) did not his faulty logic compel him to ignore it in the interests of his morphology.

Again, to take another example from ancient religion, he asserts that classical gods are all gods of the "near" and the "concrete," *numina* resident in things that are here and now, this hearth, this door, this field, this river; this act, whether the act of sowing or the act of lovemaking; always the sensuously present and near, never the distant or the future. "It is a deeply significant fact that in Hellas of all countries star gods, the numina of the Far, are wanting." (p. 402) We say nothing of the Sol Invictus, the Mithras, of Imperial Rome; for with Imperial Rome the author can play heads I win, tails you lose; in one aspect it is the decadence of the "classic," in another the rise of the "Magian," and Mithras is obviously Magian. But has he forgotten Zeus-Juppiter the sky god? Has he forgotten the stellar deities of Plato and the philosophical sky worship of Xenophanes? Has he forgotten that the adjective selected by himself as the most perfectly descriptive of the classical mind is "Apollinian"?

These are not superficial flaws. They are not minor errors or inconsistencies such as must exist in any great work. They are sacrifices of truth to method; they are symptoms of a logical fallacy which underlies the whole book and has actually been erected into a principle. The fallacy lies in the attempt to characterize a culture by means of a single idea or tendency or feature, to deduce everything from this one central idea without recognizing that a single idea, asserted in this way, calls up its own opposite in order to have something to assert itself against, and henceforth proceeds, not by merely repeating itself, but by playing a game of statement and counterstatement with this opposite. Everything in the classical mind is by Spengler deduced from the here and now of the immediate, sense-given, bodily present. But to assert the present is to deny the absent; therefore the absent must be present to the classical mind as *that which it is denying,* and it is impossible to concentrate one's mind on denying anything unless one vividly feels the need of denying it; feels that it is *there* to be denied, that someone, or some obscure force within oneself, is asserting it. Further, when one has denied it, and denied it effectively and overwhelmingly, it reasserts itself in a new form; and one has to begin over again, in order to meet this new peril. So the attempt to frame a whole life—political, artistic, religious, scientific, and so forth—by working out the implications of a single fundamental idea is foredoomed to failure; the idea can only live in conflict with its own opposing ideas or tendencies is, nowadays, one would have thought, a commonplace. Indeed, Spengler himself says it is. It is the more curious that he should not himself possess the conception; or rather, that he should base his entire system of historical cycles on denying it. For this is what, in effect, he does. It is true that classical art or thought tends to be easily intelligible, while modern or western tends to be obscure to the many and intelligible only to the few; therefore, says Spengler, this is the whole truth; "everything that is classical is comprehensible in one glance"; instead of obscure philosophers, for instance, the classical world has philosophers who can be understood by the man in the street: and in this context he actually mentions Heraclitus, without adding that he was nicknamed "the Obscure." (p. 327) Magian monotheism is dualistic, therefore the Jewish religion, being Magian, opposes to Jahweh (whom? you would never guess)—Beelzebub! (p.

32) The classical culture only cared for the present, therefore the Hellenes, unlike the Vikings, did not bury their dead in great barrows (p. 333); and what of the tombs on the Via Appia? Magian ethics, unlike Western, were mildly "recommended," not imposed as a command (p. 344); "the glad tidings of Jesus, like those of Zoroaster, of Mani, of Mahomet, of the Neoplatonists and of all the cognate Magian religions were mystic benefits *displayed* but in no wise imposed." And did Islam never appeal for its extension to the help of the sword? Classical art creates an object to be beheld, a thing standing complete here and now, not entering, therefore, into any relation with the beholder or soliciting his attention (p. 329); what of the *parabasis* of Aristophanic drama? These are merely examples of the way in which, to bring them into the scheme, facts are constantly impoverished, robbed of one element merely because it is recessive, in order that the other, dominant as it is, may be erected into a false absolute. No one, probably, will deny that the elements which Spengler identifies as characteristic of this or that culture really are characteristic of it; where he fails is in thinking out what he means by "characteristic." He thinks that the characteristic is a fundamental something whose logical consequences flow smoothly and unopposedly into all its manifestations; whereas it is really the dominant partner in a pair of opposites, asserting itself only so far as it can keep its opposite in check and therefore always colored by the hidden presence and underground activity of this opposite. To see the dominant characteristic and miss the recessive is to see history with the eye of the superficial student.

The same fault comes out in a different way in his view of the relation of cultures to one another. Vico, whose work he so curiously ignores, pointed out that the feudal barbarism of the Middle Ages differed from the Homeric feudal barbarism because it contained in itself Christianity, which summarizes and transcends ancient thought (Croce, *Vico,* p. 132). And even Spengler, when it comes to mathematics, notices that Euclidean geometry is still retained today as elementary or school geometry, so that modern mathematics contains and transcends Greek mathematics. But though he sees this fact, he does not understand it; for him, every culture is just radically different from every other, based on its own idea and not on the idea of any but itself. Each culture is wholly self-enclosed; within its limits, it proceeds on a type-pattern exactly like that of the rest, but this similarity of structure is its *only* relation to the rest. For him, therefore, it is a misfortune that our elementary geometry is still Euclidean; it gets us into bad mathematical habits and sets an unnecessary obstacle in the way of our understanding modern non-Euclidean geometry. Thus the whole idea of "classical education" is, we infer, a gigantic blunder. Similarly, it was a misfortune, he thinks, that the "Magian" culture grew up under the tutelage of decaying classical civilization, whose petrified relics prevented the new culture from rising spontaneously, because unopposed, in the Roman Imperial age. But surely it is not very hard to see that non-Euclidean geometry is based upon Euclidean even while it transcends and opposes it; and that the "Magian" culture, far from being stifled by the Roman Empire, used it as a scaffolding for its own building, a trellis for its own climbing flowers. The reason why Spengler denies these obvious facts is because he cannot grasp the true dynamic relation between opposites; his philosophical error leads him into the purely historical blunder of thinking that one culture, instead of stimulating another by its very opposition, can only crush it or be crushed by it. He thinks of cultures atomistically, each as a self-contained or closed system, precisely as Epicurus thought of the "worlds" whose plurality he asserted; and just as Epicurus could do nothing better with the spaces between his worlds than to hand them over to the gods as a dwelling, surrendering all attempt to make sense of the relation between world and world, so Spengler plugs the gap between one culture and the next with a crude, culture from its neighbors and makes it impossible to envisage an historical whole of which every culture is a part. He actually claims that the abandonment of the historical whole, and the atomistic view of cultures, is a grand merit of his system; and so it is, for it cuts out the real problem of history, the problem of *interrelating* the various cultures, which is the problem that requires profound and penetrating thought, and leaves only the problem of *comparing* them, a far easier task for those shallow minds that can accept it. And if, as Spengler says, this is the age of shallow and decadent thought, of unphilosophical philosophy and unscientific science, his philosophy of history is, as he says it is, precisely what our age needs.

The fact is that Spengler, with all his erudition and historical learning, lacks the true historical mind. Learning does not make the historian; there is a *sense* of history which is not acquired through erudition, and for this historical sense we look to Spengler in vain. History deals with the individual in all of its individuality; the historian is concerned to discover the facts, the whole facts, and nothing but the facts. Now comparative anatomy is not history but science; and Spengler's morphology is simply the comparative anatomy of historical periods. The historical morphologist is concerned not to discover what happened, but, assuming that he knows what happened, to generalize about its structure as compared with the structure of other happenings. His business is not to *work at* history, but to *talk about* it, on the assumption that someone else has already done the work—the work, that is, of finding out what the facts are, the historian's work. In this sense, Spengler nowhere shows the slightest desire to do a piece of historical work, or the slightest sign of having done one. His history consists of ready-made facts which he has found in books; and what he wants to do is to arrange these in patterns. When the man with historical sense reads a statement in a history book, he at once asks, is that really so? What evidence is there? How can I check the statement? and he sets to work doing over again, for himself, the work of determining the fact. This is because the historical sense means the feeling for historical thought as living thought, a thought that goes on within one's own mind, not a dead thought that can be treated as a finished product, cut adrift from its roots in the mind that thinks it, and played with like a pebble. Now the extraordinary thing about Spengler is that, after giving us a penetrating and vivid description of the difference between history and nature, and setting up the demand that we shall envisage "the world as history"—an admirable demand admirably stated—he goes on to consider the world not as history but precisely as nature, to study it, that is to say, through scientific and not historical spectacles, and to substitute for a truly genetic narrative, which would be history, a self-confessed morphology, which is science. And he is forced into doing this by his own philosophical errors, his errors, that is to say, concerning the structure of his own thought. He prepares us for all this, it is true, by his open scorn of logic and his statement that Goethe and Nietzsche are his only two masters; for neither Goethe nor Nietzsche, with all their poetic gifts and fine intelligence, had any grasp on the distinction between nature and history. And Spengler himself praises Goethe for confusing the two, for treating Nature as history and a culture as an organism.

The touchstone of the historical sense is the future. Science determines the future, foretells an eclipse or the like, just because the object of science is Nature and "Nature has no history." The laws of Nature are timeless truths. For history, time is the great reality; and the future is the infinite wellspring of those events which, when they happen, become present, and whose traces left upon the present enable us to reconstruct them when they are past. We cannot know the future, just because the future has not happened and therefore cannot leave its traces in the present. The historian who tries to forecast the future is like a tracker anxiously peering at a muddy road in order to descry the footsteps of the next person who is going to pass that way. All this, the historian knows instinctively. Ask him to forecast a single instant of the future, and he will laugh in your face. If anyone offers to foretell events, he speaks not as an historian but as a scientist or a clairvoyant. And if he offers to foretell events by means of historical thinking, he is either hoaxing his audience or saying historical when he means scientific. Spengler again and again claims that his morphology enables him to foretell the future. He even says that therein lies its chief merit and novelty; in which context, as usual, he refrains from mentioning his predecessors, the crowd of sociological writers, led by Marx, who have made just that claim.

But his claim to foretell the future is absolutely baseless. Just as his morphology does not work at history but only talks about it, does not *determine* the past but, assuming it as already determined, attaches labels to it, so this same method does not determine the future, but only provides a set of labels—the same old set—for a future that is undetermined. For instance,

Spengler tells us that between A.D. 2000 and 2200 someone will arise corresponding to Julius Caesar. Well, we ask, what will he do? Where will he live? What will he look like? Whom will he conquer? All Spengler can say is, he will correspond to Julius Caesar; he will do the kind of things that a person would do, who corresponded to Julius Caesar; he will live in a place corresponding to Julius Caesar's Rome; he will look like a person corresponding to Julius Caesar, and so forth. But, we must reply, this is not predetermining history. Suppose, instead, it were a question of the past: suppose we asked, who corresponded to Julius Caesar in the Egyptian culture? Suppose, now, we were told, "oh, the answer is easy: the person who corresponded to Julius Caesar." This would be *the wrong answer:* it would have determined nothing: it would be a mere confession of ignorance concerning the Egyptian past. The *right* answer (Spengler has given it) would be "Thutmosis III." This is a real answer because it names an actual concrete individual in actual concrete circumstances; and until we can do that, we have not determined any history at all. But if the past is not determined until we have said "Thutmosis III," the future is not determined until we can say "John Jones of Bulawayo," or whoever it will be. Spengler's claim to foretell the future is on a par with saying that the possession of a clock will enable its possessor to foretell the future because he can say that twelve will happen an hour after eleven. No doubt; but what will be going on at twelve?

There is another reason why the claim is wholly futile. On his own showing, the decay of classical culture in Rome synchronized with the rise of Magian culture in the very same culture area. Thus cultures may overlap both in space and in time. In Hadrian's reign, then a Spengler might have diagnosed a general petrification and decay of everything classical, and said that the Roman world was a dying world. And when someone pointed to the Pantheon, and said, "is that a symptom of decay?" the answer would be, "that is an example of imperial display by means of material and mass", and therefore it is meaningless, barren, vulgar civilization-architecture." But a counter-Spengler would retort, "not at all; the Pantheon is *the first Mosque* (pp. 72, 211, 358—as usual, he says it three times over) "and therefore belongs to the exuberant springtime of a nascent culture." Now it follows from the atomistic view of cultures that a new culture may begin anywhere, at any moment, irrespective of any circumstances whatever; and there is no possible proof that one is not beginning now. But if so, what becomes of "predetermining the future"?

It is all the more hopeless because there is no possible way, according to Spengler, of discovering what will be the fundamental idea of any hitherto undeveloped or unexamined culture. This, of course, follows from the atomistic conception; but its results are very serious. If any two cultures happened to have the same fundamental idea, they would be indistinguishable; the person corresponding to Julius Caesar would be Julius Caesar himself, repeated identically, name and all, at another date. That this possibility follows logically from Spengler's conception shows how profoundly antihistorical that conception is; that he has not observed it to follow, shows how ill he has thought out his own position. But on the other hand, if the fundamental idea of one culture differs from that of another, how can the one understand the other? Spengler unhesitatingly answers, it cannot. We do not understand the classical world; what we see in it is our own image in an opaque mirror. Very well, but how does he know this to be merely our image? How does he know that we are not understanding the past as it really was? There is no answer, and can be no answer; for the fact is, unless we understand the ancients well enough to know that we do not understand them completely, we can never have reason to suspect that our errors about them are erroneous. Spengler, by denying the possibility of understanding other cultures than our own, has denied the possibility of history itself. Here again, bad philosophy—a crude half-baked, subjective idealism—brings its own punishment. If history is possible, if we can understand other cultures, we can do so only by rethinking for ourselves their thoughts, cherishing within us the fundamental idea which framed their lives; and in that case their culture lives on within ours, as Euclidean geometry lives on within modern geometry and Herodotean history within the mind of the modern historian. But this is to destroy the idea of atomic cultures, and to assert not a mere plurality of cultures but a unity of that plurality, a unity which is the present culture, the heir of all its past. Against that conception Spengler struggles, because, having no historical sense, he does not *feel* it, and, being a bad philosopher, cannot understand it; yet that conception is presupposed on every page of his work. "The unities of place, time, and action" I read, opening it at random, "are . . . an indication of what classical man felt about life." (p. 323) And how does Spengler know what classical man felt? Only by putting himself into the position of classical man and feeling it too. Unless he has done that, he is deliberately deceiving us; no man knows what another feels if he is incapable of feeling it himself.

Spengler's so-called philosophy of history is therefore, we may repeat, lacking in orientation, because it reduces history to a plurality of cultures between whose fundamental ideas there is no relation whatever; it is unsound on fundamentals, because its purpose—that of "predetermining the future"—is impossible in itself and in any case unrealizable by his methods; it is ill thought out, because he shows no signs of having seen the fatal objections to it; and it is committed to the methodical falsification of facts because it distorts every fact falling—or alleged to fall—within a given culture, into an example of an abstract and one-sided idea which is fancied to represent the essence of that culture. In all four respects, it is an unworthy child of the historical studies of the last two hundred years. In each respect it violates elementary dictates of the historical consciousness; in each respect it is far surpassed by the cyclical doctrines of Hegel, a hundred, and Vico two hundred years ago. Vico realized that culture (to retain Spengler's term) could not arise by a miracle out of a uniform, purely cultureless, life; that barbarism contained the seeds of culture in itself, and produced culture by their germination. Thus Vico does away with Spengler's crude and superficial dualism between cultured and cultureless life. Further, granted that culture arises out of what Vico calls a "barbarism of sensation" and decays into a "barbarism of reflection" (the latter being Spengler's civilization), after having achieved a homogeneous development, economic and legal, religious and artistic, scientific and linguistic, Vico sees that this rule is merely approximate and not a priori necessary; he sees that there are exceptions to it, or, at least, that it is subject to such diversities of application in practice that it cannot serve as a basis for prophecy. This is, at bottom, because, the fundamental ideas of the various cultures being different, the cultures themselves will develop in different rhythms. Obviously, here Vico is right. What could be more ridiculous than Spengler's assumption that every idea will take the same number of years to develop through its different phases and exhaust its possibilities, no matter what idea it is? For that matter, why should it have the same phases at all? "We find," someone might plead, "that it does"; but Spengler is not entitled so to plead; for he asserts that a given culture *must* have passed through this or that phase, unknown though the phase may be, because others have done so.

Every culture, then, is surrounded not by sheer non-culture, but by other cultures, more or less perfect, perhaps, than itself; higher or lower, perhaps in the scale of value; but yet cultures. That is the first modification to be made in Spengler's doctrine. Secondly, while recognizing that a given culture has a certain self-consistent character, a fundamental idea which is working itself out into a complete social life, we must assert that this idea or character is not static but dynamic; it is not a single unchanged thing, miraculously born at one time, then persisting unaltered, and finally wiped out of existence, but a process of spiritual development, an idea which grows out of other ideas, in an environment of other ideas, which asserts itself against these other ideas through a process of give-and-take in which it modifies them and is modified by them in turn. In this process, culminating points absolute domination. Here the whole culture becomes brilliantly luminous with the light of this idea; luminous to itself, so far as its own human vehicles grasp the idea consciously, luminous to us, so far as we can re-create their idea within our minds and so see what their life meant to them. But the domination is never absolute. It is always a domination over something; there are always other ideas knocking at the gate, kept out by force, whose pressure against the ring fence of cultural life is equal and opposite to the expansive force of the life within. So the highest summits of culture reveal a contradiction between what they assert and what they deny—Greek liberty resting on Greek slavery, capitalist wealth resting on capitalist poverty—and in the long run the mere attempt to work out the cultural idea consistently to *live* it (rather than *think* it) to the full, destroys the culture. But the destruction of one culture is the birth of another; for there is no static entity called a culture, there is only a perpetual development, a development in which what has been won must be lost in order that something further may be won. And everything that is achieved in this process rests on the basis of all that has been achieved in its past phases.

Because this process is always the same, though always new, it is easy to find analogies and homologies between any part of it and any other. But when we cut it up into sections and say "here begins classical culture, and here it ends: here begins Magian culture, and here it ends," we are talking not about history but about the labels we choose to stick upon the corpse of history. Better historical thinking, deeper historical knowledge, would show us within the heart of classical culture, not a single unchanged idea, but a dynamic interplay of ideas, containing elements which even quite early, prepare it for its conversion into Magian. It is bad history and bad philosophy alike to argue that because the Pantheon is Magian it is not classical. Follow that up, and you will find that nothing is classical. It is truer to say that the classical is not a style but an age, a process, a development, which led to the Magian by its own inner logic. Thus the Pantheon is *both* Magian *and* classical; it is classical in the act of *turning into* Magian. And this conception of "turning into," the conception of becoming, is (as Spengler himself industriously asserts, and industriously forgets) the fundamental idea of all history.

What, then, remains of the conception of historical cycles? Much; for though a "period" of history is an arbitrary fabrication, a mere part torn from its context, given a fictitious unity, and set in a fictitious isolation, yet, by being so treated, it acquires a beginning, and a middle, and an end. And we fabricate periods of history by fastening upon some, to us, peculiarly luminous point and trying to study it as it actually came into being. We find our eye caught, as it were by some striking phenomenon—Greek life in the fifth century, or the like; and this becomes the nucleus of a group of historical inquiries, asking how it arose and how it passed away; what turned into it, and what it turned into. Thus we form the idea of a period, which we call the Hellenic period; and this period will resemble the Byzantine period or the Baroque period *in being a period,* that is, in having a luminous center preceded and followed by processes whose only interest to us at the moment is that they lead to and from it. From another point of view, the movement leading away from fifth-century Greece, the "decline of Hellas," will figure as the movement leading up to the Hellenistic world. Was it, then, "really" a decline or an advance? Neither, because both; it was a becoming, a change, a development; and the historian's highest task is to discover *what* developed, through *what* phases, into *what.* If anyone is not interested in that question, he is not interested in history.

Thus the historical cycle is a permanent feature of all historical thought; but wherever it occurs, it is incidental to a point of view. The cycle is the historian's field of vision at a given moment. That is why it has been so often observed that history moves in cycles; that is why, when people have tried, as many have tried, to formulate a system of cycles, that shall be "objectively valid," valid apart from any momentary point of view, they have failed with a failure whose completeness and strikingness has always been proportional to the rigor with which they have pursued the project. In a short essay, slightly written, anyone can expound a plausible system of historical cycles. Perhaps the very length of Spengler's book, and the very learning that he has lavished upon it, are well spent in revealing, as no shorter or less learned work could have done, the impossibility of the task he has attempted.

BIBLIOGRAPHY

Volume One of Spengler's *Der Untergang des Abendlandes* was published in Munich in 1918 and later revised in 1923. Volume Two was published in 1922. The two volumes were translated into English by C. F. Atkinson and are available in an edition published by Alfred Knopf. An abridged edition, prepared by Helmut Werner and Arthur Helps, was published in 1962.

DAWSON, CHRISTOPHER. "Oswald Spengler and the Life of Civilizations," *The Dynamics of World History*, New York: 1956.
GODDARD, E. H. and GIBBONS, P. A. *Civilization or Civilizations: An Essay in the Spenglerian Philosophy of History*. London: 1926.
HALE, W. *Challenge to Defeat: Modern Man in Goethe's World and Spengler's Century*. New York: 1932.
HELLER, ERICH. "Oswald Spengler and the Predicament of the Historical Imagination," *The Cambridge Journal*, 1952.
HUGHES, H. *Oswald Spengler*. New York: 1962.
MAZLISH, B. *The Riddle of History*. New York: 1966.

8 Arnold Toynbee (1881–)

Arnold Toynbee's *A Study of History* has been the most important and most widely discussed work in the philosophy of history since Hegel. The first three volumes of this mammoth study were published in 1934, the next three in 1939. Then a period of fifteen years elapsed until Toynbee published Volumes VII through X. These four volumes exhibited a marked shift in Toynbee's thought, a shift that will require some comment shortly. Two further volumes, the last entitled *Reconsiderations* (Vol. XII), completed the study. As the title of the last volume suggests, Toynbee modified a number of his earlier claims in response to criticisms.

Toynbee tells us that there were two formative influences that suggested his study to him. First, about the time World War I was beginning, he became aware of some remarkable similarities between the history of Greece-Rome and that of his own time. He began to wonder if there might be similar parallels elsewhere in history. Then at the end of the war, he came upon Spengler's *Decline of the West* which tended to confirm his earlier suspicions. Toynbee was not satisfied with Spengler's work. He thought it was too limited in scope (Spengler had examined only eight civilizations), it paid too little attention to facts, it did not offer an adequate explanation of what brought about the rise and decline of new cultures, and it was too pessimistic. Toynbee was to make much of this last difference in his later writings. He contrasted the pessimistic determinism of Spengler with his own view that man possessed the power to change the course of the future and prevent the impending destruction of Western civilization.[1]

For Toynbee, the proper units of historical study are not nation-states or periods but whole societies. Toynbee's units of history are larger than those of Spengler and Toynbee thinks he discovered more of them—twenty-one, in fact. Toynbee's purpose, at least in his first six volumes, was to study every known society to see if he could discover the factors that led to their rise and fall. His answer as to why civilizations rise is his doctrine of Challenge-and-Response. The first six civilizations arose out of primitive life by responding to challenges posed by their physical environment. For example, the civilization of Egypt was a response to the growing aridity of the Sahara Desert. Confronted by this challenge, the early Egyptians drained the marshes of the lower Nile. Thus their response to the challenge of their environment led to one of the great civilizations of world history. The challenges that confronted the fifteen civilizations that followed were less environmental and more along the line of threats of invasion or oppression. However, Toynbee explains, a challenge can sometimes be too easy or too severe. He traces a type of Golden Mean through history to

[1] See Chapter One of Toynbee's *Civilization on Trial* (Oxford: 1948) and *The Pattern of the Past* by Geyl, Toynbee, and Sorokin (Boston: 1949), pp. 73-94.

show that challenges that are too easy do not invoke sufficient response whereas challenges that are too harsh tend to stifle and smother any effective response. For example, Massachusetts posed its early settlers with a more severe challenge than South Carolina; its challenge was met by a more successful response. However, the challenge of Labrador was too severe and attempts at colonization there met with little success.

But how do we know when a civilization is growing? Is there any criterion of growth? The criterion Toynbee proposes is a special kind of change he calls etherialization. Civilizations grow by responding to a series of challenges. These challenges gradually become more spiritual in nature. As a society overcomes material obstacles and physical challenges, power is released which enables the society to respond to challenges which are internal and spiritual rather than external and material. Eventually, however, each past civilization has reached a stage where it could not advance any higher.

Every civilization rises to a Universal State in which there exists a unity of law, purpose, belief, and government. After the universal state is attained, the civilization begins to break up. Until now, the society has been led by a "creative minority," a small group of leaders who have led it during its period of growth and who have provided spiritual leadership for the masses ("the proletariat"). The creative minority gradually degenerates into a dominant minority, that is, the same leadership is still in control but it has become stagnant; it is no longer providing dynamic leadership. It retains its position of power by force. Eventually, the civilization becomes increasingly divided into three factions—the dominant minority, the internal proletariat and the external proletariat (barbarians beyond the authority of the dominant minority). Given this situation, it is inevitable that the leadership will be changed. Societies break down then, when, because of a lack of creative leadership, they become unable to respond to further challenges. The breakdowns in civilizations never spring from external causes but from inherent defects in man himself.

Toynbee ended Volume VI of his work by holding out the hope that if modern man returned to God, there was still a chance that Western Civilization might be saved. In the volumes that followed Toynbee argued that the ultimate goal of history is a new religious society based upon a universal church that would combine elements of the world's major religions. Volumes VII–X actually seem to present a new theory of history in which the cyclical or spiral pattern of the first six volumes is replaced with a linear view.

A brief comment on the selections which follow is necessary. My first plan was to include passages from Volumes I through VI of Toynbee's work that would suggest something of the pattern of his approach and the breadth of his work. However, Professor Toynbee pointed out that, given the many modifications of his position in the past twenty-five years, such selections would be quite out-of-date and rather misleading. At Professor Toynbee's suggestion, then, I have made my selections from the last volume of his work, the volume entitled *Reconsiderations*. Not only does Toynbee indicate some changes in his views, he also, in this volume, presents some interesting replies to his critics. The chapter begins with two articles by the late Harvard sociologist, Pitirim Sorokin, himself the author of an important study in the philosophy of history.[2] Sorokin's articles offer the reader a general survey of Toynbee's first ten volumes; they also give expression to some of the common objections to Toynbee's work.[3]

PITIRIM A. SOROKIN
TOYNBEE'S PHILOSOPHY OF HISTORY [*]

1. Outline and appreciation. Regardless of the subsequent criticism, Arnold J. Toynbee's *A Study of History* [1] is one of the

---

[2] Pitirim Sorokin, *Social and Cultural Dynamics,* 4 volumes (New York: 1937–1941). A shorter statement of Sorokin's views can be found in his *The Crisis of Our Age* (New York: 1941).

[3] In all fairness to Toynbee, the reader should consult the full text of his twelfth volume for his replies to Sorokin and other critics.

[*] First printed in *The Journal of Modern History,* Vol. XII, 1940, pp. 374–387. Reprinted with the kind permission of Mrs. Sorokin and the editors. The first part of Sorokin's review deals only with Vols. I–VI of Toynbee's work. His comments on Vols. VII–X begin on p. 197.

[1] Arnold J. Toynbee, *A Study of History,* 6 volumes. (Oxford University Press: 1934–39).

most significant works of our time in the field of historical synthesis. Although several volumes of it are yet to come, six published volumes display a rare combination of the thoughtfulness of a philosopher with the technical competence of a meticulous empiricist. The combination insures against the sterile scholarship of a thoughtless "fact-finder," as well as against a fantastic flight of an incompetent dilettante. Hence its significance for historians, philosophers of history, sociologists, political scientists, and for anyone who is interested in the how and why of emergence, growth, decline, and dissolution of civilizations.

Mr. Toynbee starts with a thesis that the proper field of historical study is neither a description of singularistic happenings continguous in space or time, nor a history of the states and bodies politic or of mankind as a "unity."

> The "intelligible fields of historical study" . . . are societies which have a greater extension, in both Space and Time, than national states or city-states, or any other political communities. . . . Societies, not states, are "the social atoms" with which students of history have to deal. [I, 45]

Combining religious characteristics and territorial and partly political characteristics, he takes "civilization" as the proper object of historical study, in which "civilization" is "a species of society." (I, 129 ff.) Of such civilizations, he takes twenty-one (later twenty-six) "related and unrelated" species: the Western, two Orthodox Christian (in Russia and the Near East), the Iranic, the Arabic, the Hindu, two Far Eastern, the Hellenic, the Syriac, the Indic, the Sinic, the Minoan, the Sumeric, the Hittite, the Babylonic, the Andean, the Mexic, the Yucatec, the Mayan, the Egyptiac, plus five "arrested civilizations": Polynesian, Eskimo, Nomadic, Ottoman, and Spartan. (I, 132 ff.; IV, 1 ff.) With these twenty-six civilizations at his disposal, Toynbee attacks, first, the problem of genesis of civilization: Why do some of the societies, like many primitive groups, become static at an early stage of their existence and not emerge as civilizations while other societies reach this level?

His answer is that the genesis of civilization is due neither to the race factor nor to geographic environment as such but to a specific combination of two conditions: the presence of a creative minority in a given society and of an environment which is neither too unfavorable nor too favorable. The groups which had these conditions emerged as civilizations; the groups which did not have them remained on the subcivilization level. The mechanism of the birth of civilization in these conditions is formulated as an interplay of Challenge-and-Response. The environment of the above type incessantly challenges the society; and the society, through its creative minority, successfully responds to the challenge and solves the need. A new challenge follows, and a new response successfully ensues; and so the process goes on incessantly. In these conditions no possibility of rest exists, the society is on the move all the time, and such a move brings it, sooner or later, to the stage of civilization. Surveying the conditions in which his twenty-one civilizations were born, he finds that they emerged exactly in the above circumstances. (I, 188–338; Vol. II, *passim*)

The next problem of the study is why and how, out of twenty-six civilizations, four (Far Western Christian, Far Eastern Christian, Scandinavian, and Syriac) miscarried and turned out to be abortive; five (Polynesian, Eskimo, Nomadic, Spartan, and Ottoman) were arrested in their growth at an early stage; while the remaining civilizations grew "through an *élan* that carried them from challenge through response to further challenge and from differentiation through integration to differentiation again?" (III, 128)

The answer evidently depends upon the meaning of growth and its symptoms. In Toynbee's opinion the growth of civilization is not a geographic expansion of the society and is not due to it. If anything, the geographic expansion of a society is positively associated with retardation and disintegration but not with the growth. (III, 128 ff.) Likewise, the growth of civilization does not consist in, and is not due to, technological progress and the society's increasing mastery over the physical environment: ". . . there is no correlation between progress in technique and progress in civilization." (III, 173–74) The growth of civilization consists in "a progressive and cumulative inward self-determination or self-articulation" of the civilization; in a progressive and cumulative "etherialization" of the society's values and "simplification of the civilization's apparatus and technique." (III, 128 ff., 182 ff.) Viewed in the aspect of the intrasocial and inter-individual relationship, growth is an incessant creative "withdrawal and return" of the charismatic minority of the society in the process of the ever new successful responses to ever new challenges of the environment. (III, 248 ff.) Growing civilization is a unity. Its society consists of the creative minority freely imitated and followed by the majority—the Internal Proletariat of the society and the External Proletariat of its barbarian neighbors. In such a society there is no fratricidal struggle, no hard and fast divisions. It is a solidary body. Growing civilization unfolds its dominant potentialities, which are different in different civilizations: aesthetic in the Hellenic civilization; religious in the Indic and Hindu; scientifically machinistic in the Western; and so on. (III, 128–390) As a result, the process of growth. Such is the solution of the problem of growth of civilization.

The third main problem of the study is how and why civilizations break down, disintegrate, and dissolve. They evidently do so because, out of twenty-six species of civilizations, "only four have miscarried as against twenty-six that have been born alive," and "no less than sixteen out of these twenty-six are by now dead and buried" (the Egyptiac, the Andean, the Sinic, the Minoan, the Sumeric, the Mayan, the Indic, the Hittite, the Syriac, the Hellenic, the Babylonic, the Mexic, the Arabic, the Yucatec, the Spartan, and the Ottoman). Of the remaining ten civilizations living,

> the Polynesian and the Nomadic civilizations are now in their last agonies and seven out of eight others are all, in different degrees, under threat of either annihilation or assimilation by our own civilization of the West. Moreover, no less than six out of these seven civilizations . . . bear marks of having broken down and gone into disintegration. [IV, 1–2]

Toynbee points out that the decline is not due to some cosmic necessity or to geographic factors or to racial degeneration or to external assaults of the enemies, which, as a rule, reinforce the growing civilization; neither is it caused by the decline of technique and technology, because "it is always the decline of civilization that is the cause and the decline of technique the consequence or symptom." (IV, 40)

The main difference between the process of growth and disintegration is that in the growth phase the civilization successfully responds to a series of ever new challenges, while in the disintegration stage it fails to give such a response to a given challenge. It tries to answer it again and again, but recurrently fails. In growth the challenges, as well as responses, vary all the time; in disintegration, the responses vary, but the challenge remains unanswered and unremoved. The author's verdict is that civilizations perish through suicide but not by murder. (IV, 120) In Toynbee's formulation

> the nature of the breakdowns of civilizations can be summed up in three points: a failure of creative power in the minority, an answering withdrawal of mimesis on the part of the majority, and a consequent loss of social unity in the society as a whole.

In an unfolded form this formula runs as follows:

> When in the history of any society a Creative Minority degenerates into a mere Dominant Minority which attempts to retain by force a position which it has ceased to merit, this fatal change in the character of the ruling element provokes, on the other hand, the secession of a Proletariat (the majority) which no longer spontaneously admires or freely imitates the ruling element, and which revolts against being reduced to the status of an unwilling "underdog." This Proletariat, when it asserts itself, is divided from the outset into two distinct parts. There is an "Internal Proletariat" (the majority of the members) and . . . an "External Proletariat" of barbarians beyond the pale who now violently resist incorporation. And thus the breakdown of a civilization gives rise to a class war within the body social of a society which was neither divided against itself by hard-and-fast divisions nor sundered from its neighbors by unbridgeable gulfs so long as it was in growth. [IV, 6]

This declining phase consists of three subphases: (*a*) breakdown of the civilization, (*b*) its disintegration, and (*c*) its dissolution. The breakdown and dissolution are often separated by centuries, even thousands of years, from one another. For instance, the breakdown of the Egyptiac civilization occurred in the sixteenth century B.C., and its dissolution only in the fifth century A.D. For two thousand years between breakdown and dissolution it existed in a "petrified life-in-death." In a similar "petrified" state up to the present time the Far Eastern civilization continues in China after its breakdown in the ninth century A.D. About one thousand and eight hundred years, respectively, elapsed between these points in the history of the Sumeric and Hellenic civilizations (IV, 62 ff.; V, 2 ff.); and so on. Like a petrified tree trunk, such a society can linger in that stage of life-in-death for centuries, even thousands of years. Nevertheless, the destiny of most, if not of all, civilizations, seems to be to come to final dissolution sooner or later. As to the Western society, though it seems to have had all the symptoms of breakdown and disintegration, the author is noncommittal. He still leaves a hope for a miracle: "We may and must pray that a reprieve which God has granted to our society once will not be refused if we ask for it again in a contrite spirit and with a broken heart." (VI, 321)

Such being the general nature of the decline of civilizations, a most detailed analysis of its uniformities, symptoms, and phases is developed in Volumes IV, V, and VI. Only a few of these uniformities can be touched on here. While in the growth period the Creative Minority gives a series of successful responses to ever new challenges, now, in the disintegration period, it fails to do so. Instead, intoxicated by victory, it begins to "rest on one's oars," to "idolize" the relative values as absolute; loses its charismatic attraction and is not imitated and followed by the majority. Therefore, more and more it has now to use force to control the Internal and the External Proletariat. In this process it creates a "Universal State," like the Roman Empire created by the Hellenic Dominant Minority, as a means to keep itself and the civilization alive; enters into wars; becomes slave of the intractable institutions; and works its own and its civilization's ruin.

The "Internal Proletariat" now secedes from the Minority; becomes dissatisfied and disgruntled; and often creates a "Universal Church"—for instance, Christianity or Buddhism—as its own creed and institution. While the "Universal State" of the Dominant Minority is doomed, the Universal Church of the Inner Proletariat (for instance, Christianity) serves as a bridge and foundation for a new civilization, "apparented" by, and affiliated with, the old one.

The External Proletariat now organizes itself and begins to attack the declining civilization, instead of striving to be incorporated by it. In this way the Schism enters the Body and Soul of civilization. It results in an increase of strife and fratricidal wars that work in favor of the development of the ruin. The Schism in the Soul manifests itself in the profound change of the mentality and behavior of the members of the disintegrating society. It leads to an emergence of four types of personality and "Saviors": Archaist, Futurist (Saviors by Sword), Detached and Indifferent Stoic, and finally, Transfigured Religious Savior, posited in the supersensory world of God. The sense of Drift, of Sin, begins to grow; Promiscuity and Syncretism become dominant. Vulgarization and "Proletarization" invade arts and sciences, philosophy and language, religion and ethics, manners and institutions.

But all in vain. With the exception of Transfiguration, all these efforts and "Saviors" do not stop the disintegration. At best the civilization can become "Fossilized"; and in this form, "life-in-death" can linger for centuries and even thousands of years; but its dissolution, as a rule, comes. The only fruitful way turns out to be the way of Transfiguration, the transfer of the goal and values to the supersensory Kingdom of God. It may not stop the disintegration of the given civilization, but it may serve as a seed for emergence and development of a new affiliated civilization; and through that, it is a step forward to the eternal process of elevation of Man to Superman, of "the City of Man to City of God," as the ultimate terminal point of Man and Civilization. The volumes close with an almost apocalyptic note:

> The aim of Transfiguration is to give light to them that sit in darkness . . . it is pursued by seeking the Kingdom of God in order to bring its life . . . into action . . . The goal of Transfiguration is thus the Kingdom of God. [VI, 171]

The whole human history or the total civilizational process thus turns into a Creative Theodicy; through separate civilizations and their uniform, but concretely different, rhythms, the reality unfolds its richness and leads from "under-Man" and "under-Civilization," to Man and Civilization, and finally to Superman and Transfigured Etherial Super-Civilization of the Kingdom of God.

> The work of the Spirit of the Earth, as he weaves and draws his threads on the Loom of Time, is the temporal history of Man as this manifests itself in the geneses and growths and breakdowns and disintegrations of human societies; and in all this welter of life . . . we can hear the beat of an elemental rhythm . . . of Challenge-and-Response and Withdrawal-and-Return and Rout-and-Rally and Apparentation-and-Affiliation and Schism-and-Palingenesia. This elemental rhythm is the alternating beat of Yin and Yang. . . . The Perpetual turning of a wheel is not a vain repetition if, at each revolution, it is carrying a vehicle that much nearer to its goal; and if "palingenesia" signifies the birth of something new . . . then the Wheel of Existence is not just a devilish device for inflicting an everlasting torment on a damned Ixion. The music that the rhythm of Yin and Yang beats out is the song of creation . . . Creation would not be creative if it did not swallow up in itself all things in Heaven and Earth, including its own antithesis. [VI, 324]

Such is the general skeleton of Toynbee's philosophy of history. It is clothed by him in a rich and full-blooded body of facts, empirical verification, and a large number of subpropositions. The main theses, as well as the subpropositions, are painstakingly tested by the known empirical facts of the history of the twenty-one civilizations studied. In this respect the theory of Toynbee, conceived and executed on a grand plan, is probably documented more fully than most of the existing philosophies of history. To repeat, the work as a whole is a real contribution to the field of historical synthesis.

II. Criticism. If we now ask how valid is the general scheme of Toynbee's theory of the rise and decline of civilizations as well as a number of his secondary propositions, the situation changes. Side by side with the unquestionable virtues, the work has very serious shortcomings. Among the unessential and superfluous defects, the following can be mentioned: First, the work is too voluminous and could have been compressed without losing anything in the clearness and completeness of its theory. A pronounced penchant of the author to quote abundantly from the Bible, mythology, poetry—to use overabundant poetic and symbolic images—is partly responsible for this insignificant defect.

Second, in spite of an astounding erudition, the author displays either an ignorance or a deliberate neglect of many important sociological works, which deal more fundamentally with the problems Toynbee is struggling with than other works quoted. Neither the names of Tarde, Durkheim, Max Weber, Pareto, nor those of practically any sociologist are mentioned. One of the consequences of such a neglect is that Toynbee has to write dozens and hundreds of pages on questions that were studied in such works more thoroughly and better than Toynbee does. For instance, mimesis or imitation is one of the cardinal points of his theory to which he devotes many pages. A reader who knows Tarde's *Laws of Imitation,* not to mention many later works, does not get from Toynbee's analysis anything new. More than that: Toynbee's theory of mimesis and of its uniformities has many mistakes which would have been avoided if he had studied some of the main works in this field. Similarly, he devotes several hundreds of pages—in Volumes I and II—to investigation of the influence of race and geographic environment upon societies and civilization. And yet, he does not add anything new to the existing knowledge in that field. Even more, he fails to see the demonstrated weaknesses of the claims of some of the climatic and racial theories (like that of Huntington) which he accepts to a considerable extent. A concise characterization of the existing conclusions in these fields would have permitted him to outline his theory on only a few pages and to avoid several pitfalls into which he has fallen. The same criticism can be applied to several other problems. In spite of the extraordinary erudition of the author, it shows itself somewhat onesided and inadequate.

Third, his knowledge of the history of the twenty-six civilizations he deals with is very uneven. It is excellent in the field of the Hellenic (Greco-Roman) civilization, and it is much thinner in the field of other civilizations.

Fourth, his acquaintance with the extant knowledge in the

field of such phenomena as art, philosophy, science, law, and some others with which he deals, seems also to be inadequate: little, if anything is quoted in these fields, and the conclusions of the author sound superficial and dilettante.

Fifth, the same is true of several other fields in which he makes categorical statements. For instance, he contends that "the evil of War in the eighteenth century [was reduced] to a minimum which has never been approached in . . . our Western history, either before or after, up to date." (IV, 143) As a matter of fact, our systematic study of the movement of war (see my *Social and Cultural Dynamics,* Vol. III) shows that, measured either by the number of war casualties or by the size of the armies per million of population, the centuries from twelve to sixteen, inclusive, and the nineteenth century were less belligerent than the eighteenth century. In Volume V, page 43, he himself seems to repudiate his previous statement by saying that "the life of our Western Society has been as grievously infested by the plague of war during the last four centuries as in any earlier age." As a further example: he contends that "the sense of drift" as manifested in various deterministic philosophies grows with the process of disintegration in all civilizations. (V, 422 ff.) The factual movement of deterministic conceptions versus indeterministic is very different from what he claims it is (see my *Dynamics,* Vol. II, chap. ix). A third example: he contends that in a diffusion or radiation of a given culture the alien culture is penetrated first by the economic elements; second, by the political; and third, by the cultural elements. In this way a uniformity of the order of the penetration of the alien culture by specified elements of diffusing civilization is set forth. (IV, 57) As a matter of fact, such uniformity does not exist. In some cases the economic elements penetrate first; in others, the cultural (see the evidences in Vol. IV of my *Dynamics*).

In the work there are many similar blunders and overstatements. However, in a work of such immense magnitude as *A Study of History* such shortcomings are inevitable. One should not carp at them. If the main conceptual scheme of the author is solid, such shortcomings can easily be discounted as superfluous.

Unfortunately, the work has two fundamental defects, which concern not the details but the heart and soul of Toynbee's philosophy of history. They concern, first, *"the civilization" taken by Toynbee as a unit of historical study;* second, *the conceptual scheme of genesis, growth, and decline of the civilizations put at the foundation of Toynbee's philosophy of history.* Let us look at these assumptions more closely.

By "civilization" Toynbee means not a mere "field of historical study" but a united system, or the whole, whose parts are connected with one another by causal ties. Therefore, as in any causal system in his "civilization," parts must depend upon one another, upon the whole, and the whole upon its parts. He categorically states again and again that

> civilizations are wholes whose parts all cohere with one another and all affect one another reciprocally. . . . It is one of the characteristics of civilizations in process of growth that all aspects and activities of their social life are coordinated into a single social whole, in which the economic, political, and cultural elements are kept in a nice adjustment with one another by an inner harmony of the growing body social. [III, 380, 152; see also I, 34 ff., 43 ff., 149 ff., 153 ff.]

Thus, like so-called functional anthropologists, he assumes that his "civilizations" are real systems and not mere congeries or conglomerations of various cultural (or civilizational) phenomena and objects adjacent in space or time but devoid of any causal or meaningful ties (see the analysis of sociocultural systems and congeries in my *Social and Cultural Dynamics,* Vol. I, chap. i; an unfolded theory of sociocultural systems is given in Vol. I of the *Dynamics*). If civilizations are real systems, then, as in any causal system, we should expect that when one important component of it changes, the rest of the components change too, because if A and B are causally connected, then the change of A is followed by the change of B in a definite and uniform manner. Otherwise, A and B are mere congeries but not the partners of the causal system. Is Toynbee's assumption valid? I am afraid it is not: his *"civilizations" are not united systems but mere conglomerations of various civilizational objects and phenomena* (congeries of systems and singular cultural traits) *united only by special adjacency but not by causal or meaningful bonds.* For *this reason, they are not real "species of society"; therefore they can hardly be treated as unities and can hardly have any uniformities in their genesis, growth, and decline.* These concepts cannot even be applied to the congeries, because congeries do not and cannot grow or decline. Like the components of a dumping place, they can only be rearranged, added to, or subtracted from; but we cannot talk of the growth or decline of a "civilizational dumping place" or of any merely spatial conglomeration of things and events. This diagnosis of the "civilizations" is inadvertently corroborated many times by Toynbee himself. In many places of his work he indicates that, for instance, the technique and economic life of the civilization does not change; in other cases the rest of the civilization changes while technique remains static; in still other cases, the technique changes in one way while the rest of the civilization moves in the opposite direction. (IV, 40 ff.; III, 154 ff., *et passim*) If we have A and B where the change of one of the variables is not followed by that of the other, or when it does not show any uniform variation, this means A and B are causally unrelated; therefore they are not components of the same system or parts of the same whole. Toynbee himself demonstrates—and demonstrates well—that two of the components of his civilization (technique and economy) are causally unrelated to the rest of the alleged "whole." In this way Toynbee himself repudiates his basic assumption that his "civilizations" are "the wholes whose parts all cohere together."

In fact, it is easy to show—and show convincingly—that any of his civilizations is not a "whole" or a system at all but a mere coexistence of an enormous number of systems and congeries existing side by side and not united either by causal or meaningful or any other ties (necessary for any real system) except a mere contiguity in space and time. Such a contiguity or mere spatial adjacency does not make from "a book + worn out shoes + bottle of whiskey" lying side by side any unity, whole, or system. It remains a congeries. Not only is the total civilization of such enormous "culture-areas" as the Greco-Roman, or the Sinic, or of any other of his civilizations not one whole or system, but the total civilization of even a smallest possible civilizational area—that of a single individual—is but a coexistence of several and different systems and congeries unrelated with one another in any way except spatial adjacency in a biological organism. Suppose that an individual is a Roman Catholic, Republican, professor, preferring Romantic music to Classic, Scotch to rye, blondes to brunettes. Roman Catholicism does not require, causally or logically, the Republican instead of the Democratic or other party; the Republican party is not connected logically or causally with the professorial occupation. This is true also with a preference for Scotch to rye, or Romantic music to the Classic. We have Roman Catholics who are not Republicans, and Republicans who are not Roman Catholics, professors who are neither, and many in other occupations who are Catholics or Republicans. Some Catholics or Republicans or professors prefer Scotch to rye, some rye to Scotch, some do not drink whiskey, some prefer beer to wine, and so on. This means that the total "civilization" of the same individual is not one unified system but a conglomeration of various systems and singular "civilizational" traits united only by a spatial adjacency of the same biological organism. A biological organism, being a real system, changes biologically as a whole; but its total "civilization," being congeries, does not change in togetherness, nor can the "total civilizations" of many individuals display any uniformity in their change. (See my *Dynamics,* Vol. I, chap. i; and Vol. I, for a systematic analysis of this problem.)

If, then, the total "civilization" of an individual is not one system, still less is one system the total civilization of a city block, or of the total city, of a nation, and of the still larger "civilized societies" of Toynbee. This means that Toynbee's "civilization" is not a "species" but a kind of a "large dumping place" where coexist, side by side, an enormous number of various sociocultural systems many of which are not related to one another either causally or meaningfully: the State system, the Religious systems, the Art-Ethics-Philosophy-Science-Economic-Political-Technological and other systems and congeries "dumped together" over a vast territory and carried on by a multitude of individuals. One cannot style as species of the same genus different sets of incidental congeries: "shoe-watch-bottle-*Saturday Evening Post*" here, "trousers-comb-detective story-valve-rose-automobile" there: and still less can one expect uniformities of structure and change in genesis, growth, and decline of such different congeries. Having mistakenly taken different congeries for system, Toynbee begins to treat his civilizations as "species of society" and valiantly hunts for uniformities in their genesis, growth, and decline. In this way he makes the fatal mistake of erecting an enormous building upon a foundation less stable than the proverbial sand.

All the subsequent defects of his theory follow from this "original sin." It is aggravated by another fatal mistake he commits, namely, by the acceptance of the old—from Florus to Spengler—conceptual scheme of "genesis-growth-decline," as a uniform pattern of change of civilizations. Such a conception is possibly the worst among all the existing schemes of change of civilizations; and it is doubly fatal for Toynbee's theory. Indeed, if his civilizations are mere congeries, for this reason only we cannot talk of the genesis, growth, breakdown, disintegration, and dissolution of congeries. Congeries are neither born (alive or abortively) nor can they grow or disintegrate, since they never have been integrated. Generally, this popular conceptual scheme is purely analogical and represents not a theory of how sociocultural phenomena change but an evaluative theory of sociocultural progress: how they *should* change. Therefore, Toynbee's theory is not so much a theory of civilizational change as much as an evaluative theory of civilizational progress or regress. This clearly comes out already in his formula of "growth" and "disintegration." They are evaluative formulas of progress and regress but not the formulas of change.

From these two sins follow all the factual and logical incongruities of Toynbee's philosophy of history. First, his classifications of civilizations. Many a historian, anthropologist, and sociologist will certainly object to it as arbitrary, having no clear logical *fundamentum divisionis*. Several Christian civilizations are treated as separate and different; while a conglomeration of different (religious and other) systems are united into one civilization. Sparta is arbitrarily cut out of the rest of the Hellenic civilization, while Roman civilization is made inseparable from the Greek or Hellenic. Polynesian and Eskimo civilizations or "undercivilizations" (in one part Toynbee states that they were live-born civilizations; in another he claims that they remained at "subcivilizational" level and have never reached the state of civilizations)—each is taken as a separate civilization; while all the Nomads of all the continents are united into one civilization, and so on.

Second, Toynbee's mass onslaught against civilizations in making most of them either "abortively born," "arrested," or "petrified," or "broken-down" or "disintegrating" or "dead and buried." According to Toynbee, out of twenty-six civilizations, only one—the Western—is still possibly alive at the present time, all the others being either dead or half-dead ("arrested," "petrified," "disintegrating"). Since, according to the assumed scheme, civilizations must have breakdowns, disintegration, and death, the author must either bury them or make them "abortive," "arrested," "petrified," or at least broken down and disintegrating. Since such is the demand of the scheme and since Toynbee does not have any clear criteria as to what death or breakdown or integration or disintegration of civilization really is, he willingly takes the role of an undertaker of civilizations.

Third, courageously following his scheme, he is not deterred by the fact that some of his civilizations which, according to his scheme, ought to have been dead a long time ago, after their breakdown, lived centuries, even thousands of years, and are still alive and very much so. He disposes of the difficulty by a simple device of "petrified" civilizations. So China has been petrified for thousands of years; Egypt for some two thousands of years; so the Hellenic civilization was either disintegrating or petrified after the Peloponnesian War up to the fifth century A.D. The whole Roman history was but an incessant disintegration, from the very beginning to the end; and so other civilizations. In his scheme civilizations hardly have time to live and to grow; if they are not born abortive—as some are—they are arrested; if they are not arrested, they have their breakdown almost immediately after they are born and then begin to disintegrate or are turned into a "petrified trunk." Of course, philosophically the birth is the beginning of death; but an empirical investigator of either the life of an organism or of civilization can and must be less philosophical and can and must study the process of life itself, before the real death, or paralysis, or incurable sickness occurs. And for most of the organisms and civilizations there is a great distance between the terminal points of birth and death.

This means that Toynbee studies little the greater part of the existence of the civilizations and drowns centuries and thousands of years of their existence, activity, and change in his penchant for being an "undertaker of civilizations." By this I do not deny the facts of either disintegration or even dissolution of real cultural or civilizational systems. Such facts occur, but occur with real systems, not with congeries of civilizations; and occur not immediately after the "birth" of the system but often after their long—sometimes indefinitely long—life and change. As a matter of fact, the elements of the congeries of Toynbee's civilizations still exist, even of those which he considers dead and buried a long time ago. Quite a large number of Egyptiac or Babylonic or especially Hellenic cultural systems and cultural traits (philosophy, ethics, architecture, sculpture, literature, art, and so on) are very much alive as components of the contemporary Western or other cultures. And they are alive not as objects in a museum but as living realities in our and other cultures.

Fourth, the foregoing explains why in Toynbee's work there is little of the analysis of the phase of the growth of the civilizations. There are only fairly indefinite statements that in that phase there is a Creative Minority successfully meeting the challenge, that there is no class war, no intersociety war, and that everything goes well there and everything moves and becomes more and more "etherialized." That is about all that is said of this phase. Such a characterization of the process of growth of his twenty-one civilizations is evidently fantastic in its "idyllic" and other virtues. If we have to believe it, we seemingly have to accept that in Greece before 431–403 B.C. (the breakdown of the Hellenic civilization, according to Toynbee) there were no wars, no revolutions, no class struggle, no slavery, no traditionalism, no uncreative minority, and that all these "plagues" appeared only after the Peloponnesian War. On the other hand, we expect to find that, after it, in Greece and Rome creativeness ceased, and that there was no Plato, no Aristotle, no Epicurus, no Zeno, no Polybius, no Church Fathers, no Lucretius, no scientific discovery—nothing creative. As a matter of fact, the factual situation in all these respects was very different before and after the breakdown. The indicators of war per million of the population for Greece were twenty-nine for the fifth, forty-eight for the fourth, and eighteen and three, respectively, for the third and second centuries B.C. Indicators of Internal Disturbances (revolutions) were 149, 468, 320, 259, and 36, respectively, for the centuries from the sixth to the second B.C., inclusive. This shows that the real movement of wars and revolutions in Greece was very different from what Toynbee tells us. The same is true of Rome (see the detailed data in my *Social and Cultural Dynamics,* Vol. III). The scientific, philosophical, and religious creativeness likewise reached their peak rather in and after the fifth century than before that time (see the figures of discoveries, inventions, and philosophical systems in *Dynamics,* Vol. II, chap. iii, *et passim*). In regard to the Western civilization, as mentioned, the diagnosis of Toynbee is somewhat ambiguous. In many places he says that it already had its breakdown and is in the process of disintegration; in other places he is noncommittal. Whatever is his diagnosis, the Western civilization before the fifteenth century is regarded by him as in the phase of growth. If this is so, then, according to his scheme, no revolutions, no serious wars, no hard-and-fast class divisions existed in Europe before that century. Factually, the thirteenth and fourteenth centuries were the most revolutionary centuries up to the twentieth century in the history of Europe; likewise, serfdom and other class divisions were hard and fast, and there were many wars—small and great (see the data in Vols. II and III of my *Dynamics*). Finally the medieval Western civilization of the period of growth does not exhibit many of the traits of Toynbee's growing civilizations but displays a mass of traits which are the characteristics of Toynbee's disintegrating civilizations. The same is true of his other civilizations. This means that Toynbee's uniformities of growth and decline of the civilizations are largely fantastic and are not borne out by the facts.

Fifth, a large number of the uniformities he claims in connection with his conceptual scheme are also either fallacious or overstated—for instance, his uniformity of negative correlation between the geographic expansion of civilization and its growth; between war and growth; between progress of technique and growth. Granting a part of truth to his statements, at the same time in this categoric formulation they are certainly fallacious. If Toynbee's twenty-one civilizations did not diffuse over large areas and a multitude of persons remained just the civilization of a little Sumeric, Greek, Egyptiac, or Arabic village, they could hardly become "historical" and certainly would not come to the attention of historians and Toynbee and would not become one of his twenty-one civilizations. All his civilizations are vast complexes, spread over vast areas of territory and vast populations. They did not emerge at once in such form; but in starting with a small area they expanded (in the process of their growth) over vaster and vaster areas and populations and through that became historical. Otherwise, they would not have been noticed. If Toynbee contends, as in a few places he does, that such a diffusion over vaster areas was performed peacefully, without war, through spontaneous submission of the "barbarians" to the charm of the diffusing civilization, such a statement is again inaccurate. All his twenty-one civilizations in their period of growth (according to Toynbee's scheme) expanded not only peacefully but with force, coercion, and wars. On the other hand, many of them in the period of disintegration shrank, rather than expanded, and were more peaceful than in the periods of Toynbee's growth.

Sixth, following Spengler, whose ghost weighs heavily upon the author, Toynbee ascribes different dominant tendencies to each of his civilizations: aesthetic to the Hellenic, religious to the Indic, machinistic-technological to the Western (he does not give further such dominant penchants to each of the remaining eighteen civilizations). Such a summary characterization is again very doubtful. The Western civilization did not show its alleged dominant characteristic at all up to approximately the thirteenth century A.D.: from the sixth to the end of the twelfth century the movement of technological inventions and scientific discoveries stood at about zero in this allegedly technological civilization par excellence; and from the sixth to the thirteenth century this machinistic civilization was religious through and through, even more religious than the Indic or Hindu civilizations in many periods of their history (see the data on discoveries and technological inventions in my *Dynamics,* Vol. II, chap. iii). The supposedly aesthetic Hellenistic civilization did not show its aesthetic penchant (in Toynbee's sense) before the sixth century B.C. and displayed quite a boisterous scientific and technological *élan* in the period from 600 B.C. to A.D. 200 (see the figures, Vol. II, chap. iii). The Arabic civilization (whose dominant trait Toynbee does not stress) displayed an enormous *élan* of scientific and technological penchant in the centuries from the eighth to the thirteenth —much more so than the Western civilization during these centuries (see the data, Vol. II, chap. iii). All this means that the Spenglerian-Toynbee ascription of some specific perennial tendency to this or that civilization, regardless of the period of its history, is misleading and inaccurate.

One can continue this criticism for a long time. A large part of the statements of Toynbee taken in his conceptual scheme are either inaccurate or invalid. However, many of these statements, properly reformulated and put in quite a different conceptual scheme of civilizational change, become valid and penetrating. For instance, most of the traits which Toynbee ascribes to the civilizations in their period of growth and partly in that of "petrification" are accurate for the phase of civilization dominated by what I call the "Ideational supersystem of culture" (not the total given culture in which it appears). Many of the characteristics of Toynbee's "disintegrating" period are typical for a phase of civilization dominated by what I call the "Sensate supersystem" (not the whole total culture or civilization). Many of the characteristics of Toynbee's stage of acute disorganization are but the characteristics of the period when a given culture passes from the domination of Ideational to Idealistic or Sensate supersystems, and vice versa. Such periods of shift happen several times in the history of this or that "total culture" or "civilization." They are, however, neither a death nor "petrification" nor "arrest" but merely a great transition from one supersystem to another. Put into this scheme, and reinterpreted, many pages and chapters of Toynbee's work become illuminating, penetrating, and scientifically valid. In such a setting his conception of the creative character of human history acquires still deeper meaning. Likewise, his hesitant diagnosis of the present state of the Western civilization becomes more definite and specific: as the status of the civilization entering not the path of death but the painful road of a great transition from the overripe Sensate phase to a more "etherialized" or spiritualized Ideational or Idealistic phase. Translated into more accurate terms of the real sociocultural systems and of the great rhythm of Sensate-Idealistic-Ideational supersystems of culture, *A Study of History* is a most stimulating and illuminating work of a distinguished thinker and scholar.

PITIRIM SOROKIN
COMMENTS ON VOLUMES VII–X OF TOYNBEE'S A STUDY OF HISTORY [*]

The first six volumes of Toynbee's *A Study of History* were published in 1934–39. Of the new (four) volumes completing this vast work, Volume VII gives a further analysis of the nature and role of the Universal States and the Universal Churches as phases in the growth and decline of civilizations. Volume VIII deals with the Heroic Ages and the contacts of civilizations in space. Volume IX is devoted to a study of the contacts of civilizations in time, of the law and freedom in history, and of the prospects of the Western civilization. Volume X is made up of essays on eminent historians and on chronology, of acknowledgments, and index.

Since Toynbee's fully developed "philosophy of history" was given in the first six volumes, these new volumes do not add much to his theoretical framework. Their novelty consists mainly: (*a*) of some new details concerning the Universal States, the Universal Churches, the Heroic Ages, and the interaction of civilizations in space and time; and (*b*) of the change of some of Toynbee's conclusions given in the first six volumes.

As to Toynbee's theory of history, it has its strong and weak points. In my previous criticism of his *A Study of History* I have shown that Toynbee's framework is a variation of O. Spengler's scheme which, in its turn, is a variation of N. Danilevsky's theory of history published in 1863. All three theories make a fatal error in taking a vast dump of diverse social and cultural phenomena, not integrated together by meaningful or causal ties, for a real unified system called "Culture-Historical Type," "High Cul-

[*] Reprinted with the kind permission of Mrs. Sorokin and the editors from *The Annals of the American Academy of Political and Social Sciences*, Vol. 299, 1955, pp. 144–146.

ture," or "Civilization." Not being integrated unities, such dumps of cultural and social phenomena cannot either be born or grow or disintegrate and die. For this reason, many of the conclusions of these authors concerning "the birth," "the growth," "the breakdown," "the disintegration," and "decline" of civilizations are built on a foggy foundation and crumble by themselves as soon as the fatal error is perceived.

The main changes in Toynbee's views concern two points. While in the previous volumes the Universal Religions were viewed as "the bridges" between the great civilizations, in the new volumes the great civilizations are considered as the bridges between the great Religions. While before Toynbee interpreted all great civilizations as philosophically equivalent and contemporaneous, now he classifies them in chronological and evaluative order as the progressive steps for realization of the ever greater and higher religions. Since both interpretations are not so much scientific descriptions of the empirical relationship between civilizations and religions as much as the subjective evaluations of whether civilizations ought to be the means for the end-value of religions, or religions should be the means for the bigger and better civilizations, the significance of this shift in Toynbee's views lies beyond the sphere of science.

When we turn to Toynbee's empirical generalizations, many of these appear to be either platitudinal or one-sided or fallacious. Thus he indefatigably repeats that "spiritual progress is subject to a 'law' proclaimed by Aeschylus" that we "learn through suffering," and that this "learning by suffering" is the only way to spiritual ennoblement of mankind. Stating so, he evidently forgets that suffering produces not only saints, but also criminals and "the worst of beasts"—human animals. He entirely overlooks the negative effects of suffering: suicide, mental and physical disease, aggressiveness, criminality, brutalization, which "suffering-frustration" generates more frequently rather than spiritual ennoblement. Instead of the much more adequate "law of polarization" in frustration, suffering, and calamity, he gives us a one-sided pseudolaw of the "learning through suffering" which does not stand an elementary empirical test. Another example. For corroboration of his preconceived theory that the "declining" civilizations go through the cycle of: "premonitory wars," and "general peace," he gives us five cycles of this kind for the period: 1494–1945. When, however, his data are checked by the number and duration of the wars, the size of the armies, the magnitude of war casualty for each of his cycles, several of his periods of "general peace" turn out to be as belligerent as his periods of "general war," and vice versa. His theory of the cycles of war-peace is thus clearly contradicted by the relevant empirical data. A third example of Toynbee's empirical fallacies is given by his credulous acceptance of Jung's theory of the unconscious, by the identification of this unconscious with the divine element in man, and by Toynbee's classification of the great religions (Hinduism, Christianity, Islam, and Buddhism) as "introvert" or "extrovert." Contrary to Toynbee, the future of mankind would indeed be hopeless if its spiritual and creative progress were depending upon the unconscious biological drives and their instinctive-reflexological mechanisms given in all animal species. By definition the "unconscious" activity is automatic and fixed; it cannot think and cannot create because any thinking and creative activity are always conscious or supraconscious processes. Instead of investing his hopes for the future spiritual ennoblement of man into "the supraconscious"—which is the main source of all the great creative achievements of man—Toynbee expects the salvation from the least creative unconscious forces viewed by him as the divine element in man. As a fourth sample of Toynbee's empirical errors his diagnosis and forecasting of the future of the existing civilizations can be mentioned. According to his theory practically all civilizations, except the Western one, have been either dead for many centuries, or are in a hopeless mortal agony at the present time. This equally concerns the Hindu, the Chinese, the Russian, the Arabic, and all other "fossilized" and disintegrated civilizations. The only hope for the future of mankind lies in the Western civilization which also is in a dangerous state.

If we take one by one of Toynbee's empirical generalizations, most of them will be found to be either one-sided or fallacious. This is largely due to Toynbee's poor knowledge of a vast body of sociological, psychological, and anthropological studies in the fields of social and cultural mobility, migration, diffusion, and transformation; in the field of sociocultural rhythms and periodicities, social organization and disorganization, cultural integration and disintegration, and so on. Despite vast literature quoted and referred to in Toynbee's volumes, they contain almost no references to hundreds of important studies by psychosocial scientists of the problems treated by Toynbee.

When Toynbee discusses such problems as "law and freedom in history," "the truth of science and the truth of religion," he rarely touches the fundamental points of this sort of problem. He rather goes around or dodges these points and delivers to us mainly vague generalities and unclear conclusions often backed up only by numerous quotations from the Old and the New Testaments. His footnotes in these parts show again his limited knowledge of the most important philosophical and scientific works dealing with this sort of problem.

Viewed as a whole, these volumes represent an eclectic mixture of science of history, philosophy of history, ethics and politics, theology and religion.

Side by side with these shortcomings, *A Study of History* has many strong points. It contains a multitude of remarkable insights and excellent elaborations of several basic topics of historical and social sciences. It opens new vistas on many dark problems of these sciences. Now and then it furnishes fresh and strikingly fruitful interpretations of several historical and social processes. Even when Toynbee speaks as a prophet, religious thinker, philosopher, or moralist, his utterances deserve our full attention.

To sum up: in spite of an overabundance of misreadings of historical events and other shortcomings of Toynbee's *A Study of History,* it is one of the significant works of the middle of the twentieth century in the field of historical and social science.

ARNOLD J. TOYNBEE
A STUDY OF HISTORY *

The mind's quest for explanation. One step toward explaining a phenomenon is to find its context. "Research into meaning

* The following passages are reprinted from Volume XII, *Reconsiderations*, of Toynbee's *A Study of History,* copyright © 1961

cannot be free from synthesis, for only by putting anything into a wider context can its meaning be seen." [1] A fact cannot be established or made intelligible unless it is related to other facts or is part of a larger system.

If I may venture to illustrate this point from my own work, I should say that volumes I–X of *A Study of History* hinge on two attempts to find "an intelligible field of study" as a framework for a narrower field that I had found unintelligible when taken by itself without looking beyond its limits. The starting point of the inquiry was a search for a more or less self-contained field of historical study of which the contemporary Western historians' customary national units of study would turn out to be parts. I had felt these national units to be unsatisfactory because they seemed to me to be unself-contained, which would mean that they must be fragments of something larger. I found this larger unit of study in a species of society that I labeled a "civilization." Civilizations proved, so it seemed to me, to be intelligible units of study so long as I was studying their geneses, growths, and breakdowns; but when I came to study their disintegrations I found that, at this stage, their histories—like those of the national subdivisions of the modern Western World—were no longer intelligible in isolation. A disintegrating civilization was apt to enter into intimate relations with one or more other representatives of its species; and these encounters between civilizations gave birth to societies of another species: higher religions. At the beginning of the inquiry I had tried to explain the higher religions, like the national and other varieties of parochial states, in terms of civilizations. The last stage of my survey of the history of civilizations convinced me that this way of looking at the higher religions did not, after all, give anything like an adequate explanation of them.

It was true that the higher religions had served as "chrysalisses" in which disintegrating civilizations had undergone a metamorphosis and from which new civilizations of a younger generation had emerged. It was also true that this had been the higher

---

by Oxford University Press. Reprinted with the kind permission of Professor Toynbee and Oxford University Press.

[1] M. R. Cohen, *Meaning in History*, p. 33.

religions' role in the histories of civilizations. But, in the histories of the higher religions themselves, this role turned out to have been not only an incidental one but actually an untoward accident in the sense that it had been apt to divert them from their proper task of carrying out their own missions. If I was to continue to pursue my search for some intelligible field of study that would provide an adequate context, and therefore a satisfactory explanation, for units of other species than nations and of other magnitudes—for instance, an explanation of civilizations —I now had to ask myself whether I ought not to reverse my previous plan of operations. If one species of society was to be explained in terms of another, ought not the civilizations of the first and second generations to be explained as preliminaries to the rise of the higher religions? These second thoughts about the identification of "the intelligible field" of historical study, to which I had been led in the course of my inquiry, gave me a new point of departure; and the change of outlook, demanded by the necessity for a change of explanation, was a radical one. Christopher Dawson is right in defining it as a change from a cyclical system to a progressive system.[2] It was indeed so radical that many critics have been struck by it and some of them have suggested that, at this point, I ought to have wound up my original comparative study of civilizations and to have started a new inquiry into the meaning of human history in terms of religion. . . .[3]

The need for a comprehensive study of human affairs. In a world that has been unified in both space and time, a study of human affairs must be comprehensive if it is to be effective. It must include, not only the whole of the living generation, but also the whole of the living generation's past. In order to save

[2] Christopher Dawson in *Toynbee and History*, p. 131. K. W. Thompson in *Toynbee and History*, pp. 207–212, traces my change of standpoint in greater detail. See also W. H. McNeill in *The Intent of Toynbee's History: A Cooperative Appraisal*. Geyl sees it (in *Toynbee and History*, p. 360), "the new system springs naturally from" the old one.

[3] See, for example, Hourani, "Toynbee's Vision of History," *The Dublin Review*, 1955, pp. 387–88 and 384–85; A. G. Bailey in *Queen's Quarterly*, vol. lxii, No. 1 (Spring, 1955), pp. 100–110; E. Voegelin in *The Intent of Toynbee's History: A Cooperative Appraisal*.

A STUDY OF HISTORY

mankind we have to learn to live together in concord in spite of traditional differences of religion, civilization, nationality, class, and race. In order to live together in concord successfully, we have to know each other, and knowing each other includes knowing each other's past, since human life, like the rest of the phenomenal universe, can be observed by human minds only as it presents itself to them on the move through time. Historical forces can be more explosive than atom bombs.[4] For our now urgent common purpose of self-preservation, it will not be enough to explore our common underlying human nature. The psychologist's work needs to be supplemented by the archaeologist's, the historian's, the anthropologist's, and the sociologist's. We must learn to recognize, and, as far as possible, to understand, the different cultural configurations in which our common human nature has expressed itself in the different religions, civilizations, and nationalities into which human culture has come to be articulated in the course of its history. "All of human history is relevant to present and future human needs."[5] "The knowledge of the history of mankind should be one of mankind's common possessions."[6]

We shall, however, have to do more than just understand each other's cultural heritages, and more even than appreciate them. We shall have to value them and love them as being parts of mankind's common treasure and therefore being ours too, as truly as the heirlooms that we ourselves shall be contributing to the common stock. Without the fire of love, the dangerous fissures in mankind's social solidarity cannot be annealed. Danger, even when it is as extreme as ours is today, is never a sufficient stimulus in itself to make men do what is necessary for their salvation. It is a poor stimulus because it is a negative one. A cold-blooded calculation of expediency will not inspire us with the spiritual power to save ourselves. This power can come only

---

[4] L. C. Strecchini in *Midstream*, Autumn, 1956, pp. 84–91.
[5] R. Coulborn in *Phylon*, 1940, offprint, p. 62.
[6] A fragment written by Ranke in the eighteen-sixties, printed on pp. xiii–xvi of A. Dove's preface to the Ninth Part, Second Section, of Ranke's *Weltgeschichte* (Leipzig 1881–88, Duncker and Humblot, 9 parts). The passage here quoted is on pp. xv–xvi.

from the disinterested pursuit of a positive aim that will outrange the negative one of trying to avoid self-destruction;[7] and this positive aim can be given to men by nothing but love.

In mankind's present situation a demand for a comprehensive view of human affairs is to be expected. Indirect evidence that this demand is, in fact, being made today comes to light incidentally in some of the critiques of earlier volumes of the present book. Some of this evidence carries conviction, because it is the testimony of critics who hold that the book has had a more favorable reception than it deserves. They explain this lack of judgment, as it seems to them, on the public's part by suggesting that people are now making this demand for a comprehensive view and that they have welcomed my work uncritically because they feel that it is at least giving them something of what they want.

R. V. Chase, for example, suggests[8] that "persuasive theorists do not . . . exert their strongest influence because of the logical airtightness of their theories, but rather because they fill an unconsciously felt vacuum with the force and urgency of their moral passion." Tangye Lean sees[9] me performing the role of an exponent of a particular cultural situation, embodying my contemporaries' anxiety over the problem of existence, their obsession with the spectacle of decay, which brings them face to face with death, and their burning desire to find some way of overcoming their own transitoriness and securing immortality. As A. G. Bailey sees it,[10] "clearly this book answered a deep-felt need of people beset with the anxieties and uncertainties of the twentieth century." Christopher Dawson suggests[11] that one reason why my work has found some acceptance is because it is a study of the civilizations. These have now become realities that cannot be ignored. J. F. Leddy suggests[12] that it is because peo-

---

[7] In a critique of my work, J. Romein judges that I am right in thinking that the unity of the World is now in the making. As Romein puts it, world unity has been created by the technicians; we have now to raise this technological unity to the level of creativity (*Toynbee and History*, p. 350).

[8] In *The American Scholar*, vol. 16, No. 3 (Summer, 1947), pp. 281–82.

[9] In *Toynbee and History*, pp. 35 ff., as summarized by O. F. Anderle.

[10] In *Queen's Quarterly*, vol. lxii, No. 1 (Spring, 1955), pp. 100–110.

[11] In *Toynbee and History*, p. 129.

[12] In *The Phoenix*, Vol. II, No. 4, p. 140.

ple in our time want to see the World as a whole and to find some meaning in its history. J. Romein says [13] that my work is valuable in giving a real world view, and that I have done something to help in overcoming the opposition between East and West. H. Kohn says [14] that a sense of unity will be my contribution to an understanding of things. T. J. G. Locher finds [15] that "our age is asking for a total vision, now that the World has grown together into so close a unity. This superhuman task is the one at which Toynbee has tried his hand." [16] Other critics, too, have made the

[13] In *Toynbee and History*, pp. 349–50.
[14] *Ibid.*, p. 359.
[15] In *De Gids*, May 1948, offprint, p. 30.
[16] If Pieter Geyl ever reads this page, the passages here quoted from observations made by some of his fellow critics of my work may throw light on something that has apparently puzzled him. He, too, has noticed that my work has been not badly received by the nonprofessional public, and this seems to have left him perplexed. "This chorus of praise," he remarks, "is a chastening reminder of the very restricted influence exercised by professional criticism" (*Toynbee and History*, p. 377). If the "chorus of praise" has been evoked by my attempt to take a comprehensive view of history, this gives Geyl his cue. He and my other critics have only to try their hands at the same enterprise, and the chorus will give them the same grateful welcome, even if they make no more of a success than I have made of the effort to see human affairs as a whole and to find some meaning in them.

This suggestion, will, I fancy, draw from some of these critics the retort that they do not want praise from the public at any price, and certainly not at the price of doing anything so unprofessional as to take a panoramic view of things. In their eyes popularity is incriminating. My kind interpreter Crane Brinton has done his best to exonerate me from this imputation. "It is quite clear," he testifies, "that his fame is everywhere confined . . . to highbrows and middlebrows, and has not reached the lowbrows, as it would have to do if he is to do the work of a major prophet. It is very hard indeed to think of Toynbee effectively translated to the many, as Marx has certainly been translated" (*The Virginia Quarterly Review*, Summer, 1956, pp. 361–75). Marx is vulgar indeed. His shamelessly panoramic view of human affairs has caught the *profanum vulgus*'s imagination all over the World. I have not incurred that damning degree of popularity, anyway. Yet I fear that even a modest popularity among the highbrow and middlebrow fraction of the public is enough to ruin my reputation with the professionals. E. Fiess notes disapprovingly that "popularity is no substitute for understanding," though he does concede that "all discourse is in some sense a simplification" (*Toynbee and History*, p. 378). H. J. Morgenthau and A. J. P. Taylor draw attention (*ibid.*, pp. 196–97 and 115) to the contrast between a popularity that they ascribe to me with the public and the condemnation that I have received from my fellow historians. Both of them assume, without arguing the point that I have tried to take a comprehensive view of history, without going into the question whether my work has been well received, or whether, if it has been, its attempt at comprehensiveness is what has won it favor. The purpose for which the point is made by most of them is to go on to say—as Locher does in the passage from which I have just quoted—that, in attempting this, I have obviously attempted the impossible, or that, for whatever reason, I have failed to achieve my aim. If the critics quoted in the present paragraph are right in holding that my work has been well received and that its attempt at comprehensiveness accounts for this, then the other testimonies to this attempt at comprehensiveness indirectly give further support to the view that there is a genuine demand for such attempts in the present-day world.

One of my critics has compared earlier volumes of this book to a "palace" in which "the rooms . . . are overfurnished to the point of resembling a dealer's warehouse." [17] This reviewer must

---

point, that, on any issue between public and professionals, the professionals must be right. Morgenthau chivalrously testifies that I am not being popular on purpose. "This popularity is unjust," he writes, "to Mr. Toynbee's intent, but it illuminates the weakness of his achievement" (*ibid.*, p. 197). It is true that I have never set out to win popularity, any more than I have sought to avoid it. When I am writing, the reception that is awaiting me is not in my mind. I write as the subject moves me. But surely the truth about popularity is that, in itself, it is no evidence of merit or demerit. One must know the reason why a book is popular before one can judge whether, in the particular case in point, popularity damns the author or does him credit. Morgenthau evidently holds that popularity, whatever its cause, damns an author and his work automatically. This dogma seems to rest on two assumptions: that the judgment of the public must always be wrong, and that the judgment of the professionals must always be in conflict with it.

If these are the doctrines of a professional, they are unfortunate. In what we vaguely call "the public," there are many different levels of intellectual cultivation; and, if a professional despises all these levels indiscriminately, he is putting himself in jeopardy, for at the higher levels he is likely to find his intellectual equals, and may even find his superiors in the field outside the contemptuous specialist's own chosen province. What is more, the contemptuous specialist is doing a disservice to the culture that ought to be common to the cultivated public and to him. When professional intellectual work becomes esoteric, this is a sign that culture is in a bad way. Culture flourishes only when there is an active and constant intellectual intercourse and exchange of ideas between cultivated people of all kinds.

[17] *The Listener*, 19th October, 1939, in a review of Vols. IV–VI.

also be a thought-reader; for I have often thought of myself as a man moving old furniture about. For centuries these lovely things had been lying neglected in the lumber rooms and attics. They had been piled in there higgledy-piggledy, in utter disorder, and had been crammed so tight that nobody could even squeeze his way in to look at them and find out whether they were of any value. In the course of ages they had been accumulating there—unwanted rejects from a score of country houses. This unworthy treatment of these precious pieces came to trouble me more and more; for I knew that they were not really junk; I knew that they were heirlooms, and these so rare and fine that they were not just provincial curiosities; they were the common heritage of anyone who had any capacity for appreciating beauty in Man's handiwork. At last I found that I could not bear this shocking situation any longer, so I set my own hand to a back-breaking job. I began to drag out the pieces, one by one, and to arrange them in the hall. I could not pretend to form a final judgment on the order in which they should be placed. Indeed, different orders could be imagined, each of them the right order from some particular point of view. The first thing to be done was to get as many of the pieces as possible out into the open and to assemble them in some order or other. If once I had them parked down in the hall, I could see how they looked and could shift them and reshift them at my leisure. Perhaps I should not have the leisure; perhaps the preliminary job of extracting these treasures from the lumber rooms and attics would turn out to be as much as I could manage with my single pair of hands.[18] If so, this would not matter; for there would be plenty of time afterward for other people to rearrange the pieces, and, no doubt, they would be doing this again and again as they studied them more closely and came to know more about them than would ever be known by me.

This furniture-shifting job is, of course, David's kind of work, not Solomon's; and the time when Solomon's achievement will be feasible is now only just dawning.

---

[18] "His work is a gigantic labor—the labor of a comprehensive attempt to put things in order (*Die Riesenarbeit seines Werkes ist eine umfassende Ordnungsarbeit*)." H. Werner in *Deutsche Vierteljahrsschrift für Litera-*

> There is as yet no history of humanity, since humanity is not an organized society with a common tradition or a common social consciousness. All the attempts that have hitherto been made to write a world history have been in fact attempts to interpret one tradition in terms of another, attempts to extend the intellectual hegemony of a dominant culture by subordinating to it all the events of other cultures that come within the observer's range of vision.[19]

This has certainly been true up to now. It is true, for instance, of the presentation of world history in the Old Testament, in Hellenic literature, in the Chinese dynastic histories, and in Western historians' works. If a Western historian does not fall into the egocentric error of making all history lead up to the point reached in the West in his own generation, he is likely to fall into another error, only one degree less egocentric, with which I, for instance, have been charged, with some justice, by a number of my critics. He is likely to use Hellenic history, which lies in the background of his own Western history, as an exclusive "model," not just as one out of a number of alternative possible models, for elucidating the configuration of history in general in the current age of the civilizations.

Since the World is now being unified as a result of Western inventions, and therefore, initially, within a Western framework, one or other or both of these characteristic Western distortions of the true picture of world history are likely to persist for some time and to die hard. Nevertheless, it is already possible to look forward to a time when these Western distortions of the true picture, and all other distortions of the kind, will be replaced by a new vision of the past seen from the standpoint, not of this or that nationality, civilization, or religion, but of a united human race. If mankind does respond to the challenge of its present self-imposed ordeal by saving itself from self-inflicted genocide, this will have been the reward of a common effort to transcend all the traditional divisions and to live as one family for the first time since mankind made its first appearance on this planet. This

---

turwissenschaft und Geistesgeschichte, 29. Jahrgang, xxix. Band (1955), p. 544.

[19] Christopher Dawson, *The Dynamics of World History,* p. 273.

union sacrée in the face of imminent self-destruction will be, if it is achieved, Man's finest achievement and most thrilling experience up to date. From the new position of charity and hope which Man will thereby have won for himself, all the past histories of the previous divisions of the human race will be seen, in retrospect, to be so many parts of one common historic heritage. They will be seen as leading up to unity, and as opening out, for a united human race, future prospects of which no human being could have dreamed in the age of unfettered parochialism.

Toynbee's defense of his empirical method. In this book I have claimed throughout that I am using an empirical method of inquiry. A number of my critics have taken note of this claim of mine, and most of these have contested it. I must therefore explain what I mean by the term.

I am not claiming that I approach the historical record of human experience without preconceptions; and I entirely agree with W. H. Walsh when he says that this would be "a claim which could certainly not be sustained." [20] *Some* theoretical framework and *some* working hypotheses are unavoidable," [21] because the human mind's process of thought is analytical and classificatory. If I have seemed, to so careful and discriminating a critic as Walsh, to be implying that I am approaching history without preconceptions, that must be my fault. It must mean that, in Volumes I–X of this book, I have not made it clear that I agree with Walsh on this crucial point.[22] For reasons already set out in Chapter I of this volume, I disagree with Hales, when he talks of "laws arrived at by empirical analysis." [23] I agree with E. Berkovitz that "laws" cannot be derived from facts,[24] and with Erdmann when he says, *ad hominem,* that my guiding ideas are not derived from the observation of history,[25] though I do not

---

[20] *Toynbee and History,* p. 128.
[21] *Social Science Research Council's Committee on Historiography's Report,* (1954), p. 132.
[22] For instance, I have not made this clear to Father D'Arcy, to judge by his comment that what Geyl's criticism "proves is that Toynbee should not have claimed to rest his case entirely on empirical methods" (M. C. D'Arcy: *The Sense of History,* p. 72).
[23] E. E. Y. Hales, *History To-day,* May, 1955.
[24] *Judaism: Fossil or Ferment?,* p. 10.
[25] *Archiv für Kulturgeschichte,* xxxiii. Band, Heft 2 (1951) p. 246.

agree with Mumford that my conclusions, as well as my hypotheses, "for all his empiricism, are inevitably as much the product of his own ideology as of the situations that he 'interprets.' " [26] This point has been put in telling words by H. Baudet.[27]

> Many critics have censured Toynbee's primary vision on the theoretical ground that it is "apriori." Certainly it is, as they say. But, "epistemologically," is not an "apriori" of this kind a basis [of mental operations] which speaks for itself because it is unavoidable? Is it not a compelling necessity?
>
> All vision is engendered on an "apriori," and . . . an "apriori" of this kind has its roots—as all thinking has, *au fond*—in will and passion.

The point is driven home by K. R. Popper. He rejects

> the view that science begins with observations from which it derives its theories by some process of generalization or induction.[28] I do not believe that we ever make inductive generalizations in the sense that we start from observations and try to derive our theories from them.[29] Before we can collect data, our interest in *data of a certain* kind must be aroused: the problem always comes first.[30] Theories are prior to observations as well as to experiments, in the sense that the latter are significant only in relation to theoretical problems.[31]

When Trevor-Roper says that, in my work, "the theories are not deduced from the facts," [32] the answer is that neither my theories nor anyone else's are or ever have been or ever will be generated in that way. If being "empirical" meant this, the word would have no counterpart in reality, and had better be struck out of the dictionary. On the other hand, when Trevor-Roper goes on to say that my theories are not tested by the facts either,

---

[26] *Diogenes*, No. 13, (Spring, 1956), p. 13.
[27] In *Historie en Metahistorie*, p. 46.
[28] *The Poverty of Historicism*, p. 98. Cp. p. 121.
[29] *Ibid.*, p. 134.
[30] *Ibid.*, p. 121. Cp. p. 134.
[31] *Ibid.*, p. 98.
[32] *Toynbee and History*, p. 123.

he is laying down a legitimate requirement,[33] and my claim to be using an empirical method of inquiry does stand or fall according to the verdict on this count. I agree that my claim cannot be sustained if I have not tried to test my theories and hypotheses by the facts, or if I have tried but have not done the job properly or successfully.[34] For, while it is true that theories and hypotheses can never be deduced from facts, it is also true that they can be validated only if they are confronted with relevant facts and are confirmed by them. More than that, the whole purpose of formulating a theory or a hypothesis is the heuristic one of trying to increase our knowledge and understanding by applying the theory or hypothesis to the phenomena.[35] I maintain my claim that I have tried to be empirical in this sense, which is, I believe, the correct usage of the word and does mean something that an inquirer not only can be but ought to be.

In making my claim to be empirical, I have been tacitly contrasting my approach with Dilthey's approach and with Spengler's.[36] While the plan of the present book was brewing in my mind, the first volume of Spengler's *Der Untergang des Abendlandes* was published, and, when I read it, my first impression was that, in Spengler's work, what I had been planning was already an accomplished fact. My second impression, however, was that Spengler's work suffered from being too dogmatic, in the sense that he was apt to enunciate his theories about the configuration of human affairs and to leave it at that, without putting these theories to sufficiently thorough tests on the touchstone of the phenomena.[37] Having decided to go on with my own enter-

---

[33] Baudet observes, in *loc. cit.*, p. 47, that the process of proof must be kept clearly distinct from the original vision.

[34] "Assuredly, if induction . . . were an invalid process, no process grounded on it would be valid. . . . But, though a valid process, it is a fallible one, and fallible in very different degrees," J. S. Mill, *Philosophy of Scientific Method*, ed. E. Nagel (New York: Hafner, 1950), p. 290.

[35] See Vol. XII of Toynbee's *Study of History*, pp. 22–23, 41–45, and 158–70.

[36] My wish to distinguish my approach from Spengler's has been guessed by W. H. McNeill in *The Intent of Toynbee's History: A Cooperative Appraisal*.

[37] This makes Spengler a poet, according to Holborn. "History is the reenactment of the past in the mind of the historian, and even 'facts' exist only there. But, in contrast to poetry, they call for critical verification," *The Saturday Review of Literature*, May 31, 1947, p. 29.

prise, I was told by a distinguished philosopher, the late Lord Lindsay of Birker, that I should find in Dilthey's work the very thing that I was looking for. What I was looking for was a bridge between theory and fact. But, in Dilthey's work, I did not find even theories about the configuration of human affairs. I found nothing but epistemology. I was, and am, grateful to Dilthey for that, since the relation between theory and fact cannot be studied without taking epistemology into account. But the bridge for which I was looking was not to be found in Dilthey's work, and I had to try to build it without getting help from him.

Some critics have given me credit for making this attempt. Guerard, for instance, draws the same contrast between Spengler and me that I have drawn in my own mind.[38] Feibleman says of me [39] that "he tries to analyze cultural structure, and, in doing so, takes the first step toward the establishment of the empirical field of human social structure as the empirical study of a science." To try, however, is not enough. The attempt that I have made has been criticized on at least six counts. According to the critics, the examples that I have taken as test cases have been denatured by being taken out of their context.[40] Some of these examples are ruled out of order because they are taken from phenomena of a different order of magnitude from the civilizations on which I am seeking to throw light.[41] My citation of examples, relevant to whatever the point in question may be, is not exhaustive and is therefore unrepresentative and thus misleading. Alternatively, I cite so many examples that I clutter up my argument with an indigestible mass of details.[42] Whether the number of examples that I cite is too small or too great, I am

---

[38] See Vol. XII of *A Study of History*, footnote 1.

[39] J. K. Feibleman in *Tien Hsia Monthly*, vol. xi, Nos. 1 and 2 (1940), p. 171.

[40] See Vol. XII of *A Study of History*, pp. 234–5.

[41] *Ibid.*

[42] The book is criticized in this sense by A. L. Guerard, *The Herald-Tribune*, October 28, 1934; by L. Mumford, *Toynbee and History*, p. 141; and by P. Sorokin (*ibid.*, p. 178). [See the selections by Sorokin in this chapter.] As Mumford puts it (*ibid.*, p. 142), "his Study of History . . . is . . . , in its vastness, its complexity, its impenetrability, and its magnificent profusion and confusion, an image of that great overgrown megalopolis [London], stifled by its very success."

guilty of selecting them to fit my theories.[43] When they will not fit, I force them with Procrustean violence. I have a rigid a priori scheme. If even this Procrustean treatment cannot make awkward facts conform, I ignore them.[44] Some of these charges cancel each other out, but what is left is still formidable.

The first of these indictments—that I have taken episodes out of their context—is evidently incompatible with the criticism that my work is superficial, and my spirit hybristic, because I attempt the impossible enterprise of trying to cover the whole history of the Age of the Civilizations. It is true that I have attempted to do this; and it surely follows that my work, as a whole, is likely to have suffered less from distortion as a result of taking episodes out of their context than the work of many other present-day historians. I agree that taking things out of their context does distort them. In the first chapter of this volume I have argued that it is a grievous limitation and a radical defect of the human intellect that it is incapable of apprehending Reality as a whole, and has, perforce, to take it piecemeal at the cost of failing to see it as it truly is. When we are applying our minds to study, and not to practical action, we ought to contend against this inherent infirmity of theirs as far as is humanly possible. My own criticism of the present vogue for "specialization" is that, so far from trying to combat and, to some extent, counteract this intellectual infirmity of ours, specialization gives way to it and thereby accentuates it. The charge of denaturing Reality by taking episodes out of their context does hit me, no doubt; but I should have thought that it hit, with rather greater force, the school of specialists which is the predominant school among present-day Western historians—a school in whose more polemical exponents' eyes I am something of a heretic, just because I have been unwilling to follow this current fashion.

---

[43] "He selects the instances which will support his theses, or he presents them in the way that suits him. . . . Those cases he does mention can be explained or described in a different way so as to disagree no less completely with his theses." P. Geyl in *Toynbee and History*, p. 45.

[44] "As for those items that just can't be made to fit, they are quickly tossed into the huge garbage heap of discarded facts," L. Stone in *Toynbee and History*, p. 113. I ignore exceptions to my laws, R. Pares, *The English Historical Review*, vol. lxxi, No. 279 (April, 1956), p. 262.

The charge that I draw many of my illustrations of features in the histories of civilizations from social units of a lower order of magnitude has been noticed and discussed already [45] and therefore need not be reexamined here.

The charge that my citation of examples is not exhaustive hits not only me but everyone who has ever sought to test a hypothesis by confronting it with relevant phenomena. It hits me perhaps less hard than some of my fellow prisoners in the dock, if it is true that I have surfeited my readers with examples *ad nauseam*. But it hits every student of phenomena, human or nonhuman, since phenomena, of whatever kind, are innumerable. The only class of things that could conceivably have a membership that was limited by its own nature would be some class, not of phenomena, but of mathematical abstractions that had been abstracted with the express design of creating a self-evidently closed class. Even if our momentary state of knowledge enabled us to enumerate every one of the representatives of some class of phenomena that were in existence at the moment, the exhaustive enumeration would be no better, in logic, than a "simple enumeration," as has been noticed in Chapter I.[46]

If the charge that my citation of examples is selective has to be dropped because it applies, not just to me, but to everyone who tries to test a theory, I am still confronted with the further charge that I make my selection of examples with an eye to fitting my theories. This charge, too, applies to everyone who tries to test a theory.[47] For my part I certainly have not consciously made selections to suit my purposes, and I doubt whether any other scholar ever has either. To do this might be a temptation to a company-promoter, politician, barrister, or member of some other practical profession in which this form of cheating, if the fraud remained undetected, might reap lucrative material rewards. But what interest could a scholar have in spending laborious man-hours in deliberately trying to diminish the knowledge and understanding that he is concerned to increase? The charge

---

[45] Vol. XII of *A Study of History*, pp. 234–35.

[46] *Ibid.*, pp. 23–24.

[47] "However valid this criticism may be for Mr. Toynbee's empiricism in particular, it is unerringly true with respect to empiricism in general," K. W. Thompson, *Toynbee and History*, p. 219.

is unconvincing—whoever may be the individual against whom it has been made.[48] At the same time it is hard to rebut, because it is always possible to switch the indictment from the offender's conscious self to the subconscious underworld of his psyche. However upright his conscious self may be admitted to be, his subconscious may be a rogue that has inveigled him into cheating and into doing this bona fide, inasmuch as he has never been conscious of what he is, in fact, doing.[49] I do not know how to clear myself of a charge against my subconscious; but I do know that anyone else who was arraigned on account of alleged misdoings of his subconscious would find himself in the same plight.

The same defence holds for the charge that I force facts that will not fit. I can only reply, again, that I have never done so consciously. It is true that I start with a "schema" in the sense of a formulated but still untested hypothesis or theory. But I plead "not guilty" to the charge of being "schema-bound." Where I believe that I have found some pattern or regularity or recurrence, I have always tried to ascertain the limits of the realm in which this particular "law" holds good—for instance, in Volume II, where I am dealing with a number of variations on the theme of challenge-and-response. So far from ignoring contradictory instances, I have always brought them up and discussed them when I have been aware of their existence. Of course, many will have escaped me, as also will many other instances that support my hypotheses instead of impugning them. In the numerous surveys made in the first ten volumes of this book, for the purpose of testing how far, if at all, my hypotheses might or might not be valid, I have always made my net as big, and its meshes as close, as I have been able. I am ready at any time to modify or abandon any of my hypotheses if I am given convincing reasons in the shape either of the citation of relevant phenomena previously unknown to me or of the reinterpretation of phenomena of which I am already aware.

---

[48] A propos of men, A. R. Burn observes: "It would be unjust to say that he forces facts into his mold, and much more so to imply conscious lack of integrity," *History*, (February–October, 1956), p. 3. G. J. Renier thinks that "this book cannot be a mystification," *Toynbee and History*, p. 75.

[49] "Though there is no deception of others, there is the nearest approach to self-deception." Renier, *ibid.*

The history and prospects of the West. The subject of this chapter is a big one, but the chapter need not be long, since the history and prospects of the West have been discussed at some length in a previous volume. Critics of what I have written about the West there, and in other passages, have dealt, not only with the substance of the subject, but with my views about it. These are of minor interest in themselves, but, since my critics have paid attention to them, and in some cases have apparently misunderstood them, I have dealt briefly with this personal aspect of the subject too in the Annex to Chapter II of the present volume. I therefore need not say much in this chapter about the discussion of my own views.

Unlike the histories of a majority of the civilizations known to us, the history of the West is today still an unfinished story. It is therefore hazardous to try to forecast its prospects, even in the form of suggesting a number of alternative possibilities.[50] Even if we were satisfied that the pattern of Western history, up to date, has been more or less the same as that of some other civilization—say, the Hellenic or the Sinic—whose history is over and is therefore known to us from beginning to end, we should have no warrant for forecasting that the future course of Western history will follow Hellenic or Sinic lines, if I am right —as I believe I am—in holding that patterns in the course of human affairs are not predetermined or inevitable, and that therefore past patterns afford no basis for predictions about the future.[51] If this is the truth, we cannot foretell whether or not the Western Civilization is ever going to enter into a universal state, as both the Hellenic and the Sinic did. Still less can we foretell whether, if the future course of Western affairs were to follow the pattern that is a common Helleno-Sinic one up to that point, the West's universal state would be as short-lived as the Hellenic

---

[50] *Ad hominem*, E. Gargan, writing in March, 1955, in *Books on Trial*, finds, not surprisingly, that "Toynbee, from the start of his work, has rendered judgments on the history of the West which have proved startlingly wrong" (p. 265). In general Gargan is critical of my "vision of the Western past and future."

[51] O. Halecki, in *The Intent of Toynbee's History: A Cooperative Appraisal*, has given me credit for having avoided any deterministic interpretation of the history of the West in particular and of mankind in general.

Civilization's was in the western provinces of the Roman Empire, or as long-lived as the Sinic universal state has been.

In the Atomic Age, into which the West—and, with it, the World—has entered in our lifetime, it now looks as if a universal state could not be established again—at any rate not in the standard way, and therefore not in the standard form which that way produced. In the past, universal states have been established as the result of successive wars ending in the overthrow of all great powers except one surviving victor. Even in the age of preatomic weapons this way of arriving at political unity was so destructive—psychologically still more than materially—that civilizations which had passed through this harrowing experience usually emerged from it incurably damaged. In the age of atomic weapons no power would reach the final round. There would be no victor; all belligerents alike would be vanquished; and even the first round of atomic warfare might wipe out, not only the belligerent states, but civilization, the human race, and perhaps all life on this planet. It does not follow that mankind cannot and will not attain unity. Now that, for the first time in history, the whole human race has been united on the military plane, the choice confronting us may be one between going all the way to unity or going under. What seems improbable is that a society can ever again be united by force. This seems improbable because the force used in future warfare would be atomic force, and this would annihilate the society, leaving nothing in existence to unite.

Such considerations as these have made me wary of offering predictions—above all about the future of the West. When critics point this out,[52] I take that as commendation and not as censure. And their criticism misses the mark when they go on to accuse me of inconsistency in shrinking from applying to the Western Civilization a pattern of decline and fall that, according to them, I believe to be the inevitable fate of all civilizations.[53] It

---

[52] E.g. T. J. G. Locher in *De Gids*, May, 1948, offprint, p. 26; Crane Brinton in *The Virginia Quarterly Review*, vol. 32, No. 3 (Summer, 1956), pp. 361–75.

[53] See Locher, *ibid.*, p. 27; Geyl in *Toynbee and History*, pp. 67–68; K. W. Thompson, *ibid.*, p. 216; Spate, *ibid.*, p. 303; B. Prakash in *The*

is true that I should feel rueful if I were convinced that the particular living civilization into which I have been born is bound to break down and disintegrate on the lines on which other civilizations have gone to pieces in the past. It is also true that I think that a pattern of breakdown and disintegration, common to the histories of a number of past civilizations, can be detected when we make a comparative study of them. But I do not believe that this pattern was predetermined or inevitable in any single past case; and therefore, a fortiori, I do not believe that it can be projected into a prediction about the future of a civilization that is still a going concern.[54] I do not believe, as Spengler believes, that there is a fixed pattern to which the history of every civilization is bound to conform. My unwillingness to predict that the Western Civilization will go the way that a number of its predecessors have gone is a consistent application of my conviction that the course of human affairs is not predetermined. It is not a sentimental refusal to apply to the prospects of my own civilization some pattern of breakdown and disintegration that I unavowedly believe to be every civilization's inevitable fate. I have no such cast-iron pattern in my bag of intellectual tools.

As I see it, the fact that the Western Civilization's history is still unfinished not only makes it impossible to predict its future course but also makes it difficult even to discuss the pattern of its past history as far as this has gone up to date. Sir Llewellyn Woodward has pointed out that any number of patterns can be found in history. Even if we manage to see through and discard those that are imaginary, the number of those admitted, by general consensus, to be genuine will still be great. There is room for many patterns; they are not mutually exclusive. The problem raised by their number is that of their relation to each other. When the history of a civilization, or of some greater or lesser historical episode, is complete, it may be practicable, in retrospect, to make out which of the patterns in it is the dominant pattern to which the others are subordinate. But, when the story is

---

Modern Review, (November, 1953), p. 403; Christopher Hill in *The Modern Quarterly*, (Autumn, 1947), p. 291.

[54] "Even if we could claim that all past societies have perished, it would not prove that all future ones must," J. K. Feibleman in *T'ien Hsia Monthly*, vol. xi, Nos. 1 and 2 (1940), p. 16.

still unfinished, the clue is much harder to find. If one looks at a Persian carpet at the stage at which the strip that has already been knotted runs to only a few inches out of an ultimate length of, say, twenty feet, we can perhaps identify the motifs that the total pattern of the finished carpet is going to develop; but we cannot yet single out the master-motif that is going to give form and unity to the whole.

BIBLIOGRAPHY

Arnold Toynbee's *A Study of History*, first published in twelve volumes by the Oxford University Press (1934–1961), is now available in two less expensive editions. Oxford University Press publishes a paperback edition and also an abridgment of the entire work by D. C. Somervell in two volumes. Two other works by Toynbee that are relevant to his philosophy of history are *Civilization on Trial* (Oxford: 1948) and *An Historian's Approach to Religion* (Oxford: 1956). A very helpful bibliography of books and articles on Toynbee's thought published between 1946–1960 can be found in the journal, *History and Theory* (IV, 2, 1965).

BLYTH, J. W. "Toynbee and the Categories of Interpretation," *Philosophical Review*, 1949.

BRINTON, C. "Toynbee's City of God," *Virginia Quarterly Review*, 1956.

BUTLER, J. F. "Toynbee and the Categories of Interpretation," *Philosophical Review*, 1950.

DAWSON, C. "Arnold Toynbee and the Study of History," *The Dynamics of World History*, New York: 1956.

DRAY, W. H. *Philosophy of History*. Englewood Cliffs, New Jersey: 1964.

DRAY, W. H. "Toynbee's Search for Historical Laws," *History and Theory*, 1960.

GARGAN, E. T. (ed.). *The Intent of Toynbee's History*. Chicago: 1961.

GEYL, P. *Debates with Historians*. London: 1955.

GEYL, P., TOYNBEE, A., and SOROKIN, P. *The Pattern of the Past*. Boston: 1949.

MAZLISH, B. *The Riddle of History*. New York: 1966.

MONTAGUE, A. (ed.). *Toynbee and History: Critical Essays and Reviews*. Boston: 1956.

SINGER, C. G. *Toynbee*. Philadelphia: 1964.

TREVOR-ROPER, H. R. "Arnold Toynbee's Millennium," *Men and Events*, New York: 1957.

WALSH, W. H. "Toynbee Reconsidered," *Philosophy*, 1963.

9 The Christian Understanding of History

Many of the early speculative approaches to history (those of Augustine, Joachim, Bossuet, and Vico, for example) were conscious attempts to present a Christian interpretation of history. From its beginning, Christianity has had a special interest in history. Not only does Christianity teach that God is Lord over history (in the sense that history began in His act of creation, is governed by His providence, and will end at His judgment), it also believes that in Christ God actually entered into human history. In an important sense, Christianity is grounded upon certain revelatory events (for example, the Crucifixion and the Resurrection) that took place in human history.

All the speculative theories of history studied so far suffer from the same defect—finite man's inability to ground his view of history upon an absolute historical perspective. Maurice Mandelbaum, taking note of this, has argued that no speculative system of history can be established on empirical grounds since—

> every philosopher stands in the midst of the historical process itself. It is impossible to hold that history represents a teleological development unless one knows (or believes that one knows) what the end of that process will be. But no empirical survey of the past can demonstrate the future to the philosopher of history. It therefore becomes impossible to ground historical monism upon an empirical appeal to the apparent teleology of past periods of history. In order to establish historical monism upon a teleological view of the periods of history it is therefore necessary to transcend one's temporal standpoint. In this Augustine and the entire Christian philosophy of history again represent a sounder approach to the problem of historical monism. For in Augustine and his followers we find an appeal to the nontemporal realm of God as the basis of historical monism.[1]

Because man occupies a particular place in the course of human history, he cannot know what the future will bring. Therefore, he cannot possibly demonstrate that any proposed pattern for the whole of history is valid. Furthermore, because man lacks any absolute historical perspective, he cannot really be certain as to what within history possesses lasting value. One way out of this predicament, the Christian philosopher of history claims, is to assume the truth of the Christian view of history. One advocate of this position has written, if—

> God entered the human sphere and revealed to men the origin and goal of the historical drama, the criteria for significance and value in the process, the true nature of the human participants in the drama, and the ethical values appropriate to the process; then, obviously, the question, "Where is history going" could be successfully and meaningfully answered. A gigantic If, you say. True, but

---

[1] Maurice Mandelbaum, *The Problem of Historical Knowledge* (New York: Harper and Row, 1967), p. 319.

this is precisely the central contention of the Christian religion: that God *did* enter human life—in the person of Jesus the Christ—and *did* reveal to men the nature and significance of history and human life, and *did* bring men into contact with eternal values.[2]

The selection by Kenneth Scott Latourette, first presented as his presidential address to The American Historical Association in 1948, outlines the basic tenets of the Christian view of history. Without engaging in any controversy, he reminds his fellow historians of their need for some kind of historical pattern and recommends that found in Christianity.

Many Christian thinkers (especially within Protestant Liberalism) have accepted an optimistic and progressivistic view of history influenced by such nineteenth-century idealists as Fichte, Schelling, and Hegel. Since the idealist interpretation of history in the nineteenth century was a secularized version of Christianity to begin with, there seem to be good grounds for eliminating the humanistic and pantheistic view of history found in Protestant Liberalism as a "Christian" view.

Reinhold Niebuhr, considered by many to be the most influential American theologian of the twentieth century, was a frequent critic of the progressivistic "Christian" view of history. Niebuhr argues that the Christian [3] view of history is based upon a more realistic view of man than that found in idealistic or humanistic systems. If history reveals anything and if Christianity teaches anything about man, it is the fact that man is a sinner. Reason itself can detect no pattern or meaning in history for history, according to Niebuhr, is the record of human sin. History is not progressing toward some higher goal; history is actually going nowhere. Niebuhr understands sin as "selfish pride"; it is rebellion against God. Sin is a form of idolatry inasmuch as it is always a result of man's elevation of some false center of meaning above God. Niebuhr insists that the evil revealed in history is not transient or accidental. It is a manifestation of the evil that is

---

[2] John Warwick Montgomery, "Where Is History Going?" *Religion in Life*, (Spring, 1964).

[3] The absence of quotation marks here indicates that we are referring to what Niebuhr regards as the legitimate Christian interpretation of history as opposed to the spurious view found in Protestant Liberalism.

part and parcel of human nature. The story of Adam's Sin in the book of Genesis which Niebuhr interprets as a myth is a symbolic account of the fall of all men. While Niebuhr regards sin as universal and inevitable, he still claims that it is not necessary. Man, he contends, is still free and thus must bear all responsibility for his acts.

However, it must not be thought that Niebuhr denies the presence of all meaning in history. There is unity in history but it can only be discerned by faith, not by reason. Only faith in the sovereignty of God can supply meaning for the historical process. Like Latourette, Niebuhr regards the coming of Christ as the pivotal event of history. The Christ-event has eschatological significance; it discloses the whole meaning of history. The cross reveals the depths of human sin and stands in judgment over all the idolatrous centers of meaning man worships in place of God.

KENNETH SCOTT LATOURETTE
THE CHRISTIAN UNDERSTANDING OF HISTORY *

Do patterns exist in history? All historians make selections from the multitude of happenings which constitute the quarry in which they work. Do they do so arbitrarily or in accord with what is inherent in the events? If there are patterns, can they be discerned? Is history governed by laws? If so, what are they? Does history have meaning, or is it simply sound and fury, signifying nothing? Does it have an end toward which it is moving, or is it movement without direction? These are questions which continue to trouble members of our craft. In various lands, cultures, and ages they have been repeatedly raised and many answers have been given. Whether in the ancient civilizations of the Nile and the Tigris-Euphrates Valley, in Hebrew Palestine, in China, in India, in Greece, in Rome, in the Middle Ages of Europe, or in the modern Occident, explicitly or by implication they have been posed and pondered.

---

* Presidential address delivered at the annual meeting of the American Historical Association in 1948. Reprinted by permission from *The American Historical Review* (January, 1949), pp. 259–76.

We need no full catalogue to recall how various have been the purposes which have governed selection from the fragmentary records of the past, how numerous have been the patterns which observers of man's course on this plane have seen as giving coherence to the many incidents which are the crude stuff with which historians deal, how diverse have been the laws which have been said to mold the course of events, and the meaning—or the absence of meaning—which has been thought to characterize the stream of human life. Many scribes, both ancient and modern, have centered their stories upon men and women who have loomed large in the collective life of the group—rulers, statesmen, artists, authors, scholars, religious leaders. Some of this, as in early China, has been from a mixture of reverence for ancestors and the desire of insuring prestige to a particular family. Some has been at the instance of those in the public eye who have wished to perpetuate the memory of their greatness—from some of the most ancient inscriptions and chronicles to the archives amassed and preserved by recent Presidents of the United States and the spate of autobiographies which has been mounting since the invention of the printing press. Many arrangements of events have had as their principle of selection admiration and affection for a friend, a teacher, or a saint, or concern for the perpetuation and spread of a religious or political faith—as in the case of Confucius, the Buddha, Jesus, and Lenin. Some historians have centered their narratives upon a war or series of wars—the Peloponnesian struggle, the Gallic Wars, the American Civil War, and World Wars I and II. Many have concentrated on the state and politics. Some, especially in recent times, have viewed economic factors as determinative. Others have attempted to discern a science of society. Influenced by the temper which has characterized much of the Occidental mind for the past few generations, historians have debated whether history is a science. Whatever their answer, in general they have attempted to apply scientific methods to their work. Modern historians usually believe in causation—that events and movements are in large part or entirely determined by preceding events and movements. Yet there are those who declare a time sequence to be all that can be demonstrated. For at least twenty-five hundred years there have been those who have insisted that no meanings or patterns are to be observed in history. Often, as in the case of Yang Chu, this has been in protest against those who believed such to exist. Those who have viewed this world, including human life, as illusion, as has been so widely the case in India, naturally have had little or no regard for history. Many observers across the centuries have believed that history is cyclical, repeating itself. This has been true of the Greeks, of many Buddhists, and of some of the most widely read of modern Occidental authors. Others have held that progress is discernible, whether by steady movement, by pulsations, or by the dialectical process. Some are passionately convinced that progress culminates in an ideal society in which all man's ills will have been resolved. Others, while believing in progress, do not envision mankind as ever escaping from struggle. These are merely a few of the many attitudes which men have taken as they have sought to record or to understand the past. Some contradict one another. Others can be embraced in a larger synthesis.

Faced with this multiplicity of convictions, it is not surprising that the experienced historian tends to be wary of committing himself to any of them. Yet history cannot be written without some basis of selection, whether artificial and purely subjective or inherent in man's story. A survey of the presidential addresses made before this Association reveals the fact that no one single topic has so attracted those who have been chosen to head this honorable body as have the possible patterns and meanings of history. A few of the addresses have been critical of particular interpretations or even of all interpretations of history. More have presented interpretations—although usually with such modesty and cautious tentativeness as befits those who submit themselves to the judgment of their peers. Frequently the patterns have been assumed or implied.

The historian, then, is faced with a dilemma. On the one hand he is painfully aware of the many interpretations and philosophies of history which have been put forward and is therefore hesitant to accept wholeheartedly any one of them. On the other hand he is confronted with the necessity of acting on some principle of selection, even though it be arbitrary, and is haunted by the persistent hope that a framework and meaning can be found which possess objective reality.

CHRISTIAN UNDERSTANDING OF HISTORY

This hope is peculiarly insistent in our day. We appear to be living in a time of major revolution. As historians we are familiar with many earlier periods of rapid change. Indeed, if there is one feature which we are agreed upon as characterizing history it is flux. It seems probable that no culture—if we can assent to the existence of such an entity—and no institution remains permanently unaltered. Yet so far as we are aware, never before has all mankind been so drastically on the march. Never at any one time have so many cultures been in what appears to be disintegration. In no other era have all men been faced with such colossal possibilities of what they deem good and ill. Never before has the race as a whole been so assailed by those who urge upon it dogmatically one or another interpretation of the historical process to explain and to guide in humanity's painful transition.

May I make bold under these circumstances to invite your consideration to one of the oldest interpretations of history, the one which bears the name Christian? I do so realizing that many now regard it as quite outmoded, as associated with a stage of thinking which mankind is discarding, and as being held only by those who are victims of what is indulgently denominated social lag. I do so as one who accepts the Christian understanding of history and is more and more attracted by what he believes to be the accuracy of its insight. But it is not as an advocate, as one in the long succession of those who would seek to justify the ways of God to men, that I would once more draw your attention to it. I would, rather, raise with you the question of whether the Christian understanding of history may not offer the clue to the mystery which fascinates so many of our best minds.

May I first outline what the Christian understanding of history is? Then may I go on to suggest the degree to which it eludes testing by the methods employed by historians of our day? May I next note the ways in which it can be approached by these methods and indicate possible conclusions from these tests? The subject is rendered pertinent partly by reason of the claims which continue to be made for the Christian understanding of history, partly because, through the geographic expansion of Christianity, the Christian view is held by individuals and groups in more and more peoples and is, indeed, more widely spread than any other, in part from the challenges, some old and some new, to which the view is submitted, and because recent experience may shed fresh light on a familiar question.

What is the Christian understanding of history? At first sight there may seem to be no single view held by all Christians and given the Christian name, but rather a number of views, related but reciprocally contradictory and having little in common. Some differences are to be found near the very beginning of Christianity and are embedded in the earliest documents of the faith, those assembled in the New Testament. Most of the others arise from varying interpretations of these documents.

The chief differences are quickly summarized. Jesus had much to say of what he called the Kingdom of Heaven or the Kingdom of God. Presumably he meant by this the doing of God's will, for one of the central petitions of the prayer which all Christians agree to have been taught by him, "Thy Kingdom come, thy will be done on earth as it is in Heaven," in the fashion of Hebrew poetry makes the second part repeat in different words the idea in the first part. But Christians disagree as to how and when that petition is to be answered. Is the Kingdom of God to come by slow stages and by the cooperation of men until God's will is perfectly accomplished—within history? This view was widely cherished in Protestant circles late in the nineteenth century and in some quarters survives today. It is believed to have support in the words of Jesus. This, obviously, is akin to evolution and has been congenial to many who have accepted the evolutionary hypothesis. The opposite view has been held that the world is becoming no better, and, indeed, may even be deteriorating, and that God by His own unaided act will bring history to a sudden dramatic end and will then accomplish His perfect will. Eminent scholars have contended that Jesus himself expected this consummation and very soon. From time to time through the centuries there have been those who have believed the end of history to be imminent. Indeed, we have them with us today. Some Christians identify the Kingdom of God with the Church. Others would not so identify it. Some have held that the human will is so hopelessly corrupted by sin that every effort by man to better his condition is foredoomed and that we must quietly wait for God to accomplish His purposes. Others, with

CHRISTIAN UNDERSTANDING OF HISTORY

more confidence in human ability, make God dependent on man's efforts in bringing in the Kingdom.

Striking and important though these differences are, they occur within a framework to which most informed Christians give general assent. They state their faith in a wide variety of ways, but back of the many formulations lies a large measure of agreement. Christians believe that God is the creator of the universe and rules throughout all its vast reaches, whether, to man, the unimaginable distances and uncounted suns or the inconceivably minute world of the atom, whether in what men call matter or in what they call spirit. This means that man lives and history takes place in a universe, that all of reality is one and under the control of God, and that the human drama is part and parcel of the far larger unity of God's creation. Ultimately and in His own way, so the Christian view maintains, God is sovereign in the affairs of men. Physically frail though he is, man, the Christian declares, was created in the likeness of God and with the possibility of fellowship with God. For this reason, as the Christian sees it, mankind is one; history embraces all mankind and is universal. In creating man in His image, God gave to man a certain measure of His own free will. Man's freedom is limited by various factors, among them heredity and physical and social environment, but his freedom is still real. Human history is in large part tragedy, and the tragedy consists in man's abuse of his freedom. Man is prone to ignore the fact that he is a creature. In one fashion or another he arrogates to himself full autonomy and seeks to do not God's will but his own will. He places other loyalties above his loyalty to God and gives to them the allegiance due to God. Thus one's own fancied security and pleasure, the family, a set of ideas, the state or some other organization, even a church, may be given priority. God, who is always working in the universe and in history, meets this perversion of man's will, so the Christian goes on to say, in two ways, by judgment and by mercy. Through what are sometimes described as His inexorable laws written into the structure of the universe and so in man's own constitution and environment, God judges man and whatever man sets up in place of God. Hence comes most of man's misery and frustration. But God wishes man to repent, and as often as men truly repent, whether individually or in groups, He forgives them and gives them fresh opportunity to grow toward the purpose which He has for them. Ultimately God will triumph. History moves toward a culmination. Whether within or beyond time God's will is to be accomplished and His full sovereignty will be seen to have prevailed.

Thus far the Christian understanding of the universe and of history resembles several non-Christian views. What is here outlined is largely true of Judaism, to a certain extent of Islam, and has partial parallels in theistic or near theistic systems in China, ancient Persia, and elsewhere.

The distinctively Christian understanding of history centers upon historical occurrences. It has at its heart not a set of ideas but a person. By a widespread convention historians reckon history as B.C. and A.D. They are aware of many other methods of recording dates and know that this particular chronology has acquired extensive currency because of the growing dominance during the past few centuries of a civilization in which Christian influences have been potent. To the Christian, however, this reckoning of time is much more than a convention. It is inherent in history. In Jesus of Nazareth, so the Christian holds, God once for all disclosed Himself and acted decisively. The vast majority of Christians believe that Jesus was God incarnate. Historians are well aware of the long debates and the ecclesiastical struggles, some of them in stark contradiction to the love which is the supreme Christian virtue, over the relation of the divine and human in Jesus. That so many of the debates should have been an occasion for this temper is part of a larger problem to which we must later recur and which had its most dramatic and, so Christians believe, its decisive expression in the crucifixion of Jesus. In spite of and, perhaps, in part because of their acrimony, the controversies over the relation of the human and divine in Jesus are evidence of the struggle of the human mind and spirit to comprehend what Christians hold to have been a quite unique event. The large majority of Christians agree with the conviction expressed in one of the early Christian documents, that in Jesus the eternal Word which was and is God became flesh. In Jesus, so Christians maintain, God's Kingdom began in a fresh way. This was partly because Jesus, being both God and man, disclosed by

CHRISTIAN UNDERSTANDING OF HISTORY

his life and his teachings what God intended man to be and what man might become. It was also because in and through Jesus God revealed His inmost nature and accomplished a work of central and supreme importance.

God, so the Christians declare, is love. The English word "love" is clumsy and ambiguous. It is used to cover a wide range of meanings. The Greek which the early Christians employed was more discriminating. But even that was inadequate. In "love," as that term is applied to God, the Christian discerns a self-giving which can never be perfectly described in words but which was disclosed in Jesus. This love was especially seen in the death of Jesus. Here, as one of the earliest Christians declared, although it appeared to be weakness and folly, were displayed both the power of God and the wisdom of God.[1] The crucifixion was followed by the resurrection. Through the resurrection, so Christians believe, God demonstrated that physical death not only does not end all but that it may be a stage in an endless life beyond history which is not merely continued existence—this might be and presumably will for some men be extraordinarily unhappy—but which is one of growing fellowship with God, God who is love. In the earliest documents the name for what God did in Jesus is not Christianity: it is Gospel, "Good News." The Gospel judges man by making clear as in no other way man's perversity and sin. It also releases life to overcome that perversity and sin. The purpose of God in history is that men shall be "conformed to the image of His son."[2]

The Christian understanding of history goes on to say that following the crucifixion and the resurrection God continued to operate through what Christians call the Holy Spirit. Through the Holy Spirit men can be remade and can enter upon the radiant, eternal life which from the beginning was God's plan for men. Those who have that life are characterized by faith, hope, and especially love, the kind of love which is of the very nature of God. They form a fellowship, the Church, which takes on a visible form or forms within history but which is never completely identical with any historic expression and continues beyond his-

---
[1] I Cor. 1:18–25.
[2] Rom. 8:29.

tory. The course of history is God's search for man. God is judge, but He judges man that He may save him and transform him. God's grace, the love which man does not deserve and cannot earn, respects man's free will and endeavors to reach man through the incarnation, the cross, and the Holy Spirit. Here, to the Christian, is the meaning of history and its unifying core.

From the outset, the Christian view of history has embraced all men. From the Christian standpoint man is not necessarily central in the universe. There may be many other beings on other planets or in other stellar systems whom God creates in His likeness, to whom He gives free will, and who abuse that free will. If so, His love also seeks them. If God is love, His love must be at work in all the universe. Yet on this planet God's love certainly includes all men. The early disciples were commanded to be "witnesses" "unto the uttermost parts of the earth," [3] to "make disciples of all nations," baptizing them, and teaching them to observe all that Jesus had commanded his original followers.[4] This, presumably, also becomes the obligation of all subsequent Christians. It implies that the Christian goal can be nothing short of the full obedience of all men to God as He disclosed Himself in Jesus. This would entail the complete transformation of human society to bring society into entire conformity with God's will for man. Yet it seems clear that neither Jesus nor the early Christians expected within history the full conformation of mankind to the "measure of the stature of the fullness of Christ." [5] Both the wheat and the tares, the good and the evil, were expected to "grow" until the consummation of history.[6] Beyond history, presumably outside of time, God is "to gather together all things in one in Christ, which are in heaven and which are on earth." [7] God has always been sovereign, and in the cross and the resurrection He signally triumphed,[8] but beyond history His sovereignty is to be seen as complete.

The Christian understanding of history differs radically from

[3] Acts 1:8.
[4] Matt. 28:19, 20.
[5] Eph. 4:13.
[6] Matt. 13:24–30.
[7] Eph. 1:10.
[8] Col. 2:15.

CHRISTIAN UNDERSTANDING OF HISTORY

other views. It is in contrast with the ancient Persian dualism, for the latter implies separate origins of good and evil. This dualism means that the good God is not sovereign in history, because He has not created the universe as a whole, whereas Christianity regards God as creator and lord of all. Only a sovereign God can forgive sins as the Christian believes Him to do. Nor is Christianity pantheistic, as is so much of Indian philosophy, for it does not make God the author of what men call evil. Man's misery, so Christianity declares, arises from the abuse of the free will which God has given him. The Christian understanding of history is not exclusively cyclical. It recognizes eras and ages, but it holds that novelty enters, that new things happen. The great event, as the Christian sees it, was Jesus and Jesus was without precedent. So, too, the consummation will be new. Some interpretations of history seem to expect perfection within history, the coming of the ideal human society. This is the communist message. It appears to have been true of Comte and of Hegel. The Christian understanding of history does not necessarily deny progress. Obviously, the criteria for measuring advance must be established before we can say whether progress has occurred, and the Christian criteria are peculiarly Christian—growth in the likeness of God as God reveals Himself in Jesus. Christians are not agreed as to whether progress occurs in history. Some affirm it and others deny it. Yet few if any Christians have maintained that man will attain his full destiny within history.

All this is, or should be, a commonplace to historians. It is simply an attempt at a restatement of what the majority of Christians have always believed. Many Christians would add to this or would amplify it. Many would regard it as inadequate and incomplete. Yet the overwhelming proportion would say that so far as it goes it is a summary of what Christians have held and hold today to be the Christian view of history. I would apologize for repeating it were it not necessary for any assessment of the Christian understanding of history.

Several features of the Christian outlook must be especially noted if the historian would seek an appraisal by the standards which the members of his craft are currently inclined to apply.

First of all, he must be clear that here are frankly a perspective and a set of values which are the complete reverse of those which mankind generally esteems. We are told that unless a man is born again not only can he not enter, but he cannot even see (or presumably recognize) the Kingdom of God.[9] On one memorable occasion the "prince of the apostles" was rebuked by Jesus for thinking like man and not like God.[10] This was because he was shocked by the prospect of the crucifixion and sought to dissuade his master from it. Centuries before Jesus a famous story of the one of the prophets who was counted as among his greatest predecessors declared that God was not in the thunder nor in a mighty wind, where He was expected, but in a still small voice.[11] Another of the prophets in whose succession Jesus stood was emphatic that God's thoughts are not man's thoughts nor man's ways God's ways.[12] Of the crucifixion Paul declared that the "wise man" and the "scribe," namely the scholar, completely miss its significance and that God makes foolish the wisdom of this world.[13] In other words, if he is to understand history as God sees it, the historian must focus his attention upon events which he would normally ignore. From the Christian standpoint, the usual historian has an entirely distorted view of history and misses the most important features. This, may we add parenthetically, may be true of those who deal with ecclesiastical as well as with political, economic, or intellectual history.

Even when the historian gives attention to the events which the Christian understanding deems most significant he may miss their real import. There is deep meaning in the plea, "Father forgive them for they know not what they do." [14] Had those who crucified Jesus dreamed that they were executing the Son of God they would, presumably, have drawn back in terror or in horror.

In the second place, the historian must recognize that from the viewpoint of Jesus the individual is of outstanding importance. In this he declared that he was expressing the mind of God. The Christian faith exalts the individual. Each human being, as we have said before, is regarded as intended for fellowship with the

---

[9] John 3:3, 5.
[10] Matt. 16:23.
[11] I Kings 19:11–13.
[12] Isaiah 55:8.
[13] I Cor. 1:20.
[14] Luke 23:34.

eternal God Who is love. It was to individuals that Jesus gave his attention. He healed men one by one. Some of his best remembered sayings and parables were to single persons. He spoke again and again of the value which God places on individuals. The concern of God for the erring, so he said, is like that of the shepherd who leaves the ninety and nine who are safe in the fold and seeks for the one sheep who is lost until he finds it,[15] or like the father who longs for the return of a wayward son and rejoices when he appears, repentant.[16]

Jesus was deeply concerned for the fate of his people. In his day Palestine was seething with unrest which a few years later broke out in open revolt and was followed by the destruction of Jerusalem. He clearly foresaw what was coming, as must any intelligent, well-poised observer who took account of the mounting nationalistic and religious fanaticism and who knew the power of Rome. He believed that the destruction had not been unavoidable, that had its inhabitants been willing to heed him Jerusalem might have escaped, but that they were so blind that the doom of the city was sealed. So deeply pained was he by the prospect that he wept.[17]

Yet so far as we know Jesus never engaged in politics. Indeed, at the outset of his public career he had put aside as a palpable temptation the suggestion that he enter the political arena.[18] To be sure, he was accused of treasonable aspirations and was crucified derisively as "the King of the Jews," [19] but it is quite clear that he believed his kingdom to be "not of this world" [20] and that as applied to what he had in mind and what he believed to be God's purpose, the term had for him far other significance than that given it by men. From the standpoint of political wisdom and when viewed prudently the program which Jesus followed seemed the sheerest madness. On the visit to Jerusalem which issued in his death he pursued a course which could not but bring down on his head the wrath of the established authorities of reli-

---

[15] Luke 15:3–6.
[16] Luke 15:11–24.
[17] Luke 19:41–44.
[18] Luke 4:5–8.
[19] Mark 15:18, 26; Luke 23:1, 2.
[20] John 18:36.

gion and the state and yet he declined either to flee or to permit his followers to organize or to use armed force to defend him and his cause.

However, in the third place, Jesus did not ignore the social structures of mankind. He said much of the relation of individuals to other individuals and declared that the corollary of love for God is love for one's neighbor.[21] The Kingdom of God, of which he so often spoke, is a society. Men are to meet that Kingdom one by one. When they enter it, as they can here and now, they are to act as its members and as though the Kingdom were already here. The standards of that Kingdom are so far above the actual attainments of any other society that Christians as members of the Kingdom are always a revolutionary force. It is not the purpose of the Gospel to save any culture. The rise and fall of cultures and empires are important in so far as they affect individuals, but the rise and fall may harm the individual no more than do the cultures and empires themselves. There is that in the Gospel, so Christians maintain, which enables individuals to pass through such experiences triumphantly, centers of healing and strength. Indeed, the collapse of an empire or a culture may make it possible to build what, from the Christian standpoint, is better. Christians must always challenge any civilization in which they are set. Yet they are not to be primarily destructive but constructive. They are to be "the salt of the earth" and "the light of the world." [22]

Here at last appears to be something tangible on which the historian would like to believe that he can lay his hand and begin to measure. Surely he can determine where Christians, because of their faith, have been a molding force in history. Yet he is warned that, since the Christian set of values is different from that of the rank and file of men, the record of the accomplishments of Christians may not be preserved in the documents on which he rules. "The last shall be first and the first last." [23] The Kingdom of God, he is told, comes not by observation. Neither can men say about it "lo here and lo there." [24]

[21] Matt. 22:34–40.
[22] Matt. 5:13, 14.
[23] Matt. 19:30.
[24] Luke 17:20, 21.

CHRISTIAN UNDERSTANDING OF HISTORY

In the fourth place, the Christian understanding of history regards history and time as surrounded by eternity. Christianity centers upon historical events and views God as acting in history. Yet it holds that the human drama is not completed in time, and that one must go beyond the events with which the historian deals and even beyond what is still to occur in time in order completely to see God's dealings with man. Of necessity and by its very nature history deals with time. Christianity centers upon events in time and also transcends them.

When he is confronted with the Christian understanding of history the historian may well feel baffled and even impatient. He may say with a wry smile that the Christian is like the Taoist who declared that those who know do not speak and that those who speak do not know.[25] Some of the key Christian convictions about history are not and cannot be subject to the tests which the historian is able to apply. For instance, the historian can neither absolutely prove nor disprove that God created man in His own image. Obviously he cannot reach beyond time and verify the Christian conviction concerning the goal of history. God cannot be fully known within history. If He could, He would be limited and would cease to be what the Christian faith believes Him to be.

The difficulty is inherent in the methods to which the historian is confined. He must deal with records. Through whatever channels are open to him he must attempt to determine what actually happened. The records which are accessible to the historian are usually very faulty. In appraising them and in arranging and interpreting events the historian relies on his reason. He knows that in most of the records and in his arrangement and interpretation of them there is subjectivity, a subjectivity from which he can never be entirely emancipated. He seeks through reason to reduce the subjective elements to a minimum, but if he is honest and well equipped he knows something of the limitations of reason and also suspects that the subjective element can never be completely eliminated. The historian is himself part of history. He is caught in it and cannot fully stand apart from it or view it with undiluted objectivity.

[25] *Tao Tê Ching*, 56.

These limitations on his work handicap the historian in all his endeavors, including his attempt to appraise any interpretation of history. It is not merely when he applies his tools to the Christian understanding of history that he is hampered. The historian is dealing with visible events, but there are also invisible forces which he cannot measure. If he is not to do violence to history the historian can never abstract fact from value. Yet his training at least as usually given in our day, does not equip him to deal with the latter. Unless he is a thoroughgoing skeptic, the historian tries to discover a standard of values. Christianity professes to provide him with an absolute criterion. Yet by the processes which he normally employs the historian is clumsy and baffled when he comes to appraise the Christian or any other set of values.

However, limited though they are, the historian must employ such tools as he possesses. When he does so, much comes to light which tends to support the Christian understanding of history. The historian as historian can neither refute nor demonstrate the Christian thesis, but he can detect evidence which suggests a strong probability for the truth of the Christian understanding.

Increasingly it is apparent that history must be seen in its entire setting and that that setting is the universe. This is what the Christian has all along contended. More and more man by the scientific method is recognizing that the universe is orderly. This supports theism. An orderly universe which can be explored by human reason implies a reason and a will controlling that universe to which the human mind is akin.

In the development of life on the earth there seems to be purpose. Man appears to be the culmination, at least at this stage, of the life process on the planet. So far as we know, man is the only creature who is interested in his own past and in seeking to understand the universe. It is quite unlikely that this is the outcome of blind chance. Moreover, in support of the Christian conviction, as life reaches what we believe to be higher stages, the biological process appears to be increasingly interested in the individual rather than the mass. Certainly individuals are more and more differentiated from one another.

The Christian belief about what happens beyond history gives relevance to the development of life on the earth. As we have said, it appears to be true that this development issues in ever higher forms of life of which man is, at least in the present stage, the highest. But man is obviously incomplete within history. He has longings which cannot be satisfied in the brief span of the existence of individuals in this flesh. The Christian view of history regards what occurs beyond physical death as essential to the realization of man's capacities and holds out confident hope of that fulfillment. This is what is embraced in what the theologian terms apocalypticism and eschatology.

The Christian conception of man provides an intelligible and reasonable explanation of the tragic dilemma in which man increasingly finds himself. On the one hand man aspires to understand the universe and adds more and more to his fund of knowledge. This is what we would expect of man, as the Christian faith declares, as created in the image of God. Man is thinking God's thoughts after Him. It is clear, too, that were man to follow the law of love which the Christian declares is written by God in man's nature, he would be freed from the ills which he now brings on himself. He would be in reverence and love of God and of his neighbor. War would be banished. Men would cooperate the globe over in utilizing the resources of their environment for the physical and spiritual well-being of all. Just as clearly through his departure from this law man brings on himself misery. The more his knowledge and mastery of his physical environment increase, the more man employs them on the one hand for his benefit and on the other for his woe. Indeed, through his misuse of that knowledge he threatens the existence of the civilization which he has created and even the race itself. In this the Christian sees the judgment by which God seeks to constrain man to do His will.

But what of the redeeming love which the Christian believes God to have displayed in Jesus? What evidence, if any, is there that this is present and is proving effective? It is, of course, clear that Jesus lived, that he taught and was crucified, that his disciples were profoundly convinced that he was raised from the dead and in the strength of that conviction set out to win the world to allegiance to him. As the centuries pass the evidence is accumulating that, measured by his effect on history, Jesus' is the most influential life ever lived on this planet. That influence appears to be mounting. It does not increase evenly but by pulsations of advance, retreat, and advance. It has had an unprecedented growth in the past four and a half centuries and especially in the last century and a half. Christianity is now more widely spread geographically than it or any other religion has ever been. Only a very few peoples and tribes exist where it is not represented by organized groups.

This advance has been associated with the expansion of the Occident. As we all know, that expansion is a recent historical phenomenon. As we also know, Western Europe, from which that expansion stemmed, appears to be waning and at times it seems that in Western Europe itself Christianity is declining. Yet nations, notably the United States, which trace their source to Western Europe, are still continuing the expansion of the Occident, and the culture which had its origin in the West spreads ever more widely and rapidly. It has become global. That Occidental civilization is in part the product of Christianity is obvious. In art, literature, thought, education (for universities and many other new types of schools have owed to it an incalculable debt), in morals, and in social, economic, and political institutions Christianity has been a major factor. Democracy as the West understands that term is largely its child. A case can be made for the claim that science sprang from Christianity. Precisely to what degree Jesus is responsible for Western culture is by no means clear. On that question large volumes could be written and the answers would not be definitive. Now the expansion of the Occident and its culture has by no means been an unmixed blessing to mankind. If Jesus has had a major share in the development of that culture and in its dynamic spread, we may well ask whether the redemption which the Christian declares that God wrought through him has been sufficiently potent to offset the ills that have accompanied the growth of what is often described as Christendom.

As the influence of Jesus has spread geographically, various results have followed which are evidence that the transforming power which Christians claim for it is at work. Because of it more languages have been reduced to writing than through all other agencies in the history of mankind. Literacy is not an unmixed blessing, but it can be and has been used to further the enrichment of man's life. Through the expansion of Western Peoples and their culture, mankind has for the first time been brought together. To the degree that this is the result of the influence of Jesus it is a partial implementation of the dream of the unity of mankind which is a feature of the Christian understanding of history. The struggle to regulate and eventually to eliminate the wars which make our shrinking globe so perilous a neighborhood owes much to Jesus. That he was potent in such pioneers of international law as Francisco de Vitoria and Hugo Grotius is well attested. He can also be shown to have had a part in the initiation of the Hague conferences of the last generation. Such attempts at world-wide cooperation as the League of Nations and the United Nations are demonstrably to some extent from him. However, just how large his share has been in these achievements cannot be accurately measured.

Much clearer is the decisive part which Jesus has had in the efforts to combat slavery and other forms of the exploitation of men by their fellows. It is significant that the first Christian priest ordained in the New World, Bartolomé de Las Casas, was the chief pioneer in the struggle to protect the Indians against the cruelties of the Spaniards, to write humane statutes in the Laws of the Indies, and to seek their enforcement. The list is long of the Spanish and Portuguese laymen and clergy who, inspired and sustained by their Christian faith, labored to guard the non-Europeans in the colonies in both hemispheres from the callous selfishness of their fellow countrymen. The place of his Christian faith in impelling Wilberforce in his campaign against the Negro slave trade is well known. So, too, is the role of the Quakers, Samuel Hopkins, and those touched by the Finney revival, consciences made sensitive by commitment to the Christian faith, in the movement for the emancipation of Negro slaves in the United States. We are all aware of the efforts of the Christian missionary, David Livingstone, to curb the slave trade in Africa itself. Less familiar is the share of such Christian missionary leaders as John Philip and Cardinal Lavigerie in the campaign against African slavery. Christianity has been one of the most potent forces making for the liberation and advance of the depressed classes of India. Jesus was a major inspiration of Gandhi. In land after land he has contributed to the emancipation of women. In the impact of Occidental upon non-Occidental peoples Christian missions and other agencies inspired by him have made for improved medical care, for public health, for better methods of agriculture, and for schools and universities better adapted to the new day than were their predecessors. Increasingly these features of the influence of Jesus have been spreading and now in varying measure embrace mankind.

More and more the ecclesiastical organizations which we call churches are becoming worldwide. They seek, not unsuccessfully, to perpetuate the influence of Jesus and to incarnate the self-giving and the fellowship which are of the essence of the Christian Gospel. Their divisions and quarrels are familiar to the historian, but in spite of them the churches have become global. The largest, the Roman Catholic Church, is to be found in almost every land and people. The non-Roman Catholic churches are fully as widely distributed and have been drawing together through new types of organizations, several of which include some Roman Catholics.

The transforming love of God through Jesus is seen, so the Christian believes, not only in collective movements but also and primarily in individuals. Some of these individuals loom large in the records which are at hand for the historian. Among these are Paul of Tarsus, Augustine of Hippo, Francis of Assisi, Martin Luther, Ignatius Loyola, George Fox, and John Wesley. Indeed, the list could be extended to many pages. What from the Christian standpoint would be a full and therefore an accurate list can never be compiled, for it would need to include untold millions for whom no record survives. Moreover, for those whose records we have, we cannot determine with complete accuracy just which qualities and changes of character are due to the Christian faith and which to other factors. For the qualities of character, too, which the Christian view prizes no accurate measurements are possible. They are real, but are not capable of being plumbed by the methods which are at the historian's disposal. Nor can we judge their full effects on other lives and upon human society as a whole. Yet we have enough information to permit some generalizations which possess rough accuracy. We know that under Christian influence changes in character take place. Sometimes these appear to be sudden. More often they come by gradual, almost imperceptible stages. In some lives they are outstanding. In many they are slight. Yet when we see them we recognize them. They are the qualities commended in the Sermon on the Mount and in other parts of the Gospels and in the Epistles of the New Testament. Often we find them nourished in small groups of those who have sought to commit themselves fully as Christians. Indeed, those in whom the Christian faith predominates as a transforming force have always been small minorities. Yet often they have had effects which far outstrip their own borders.

These many results of Christianity, in society at large, in individuals, and in groups, are what we would expect from what the Christian calls the Holy Spirit. They are, so the Christian maintains, in consequence of stimuli issuing from the divine initiative, stimuli marked by the characteristics displayed in Jesus and tied up historically with him. Yet they are more than the lengthened influence of a great life. The Christian understanding of history is that it is through the Holy Spirit which is God himself that God continues to work in history. Thus God respects man's will but continuously brings His love to bear on man. It is through the Holy Spirit, the Christian believes, that as the centuries pass the influence of Jesus grows rather than wanes.

Somewhere in this region lies a possible explanation of one of the most perplexing questions provoked by the Christian understanding of history. Why is it that what the Christian deems evil and good continue side by side in individuals and in groups? Why do even ecclesiastical bodies display both, bodies presumably the result of God's love, the embodiment of the Christian community of love? Why do some of the chronic ills of mankind, notably war, attain their most colossal dimensions in lands and through peoples that have long been under Christian influence? Why are some of what seem to be the gifts of God and the effects of Christianity twisted to man's hurt. Here we recall the fashion in which science and its fruits are so often turned to man's destruction. Has God failed? Is His sovereignty compromised? Is His salvation through Jesus frustrated? Is the influence of Jesus, though growing, always to be a minority force, outstripped by the forces opposed to it and perhaps even provoking them to greater activity? Is, therefore, the Christian view of history an illusion?

As we meditate on these persistent questions we need to remind ourselves again that the Christian understanding of history presupposes a degree of freedom of man's will, sufficient for man to accept or reject God's love. We must also recall that the issues are not new. They are posed in their most vivid form in the crucifixion of Jesus. Here, as the Christian sees it, man's blindness to God's purpose and man's self-assertiveness were at stark contrast with the seeming weakness and futility of God's chosen way of showing His love. Indeed, this is what we should expect if the Christian teaching of man and God is in accord with the facts. Man's rebellion becomes most marked when God's love is most clearly displayed. In the cross and the other perversions of God's gifts is seen the judgment as well as the love of God.

Yet, if God is love and is sovereign, His judgments must be a way to the triumph of His love. It is, therefore, not surprising that following the crucifixion there came a fresh release of power in the lives of those who began to see something of the significance of the death of Jesus and freely accepted the forgiveness and love of God. It is understandable that the cross became the symbol of the Christian faith and has been the confidence and inspiration of millions to face triumphantly the evil in them and about them. Similarly the abuses of God's love which have followed the crucifixion and have been painfully apparent in those cultures where the influence of Jesus has been most marked have been the occasion for millions to seek to eliminate the evils of which they are the symptoms and thus have given rise to something better than had been there before, both in individual lives and in the collective life of mankind.

The struggle continues. Civilization becomes more complex. All mankind is bound together ever more closely in the bundle of life and the disorders of one segment affect the whole. Yet the efforts to combat these disorders mount and more and more make themselves felt throughout the earth. Increasingly they have a major source in Jesus, and what Christians have believed about his birth, his life, his death, and his resurrection. Here is one of the strongest reasons for confidence in the accuracy of the Christian view of history. The historian, be he Christian or non-Christian, may not know whether God will fully triumph within history. He cannot conclusively demonstrate the validity of the

Christian understanding of history. Yet he can establish a strong probability for the dependability of its insights. That is the most which can be expected of human reason in any of the realms of knowledge.

REINHOLD NIEBUHR
FAITH AND HISTORY [*]

Christianity embodies the whole of history in its universe of meaning because it is a religion of revelation which knows by faith of some events in history, in which the transcendent source and end of the whole panorama of history is disclosed. Christian faith fully appreciates the threat of meaninglessness which comes into history by the corruption of human freedom. But it does not succumb to the despairing conclusion that history is merely a chaos of competing forces. It has discerned that the divine power which is sovereign over history also has a resource of mercy and love which overcomes the rebellion of human sin, without negating the distinctions between good and evil, which are the moral content of history. The revelations of God in history, are, in fact, according to the Biblical faith, evidences of a divine grace which both searches out the evil character of human sin and overcomes it. . . .

The universality of this corruption of evil raises the question whether history has any moral meaning. Do not the strong men and nations regard their own will as the source of law and their own interests as the criterion of right? Is there any sovereignty over history strong enough to overcome this rebellion against the moral content of life? And is there any love great enough to give meaning to the life of the innocent victims of the cruelties and the contumelies of proud men and nations? These questions were asked more and more searchingly by the Old Testament prophets; and they looked for an answer to the questions in a future messianic reign.

The Christian faith begins with, and is founded upon, the

[*] Reprinted with the permission of Charles Scribner's Sons from pages 22, 26–29, 113–19, 120–21, 136–38, 139, 214–15, and 231–34 of *Faith and History* by Reinhold Niebuhr. Copyright 1949 Charles Scribner's Sons.

affirmation that the life, death, and resurrection of Christ represent an event in history, in and through which a disclosure of the whole meaning of history occurs, and all of these questions are answered. The interpretation of history in the light of this event creates a structure of meaning in which the history of a particular nation, as the center of the whole of history is unequivocally transcended. This "second covenant" between God and His people is not between God and any particular people but with all of those of any nation who are "called," that is, who are able to apprehend by faith that this person, drama, and event of history discloses the power and the love which is the source and the end of the whole historical drama. Insofar as this is an event, the revelatory depth and height of which must be apprehended by faith, it is not the basis of a "philosophy of history" at which one might arrive by analyzing the sequences and recurrences, the structures and patterns of history. But insofar as history becomes meaningful by being oriented toward the revelation of this event, the event is the source of "wisdom" and of "truth."

The conception of a divine sovereignty over history which is not immediately apparent in the structures and recurrences of history establishes a dimension in which there can be meaning, though the facts of history are not related to each other in terms of natural or logical necessity. The freedom of God over and beyond the structures of life makes room for the freedom of man. All forms of naturalistic or spiritualistic determinism are broken. History is conceived meaningfully as a drama and not as a pattern of necessary relationships which could be charted scientifically. The clue to the meaning of the drama is in the whole series of revelatory events, "God's mighty acts," culminating in the climax of revelation in the life, death, and resurrection of Christ. In these mighty acts the mysterious design of the sovereignty which controls historical destiny is clarified.

The interpretation of history from the standpoint of this revelation leads to a full understanding of the reality of evil. Evil is a force within history itself and not the intrusion of the necessities of nature into the historical. The drama of history contains a subordinate conflict between good and evil forces in history. Ultimately the drama consists of God's contest with all men, who are all inclined to defy God because they all tend to make their own

FAITH AND HISTORY

life into the center of history's meaning. An outer limit is set for this human defiance of the divine will by the fact that God's power, revealed in the structures of existence, leads to the ultimate self-destruction of forms of life which make themselves into their own end by either isolation or dominion. But it is not denied that any particular period of history is morally obscure because of the seeming impunity of the proud and the powerful who exploit the weak, and the general self-seeking of all men who defy the sovereignty of God. Ultimately this rebellion of man against God is overcome by divine power, which includes the power of the divine love. The "foolishness of the Cross" as the ultimate source of wisdom about life consists precisely in the revelation of a depth of divine mercy within and above the "wrath" of God. By this love God takes the evils and sins of man into and upon Himself. Whenever men penetrate through the illusions and self-deceptions of life to confront this God, as revealed in Christ, finding His judgment upon their sin not less but more severe, because of the disclosure of the love which prompts it, they may be converted and renewed. History is thus a realm of endless possibilities of renewal and rebirth. The chain of evil is not an absolute historical fate.

Yet even men and nations, thus redeemed, are never free of the taint of rebellion against God. Ultimately, therefore, only the divine forgiveness toward all men can overcome the confusion of human history and make this whole drama meaningful. According to the New Testament, men who are armed with this clue to the meaning of the whole of life and history will face all the future possibilities and perils of history without fear. They will not be surprised or dismayed by anything, knowing "that neither life nor death . . . will separate them from the love of God which is in Christ Jesus our Lord." The New Testament faith anticipates that man's defiance of God will reach the highest proportions at the end of history. Precisely in "the last days perilous times will come" when men shall be "lovers of their own selves, covetous, boasters, proud, blasphemers, disobedient to parents, unthankful, unholy . . . traitors, heady, highminded, lovers of pleasure rather than lovers of God" (II Timothy 3:2, 4). This expectation of heightening forms of human defiance of God in history, which is also clearly expressed by Jesus himself in his warning of false

Christs and false prophets (Matthew 24) is a symbol of the tremendously wide frame of meaning which the Christian faith has for the stuff of history. It envisages antinomies, contradictions, and tragic realities within the framework without succumbing to despair. . . .

The second contribution of the Biblical idea of divine transcendence to the concept of universal history is contained in the rigor with which the inclination of every human collective, whether tribe, nation, or empire, to make itself the center of universal history is overcome in principle. The God who has chosen Israel promises peril, rather than security, as the concomitant of this eminence. The God who is revealed is Christ brings all nations under His judgment. The majesty of a suffering servant and crucified Savior will cast down "every high thing that exalteth itself against the knowledge of God" (2 Corinthians 10:5).

It is through the judgment of God, who stands against all human pride and pretension, that the inclination of men and nations to make themselves the false center of universal history is broken in principle. The scandal that the idea of universal history should be the fruit of a particular revelation of the divine, to a particular people, and finally in a particular drama and person, ceases to be scandalous when it is recognized that the divine Majesty, apprehended in these particular revelations, is less bound to the pride of civilizations and the hopes and ambitions of nations, than the supposedly more universal concepts of life and history by which cultures seek to extricate themselves from the historical contingencies and to establish universally valid "values."

Biblical faith must be distinguished on the one hand from the cultures which negate the meaning of history in the rigor of their effort to find a transcendent ground of truth; and on the other hand from both ancient and modern affirmations of the meaning of life and history, which end by giving history an idolatrous center of meaning. In the first category we must place not merely the classical culture of the western world, whose ahistorical character we have previously analyzed; but also the high religions of the Orient. In the second category belong not merely the imperial religions of the ancient civilizations of Egypt, Babylon, Persia, etc.; but also modern secularized idolatries, in which some powerful nation, whether Germany, Russia, America, Britain, or any other nation, conceives itself as the center of historical meaning; or in which a culture, such as the bourgeois culture of the nineteenth century, imagines itself the culmination of historical progress.

In contrast to ahistorical cultures, Biblical faith affirms the potential meaning of life in history. It is in history, and not in a flight from history, that the divine power which bears and completes history is revealed. In contrast to idolatrous historical cultures the relation of the divine, which manifests itself in history, casts down everything which exalteth itself against the knowledge of God.

According to Biblical faith, the tendency toward idolatry in the interpretation of history is a part of the phenomenon of original sin; that is, of the inclination of the human heart to solve the problem of the ambiguity of human existence by denying man's finiteness. The sin is particularly evident in the collective life of mankind because nations, empires, and cultures achieve a seeming immortality, a power and a majesty which tempts them to forget that they belong to the flux of mortality.[1] This inclination could be interpreted provisionally as the fruit of human ignorance. It would seem that the individual man is fooled by the greater majesty and the seeming immortality of collective man's achievements. Therefore he worships his nation as god. But there is always an element of perversity as well as of ignorance in this worship. For other nations and cultures are perversely debased and become merely the instruments or tools, the victims or allies of the nation of one's worship. There are no strictly pluralistic conceptions of history after the primitive period of culture, when every tribe remembers its own story without reference to any other story or tribal destiny. Since the beginning of ancient civilizations history is interpreted, not pluralistically, but in terms of false conceptions of universal history. The culture which elaborates the scheme of meaning makes its own destiny into the false center of the total human destiny.

Neither secular nor Christian nations are immune from the temptation to such idolatry. The history of Christian nations

[1] Cf. Ezekiel 28–32.

abounds in ridiculous conceptions of nationalistic messianisms, in which a particular nation is regarded as the instrument or agent of the culmination of history.[2] In Nicolai Berdyaev's *The Russian Idea* this Christian theologian examines the various Messianic ideas in the history of Russian culture. Instead of dismissing the very concept of nationalistic messianism as heretical from the Christian standpoint, he labors diligently to find the most adequate expression of it and comes to the conclusion that the modern secularized version of messianism, as expressed in Russian Communism, though not completely adequate, comes closer to the truth than previous messianic ideas. It evidently has not occurred to Berdyaev that one of the most tragic aspects of human history is that a "final" form of evil should periodically come into history by the pretension of a nation, culture, or class that it is the agent of a final form of redemption.

The virulence and truculence which flows from the Russian illusions are important reminders of the fact that secular civilizations do not escape religious idolatries by a formal disavowal of religion. A secular age spawns these idolatries more readily, in fact, because it has lost every sense of a divine majesty "that bringeth the princes to nothing" and "maketh the judges of the earth as vanity" (Isaiah 40:23). The concept of the "American dream" according to which America is a kind of second chosen nation, ordained to save democracy after the effete nations of Europe proved themselves incapable of the task, is a milder form of such nationalistic messianism.

While these nationalistic and imperial corruptions of the idea of universal history are the most vivid examples of the inclination of men and nations to make themselves into the false center of the vast panorama of history, they are nevertheless merely one aspect of the whole problem of historical relativism, which remains one of the unsolved problems of modern culture. The problem forces modern man, who claims to be increasingly the master of historical destiny, into periodic moods of scepticism as he analyzes his dubious position as observer of history. The problem is, how a man, nation, or culture involved in the muta-

[2] For examples of such nationalistic messianism in the history of Christian nations see Salo Baron, *Modern Nationalism and Religion* (New York: Harper Torchbooks, 1960).

bilities of history can achieve a sufficiently high vantage point of wisdom and disinterestedness to chart the events of history, without using a framework of meaning which is conditioned by contingent circumstances of the class, nation, or period of the observer.

In Dilthey's profound study of historical relativism he finds escape from scepticism by the assumption that a common participation in "objective spirit" allows the observer of historical phenomena an affinity with the observed phenomena, transcending the different contingencies in which the observers and the observed are involved.[3] Kant has no difficulty with the problem because for him, history as observed belongs to the realm of nature, while the observer of history, insofar as he is rational, transcends the world of nature.

Karl Mannheim's solution of the problem of historical relativism is influenced by the modern confidence in science. He believes that it is possible to develop a "sociology of knowledge" which will, in infinite regression, refine historical knowledge by isolating and excluding the conditioned perspectives of persons, classes, interests, and periods until the real truth is reached.[4] An American philosopher, Maurice Mandelbaum, seeks to escape historical relativism by exalting "facts" and minimizing their valuation, through which the historian betrays his own relative viewpoint. "Every historical fact," he declares, "is given in some specific context in which it leads to some other fact. . . . Thus when a historian makes a statement of fact it is not with an isolated fact but with a fact in a given context that he is concerned. And in that context the fact leads on to further facts without any intermediation or selection, based on the historian's valuational attitudes, class, interests, or the like." [5]

The difficulty with this solution is that every fact is both the fruit of a dozen or a hundred different historical pressures, forces, and tendencies and the root of a dozen or a hundred historical consequences. The "bare" fact is little more than a date in history. A victory or defeat in battle may be an explicit event, subject to an unambiguous description; but usually even military

---

[3] Wilhelm Dilthey, *Gesammelte Werke*, VII.
[4] Karl Mannheim, *Ideology and Utopia*.
[5] *The Problem of Historical Knowledge*, pp. 200–201.

victories and defeats are not so explicit as to obviate conflicting interpretation. In the vast complexities of political defeats and victories, interpretations of the events depend even more obviously upon the framework of meaning from which they are observed. The larger the area of historical events which is surveyed, the more obvious is it that events in it can be correlated only within a framework of meaning, to which the viewpoint of an age, a class or a nation contributes as much as the facts themselves. There is, of course, a difference between an honest historian who changes his frame of meaning if he finds that he cannot correlate the facts within it and a dishonest historian who suppresses the facts in order to preserve his frame of meaning. But when the area of inquiry is sufficiently wide and complex, even the most scrupulous honesty on the part of the historian cannot prevent his viewpoint from coloring the historical picture. Historical relativism is overcome too easily if, as in the thought of Dilthey, or Kant, the involvement of the observer of history in historical mutability is denied; or if, as in the thought of Mannheim, a final scientific triumph over historical "ideologies" is presumed to be possible; or if, as in the thought of Mandelbaum, historical events are reduced to "facts" which are immune to evaluational distortion.

There is, in short, no complete rational solution for the problem of historical relativism. Insofar as the human mind in both its structure and in its capacities of observation has a vantage point over the flux of historical events, it is possible to achieve valid historical knowledge though this knowledge will never have the exactness of knowledge in the field of natural science. But insofar as men, individually or collectively, are involved in the temporal flux they must view the stream of events from some particular locus. A high degree of imagination, insight, or detachment may heighten or enlarge the locus; but no human power can make it fully adequate. That fact is one of the most vivid examples of the ambiguity of the human situation. The pretension that this is not the case is an aspect of the "original sin" which infects all human culture. Its essence is man's unwillingness to acknowledge his finiteness.

Men must observe and interpret the flow of historical events with as much honesty and wisdom as possible. Historical sciences will continue to be elaborated and scientific schemes invented to reduce conscious and unconscious ideological taints in historical observations. Philosophical disciplines will be judged and scrutinized on the basis of the adequacy of their guard against the temptation of the observer to pretend to more absolute knowledge than a finite creature has the right to claim. All such efforts belong to the legitimate improvement of human culture. But none of them can obviate the necessity of using a scheme of meaning for the correlation of the observed data of history, which is not the consequence but the presupposition of the empirical scrutiny of historical data. The more the whole panorama of history is brought into view, the more obvious it becomes that the meaning which is given to the whole is derived from an act of faith. History may have a minimal unity by reason of the fact that all of its events are grounded in the flow of time in a single world. But this minimal unity gives no key for correlating the wide variety of cultural and political configurations which distinguish history from the flow of natural events. History in its totality and unity is given a meaning by some kind of religious faith in the sense that the concept of meaning is derived from ultimate presuppositions about the character of time and eternity, which are not the fruit of detailed analyses of historical events.

Whether these ultimate presuppositions of meaning constitute an adequate framework for the correlation of all relevant historical facts is a question which can be approached rationally. It is possible, at least, to reject all concepts of the unity of history which make some vitality, event, or value within history itself into a premature and idolatrous center of its meaning. If such idolatries are rejected it will become apparent that the real center of meaning for history must transcend the flux of time. To believe that the story of mankind is one story because the various disparate stories are under one divine sovereignty is therefore not an arbitrary procedure. On the contrary it prevents ages and cultures, civilizations and philosophies, from arbitrarily finding the center of history's meaning within their own life or achievements and from seeking the culmination and fulfillment of that meaning prematurely in the victory of their cause or the completion of their particular project.

Every large frame of meaning, which serves the observer of historical events in correlating the events into some kind of pattern, is a structure of faith rather than of science, in the sense that the scientific procedures must presuppose the framework and it can therefore not be merely their consequence. The difference between structures of meaning is therefore not between supposedly "rational" and supposedly "irrational" ones. Supposedly rational frames of meaning may be irrational in the sense that an implicit and unacknowledged center and source of meaning may be inadequate to do justice to every dimension of human existence and every perplexity and antinomy in the stuff of history. A supposedly "irrational" frame of meaning may be rational in the sense that it acknowledges a center and source of meaning beyond the limits of rational intelligibility, partly because it "rationally" senses the inadequacy or idolatrous character of centers and sources of meaning which are within the limits of rational intelligibility. . . .

The sovereignty of God establishes the general frame of meaning for life and history, according to Biblical faith. But the first specific content of the drama of history is furnished by the assertion of divine sovereignty against man's rebellious efforts to establish himself as the perverse center of existence. Biblical faith does not deny the fact of evil in history. On the contrary it discerns that men are capable of such bold and persistent defiance of the laws and structures of their existence that only the resource of the divine power and love is finally able to overcome this rebellion. The patterns of human existence are filled with obscurities and abysses of meaninglessness because of this possibility of evil in human life.

The obscurities and incoherences of life are, according to Biblical faith, primarily the consequence of human actions. The incoherences and confusions, usually defined as "natural" evil, are not the chief concern of the Christian faith. Natural evil represents the failure of nature's processes to conform perfectly to human ends. It is the consequence of man's ambiguous position in nature. As a creature of nature he is subject to necessities and contingencies, which may be completely irrelevant to the wider purposes, interests, and ambitions which he conceives and elaborates as creative spirit. The most vivid symbol of natural evil is

FAITH AND HISTORY

death. Death is a simple fact in the dimension of nature; but it is an irrelevance and a threat of meaninglessness in the realm of history. Biblical faith is, however, only obliquely interested in the problem of natural evil. It does not regard death, as such, as an evil. "The sting of death," declares St. Paul, "is sin." [6]

Nor does it regard moral evil as due to man's involvement in natural finiteness. On the contrary, moral or historical evil is the consequence of man's abortive effort to overcome his insecurity by his own power, to hide the finiteness of his intelligence by pretensions of omniscience and to seek for emancipation from his ambiguous position by his own resources. Sin is, in short, the consequence of man's inclination to usurp the prerogatives of God, to think more highly of himself than he ought to think, thus making destructive use of his freedom by not observing the limits to which a creaturely freedom is bound.

Man is at variance with God through this abortive effort to establish himself as his own Lord; and he is at variance with his fellowmen by the force of the same pride which brings him in conflict with God. The prophets of Israel seemed to sense this primary form of historical evil most immediately in its collective form. They felt that Israel was guilty of it, because it drew complacent conclusions from the fact of its special covenant with God. The great nations and empires which encircled Israel were guilty because they imagined that their power made them immortal and secure. The myth of the Fall of Adam universalizes, as well as individualizes, this theme of man's revolt against God. The influence of this myth upon the Christian imagination is not primarily due to any literalistic illusions of Christian orthodoxy. The myth accurately symbolizes the consistent Biblical diagnosis of moral and historical evil. Adam and, together with him, all

---

[6] Ritschl, in common with many liberal theologians of the nineteenth century, made the mistake of believing that the Christian faith, in common with other high religions, is a way of gaining "assurance that man is not a part of the natural world, but is a cooperator with the divine purpose in the world." Faith is thus a method of man's being "sure of his spiritual uniqueness despite his subordination to the world of nature." From unpublished "Dogmatik" quoted by Goesta Hök, *Die Elliptische Theologie Albert Ritschls*, p. 28. Hegel's definition of evil as the "discord between the inner life of the heart and the actual world" is prompted by the same logic.

men seek to overstep the bounds which are set by the Creator for man as creature. . . .

Thus the final revelation of the divine sovereignty in New Testament faith transfigures the moral perplexity about suffering innocence into the ultimate light of meaning. It gives life a final meaning without promising the annulment of history's moral obscurities. Above all it holds out the hope of redemption from evil, upon the basis of a humble acceptance of human finiteness and a contrite recognition of the evil in which men are involved when they seek to deny their finitude.

The points of reference for the structure of the meaning of history in the Christian faith are obviously not found by an empirical analysis of the observable structures and coherences of history. They are "revelations," apprehended by faith, of the character and purposes of God. The experience of faith by which they are apprehended is an experience of the ultimate limits of human knowledge; and it requires a condition of repentance which is a possibility for the individual, but only indirectly for nations and collectives.

The character of these points of reference or these foundations for a structure of meaning make it quite clear that it is not possible to speak simply of a "Christian philosophy of history." Perhaps it is not possible to have any adequate "philosophy" of history at all because a philosophy will reduce the antinomies, obscurities, and the variety of forms in history to a too simple form of intelligibility. Yet a Christian theology of history is not an arbitrary construct. It "makes sense" out of life and history.

That the final clue to the mystery of the divine power is found in the suffering love of a man on the Cross is not a proposition which follows logically from the observable facts of history. But there are no observable facts of history which cannot be interpreted in its light. When so interpreted the confusions and catastrophes of history may become the source of the renewal of life.

That life in history is meaningful though the historic growth of human power may sharpen rather than mitigate the struggle between good and evil, and may accentuate rather than modify the inclination of the human heart to idolatry, is also not a proposition which follows inevitably from an observation of the historical drama. The sense of meaning is derived from the conviction that no human rebellion can rise so high as to challenge the divine sovereignty essentially. While this confidence in the final source and end of human life is not a fruit of empirical observation, it is worth noting that the philosophies which are the fruit of empirical observation either drive men to despair by charting the growing antinomies of life or they prompt complacency by obscuring the obvious tragic aspects of life and history.

The final vision of the fulfillment of life and history in Christian eschatology transcends the canons of reason and common sense even more explicitly. Christian eschatology looks forward to an "end" of history in which the conditions of nature-history are transfigured but not annulled. This picture of the fulfillment of life involves the rational absurdity of an eternity which incorporates the conditions of time: individuality and particularity. But the alternative faiths by which men live envision an eternity which either (1) annuls the whole of history and thereby denies the significance of human life in history; or (2) falsely reduces the whole dimension of history with its partial and fragmentary meanings to the level of nature; or (3) assumes that a progressive history ceases at some point to be a history in time and culminates in an incredible utopia where unconditioned good is realized amidst the contingencies of history.

The Christian philosophy of history is rational, therefore, only in the sense that it is possible to prove that alternatives to it fail to do justice to all aspects of human existence; and that the basic presuppositions of the Christian faith, though transcending reason, make it possible to give an account of life and history in which all facts and antinomies are comprehended.

The foolishness of the cross and the sense of history. The New Testament makes the startling claim that in Christ history has achieved both its end and a new beginning. The affirmation that Christ is the end of history signifies that in His life, death, and resurrection the meaning of man's historic existence is fulfilled. The divine sovereignty, which gives it meaning, is revealed to have an ultimate resource of mercy and forgiveness, beyond judgment, which completes history despite the continued fragmentary and contradictory character of all historic reality. The affirmation that in Christ there is a new beginning, that a "new age" has been initiated in the history of mankind, means that the wisdom of faith which apprehends the true meaning of life also contains within it the repentance which is the presupposition of the renewal of life. . . .

Fulfillments in history and the fulfillment of history. The fact that the grossest forms of evil enter into history as schemes of redemption and that the Christian faith itself introduces new evils, whenever it pretends that the Christian life, individually or collectively, has achieved a final perfection, gives us a clue to the possibilities and limits of historic achievement. There are provisional meanings in history, capable of being recognized and fulfilled by individuals and cultures; but mankind will continue to "see through a glass darkly" and the final meaning can be anticipated only by faith. It awaits a completion when "we shall know even as we are known." There are provisional judgments upon evil in history; but all of them are imperfect, since the executors of judgment are tainted in both their discernments and their actions by the evil, which they seek to overcome. History therefore awaits an ultimate judgment. There are renewals of life in history, individually and collectively; but no rebirth lifts life above the contradictions of man's historic existence. The Christian awaits a "general resurrection" as well as a "last judgment."

These eschatological expectations in New Testament faith, however embarrassing when taken literally, are necessary for a Christian interpretation of history. If they are sacrificed, the meaning of history is confused by the introduction of false centers of meaning, taken from contingent stuff of the historical process; new evil is introduced into history by the pretended culminations within history itself; and tentative judgments are falsely regarded as final. Whether dealing with the Alpha or the Omega of history, with the beginning or with the end, the Christian faith prevents provisional meanings, judgments, and fulfillments from becoming ultimate by its sense of a final mystery of divine fulfillment beyond all provisional meanings. But it does not allow this ultimate mystery to degenerate into meaninglessness because of its confidence that the love of Christ is the clue to the final mystery.

There are forms of the eschatological hope which tend to deny the moral judgments of history. They reduce historical existence to complete darkness, illumined only by a single light of revelation; and they reduce historical striving to complete frustration, relieved only by the hope of a final divine completion. This type of Christian eschatology is as false as the optimism which it has displaced; for it destroys the creative tension in Biblical faith between the historical and the transhistorical. When followed consistently, the Biblical faith must be fruitful of genuine renewals of life in history, in both the individual and the collective existence of man. These renewals are made possible by the very humility and love, which is derived from an awareness of the limits of human virtue, wisdom, and power.

We have previously considered the Christian interpretation of the possibility and necessity of the renewal of the life of the individual. Christian faith insists that "except a man be born again . . . he cannot enter into the kingdom of God." (John 3:5) The question to be answered is what light this Christian doctrine of the renewal of life throws upon the fate of civilizations and cultures. Can they escape death by rebirth? Is the renewal or rebirth of individual life an analogy for the possibilities of man's collective enterprises? The individual is promised new life if he dies to self, if he is "crucified with Christ." The self which seeks the realization of itself within itself destroys itself. Does this fate of self-seeking individuals give us a clue to the self-destruction of cultures and civilizations? And does the promise of a new life through the death of the old self hold also for the life of nations and empires. . . .

The knowledge that "the world passeth away and the lusts thereof" and that every *civitas terrena* is a city of destruction does not, however, negate the permanent values which appear in the rise and fall of civilizations and cultures. A feudal civilization may be destroyed by its inability to incorporate the new dynamism of a commercial and industrial society. But there are qualities of organic community, including even the hierarchical organization of the community, in a feudal society, which transcend the fate of such a civilization. In the same manner a bourgeois society, though involved in a self-destructive individualism, also contributes to the emancipation of the individual in terms of permanent worth. There are thus facets of the eternal in the flux of time. From the standpoint of Biblical faith the eternal in the temporal flux is not so much a permanent structure of existence, revealed in the cycle of change, as it is a facet of the *Agape* of Christ. It is "love which abideth." An organic society may achieve a harmony of life without freedom, insofar as it is without freedom it is not a perfect incarnation of *Agape*, but insofar as it is a harmony of life with life it is an imperfect symbol of the true *Agape*. A libertarian society may sacrifice community to the dignity of the individual. But insofar as it emancipates the individual from social restraints which are less than the restraints of love, it illustrates another facet of the full dimension of *Agape*. Thus, the same civilizations which perish because they violate the law of love at some point may also contribute a deathless value insofar as they explicate the harmony of life with life intended in creation.

If this be so, the question arises why the process of history should not gradually gather up the timeless values and eliminate the worthless. Why should not history be a winnowing process in which truth is separated from falsehood; and the falsehood burned as chaff, while the wheat of truth is "gathered into the barn." In that case *die Weltgeschichte* would, after all, be *das Weltgericht*. There is one sense in which this is true. Yet this conception of history as its own judge is finally false. It is true in the sense that history is actually the story of man's developing freedom. Insofar as increasing freedom leads to harmonies of life with life within communities and between communities, in which the restraints and cohesions of nature are less determinative for the harmony than the initiative of man, a positive meaning must be assigned to growth in history. There is, certainly, positive significance in the fact that modern man must establish community destroyed even on the level of the local village. To establish community in global terms requires the exercise of the ingenuity of freedom far beyond the responsibilities of men of other epochs, who had the support of natural forces, such as consanguinity, for their limited communities. The expansion of the perennial task of achieving a tolerable harmony of life with life under even higher conditions of freedom and in even wider frames of harmony represents the residual truth in modern progressive interpretations of history.

But this truth is transmuted into error very quickly if it is assumed that increasing freedom assures the achievement of the wider task. The perils of freedom rise with its promises, and the perils and promises are inextricably interwoven. The parable of the wheat and the tares expresses the Biblical attitude toward the possibilities of history exactly. The servants who desire to uproot the tares which have been sown among the wheat are forbidden to do so by the householder "lest while ye gather up the tares, ye root up also the wheat with them. Let both grow together until the harvest: and in the time of harvest I will say unto the reapers, Gather ye together first the tares, and bind them into bundles to burn them: but gather the wheat into my barn." (Matthew 13:29-30.)

There is, in other words, no possibility of a final judgment within history but only at the end of history. The increase of human freedom over nature is like the advancing season which ripens both wheat and tares, which are inextricably intermingled. This simple symbol from the sayings of our Lord in the Synoptics is supplemented in the eschatology of the Epistles, where it is Christ himself who becomes the judge at the final judgment of the world.

History, in short, does not solve the enigma of history. There are facets of meaning in it which transcend the flux of time. These give glimpses of the eternal love which bears the whole project of history. There is a positive meaning also in the ripening of love under conditions of increasing freedom; but the possibility that the same freedom may increase the power and destructiveness of self-love makes it impossible to find a solution for the meaning of history within history itself. Faith awaits a final judgment and a final resurrection. Thus mystery stands at the end, as well as at the beginning of the whole pilgrimage of man. But the clue to the mystery is the *Agape* of Christ. It is the clue to the mystery of Creation. "All things were made by him; and without him was not anything made that was made." (John 1:3) It is the clue to the mystery of the renewals and redemptions within history, since wherever the divine mercy is discerned as within and above the wrath, which destroys all forms of self-seeking, life may be renewed, individually and collectively. It is also the clue to the final redemption of history. The antinomies of good and evil increase rather than diminish in the long course of history. Whatever provisional meanings there may be in such a process, it must drive men to despair when viewed ultimately, unless they have discerned the power and the mercy which overcomes the enigma of its end.

The whole history of man is thus comparable to his individual life. He does not have the power and the wisdom to overcome the ambiguity of his existence. He must and does increase his freedom, both as an individual and in the total human enterprise; and his creativity is enhanced by the growth of his freedom. But this freedom also tempts him to deny his mortality and the growth of his freedom, and power increases the temptation. But evils in history are the consequence of this pretension. Confusion follows upon man's effort to complete his life by his own power and solve its enigma by his own wisdom. Perplexities, too simply solved, produce despair. The Christian faith is the apprehension of the divine love and power which bears the whole human pilgrimage, shines through its enigmas and antinomies and is finally and definitively revealed in a drama in which suffering love gains triumph over sin and death. This revelation does not resolve all perplexities; but it does triumph over despair, and leads to the renewal of life from self-love to love.

Man, in both his individual life and in his total enterprise, moves from a limited to a more extensive expression of freedom over nature. If he assumes that such an extension of freedom insures and increases emancipation from the bondage of self, he increases the bondage by that illusion. Insofar as the phenomenal increase in human power in a technical age has created that illusion, it has also involved our culture in the profound pathos of disappointed hopes, caused by false estimates of the glory and the misery of man.

To understand, from the standpoint of the Christian faith, that man cannot complete his own life, and can neither define nor fulfill the final mystery and meaning of his historical pilgrimage, is not to rob life of meaning or responsibility.

The love toward God and the neighbor, which is the final virtue of the Christian life, is rooted in a humble recognition of the fragmentary character of our own wisdom, virtue, and power. The forgiveness which is the most perfect expression of that love, is prompted by a contrite recognition of the guilt with which our own virtue is tainted. Our faith in the faithfulness of God, and our hope in His triumph over the tragic antinomies of life do not annul, but rather transfigure, human wisdom. For they mark the limit of its power and purge it of its pretenses. For "God hath chosen the foolish things of the world to confound the wise; and God hath chosen the weak things of the world to confound the things that are mighty . . . that no flesh should glory in His presence."

BIBLIOGRAPHY

ALBRIGHT, W. F. *From Stone Age to Christianity.* Baltimore: 1946.
BERDYAEV, N. *Destiny of Man.* New York: 1937.
BERDYAEV, N. *The Fate of Man in the Modern World.* London: 1935.
BERDYAEV, N. *The Meaning of History.* London: 1936.
BERKHOF, H. *Christ the Meaning of History.* Richmond, Va.: 1966.
BERKOUWER, G. C. *The Providence of God.* Grand Rapids, Mich.: 1952.
BULTMANN, RUDOLF. *The Presence of Eternity: History and Eschatology.* New York: 1957.
BUTTERFIELD, H. *Christianity and History.* London: 1950.
BUTTERFIELD, H. *History and Human Relations.* New York: 1952.
CASSERLEY, J. V. L. *Toward a Theology of History.* New York: 1965.
CLARK, G. H. *Christian View of Men and Things.* Grand Rapids, Mich.: 1952.
CLARK, G. H. "Bultmann's Historiography," *Jesus of Nazareth: Savior and Lord,* ed. C. F. H. Henry. Grand Rapids, Mich.: 1966.
CONNOLLY, J. M. *Human History and the Word of God.* New York: 1965.
CULLMANN, OSCAR. *Christ and Time.* Philadelphia: 1950.
DANIELOU, JEAN. *The Lord of History.* London: 1958.
DAWSON, CHRISTOPHER. *Enquiries into Religion and Culture.* New York: 1943.
DAWSON, CHRISTOPHER. *The Dynamics of World History.* New York: 1962.
DRAY, WILLIAM. *Philosophy of History.* Englewood Cliffs, N. J.: 1964.
FITCH, R. E. "Reinhold Niebuhr's Philosophy of History," *Reinhold Niebuhr: His Religious, Social and Political Thought,* ed. C. W. Kegley and R. W. Bretall. New York: 1961.

GUILDAY, PETER. (ed.). *Catholic Philosophy of History*. New York: 1936.

HARLAND, G. *The Thought of Reinhold Niebuhr*. New York: 1960.

JASPERS, KARL. *The Origin and Goal of History*. New Haven: 1953.

LATOURETTE, K. S. *A History of the Expansion of Christianity*. New York: 1938.

LÖWITH, KARL. "History and Christianity," *Reinhold Niebuhr: His Religious, Social and Political Thought*, ed. Kegley and Bretall (cited above).

LÖWITH, KARL. *The Meaning of History*. Chicago: 1949.

MARITAIN, J. *On the Philosophy of History*. New York: 1957.

MONTGOMERY, J. W. *The Shape of the Past: An Introduction to Philosophical Historiography*. Ann Arbor: 1962.

MONTGOMERY, J. W. "Towards a Christian Philosophy of History," *Jesus of Nazareth: Savior and Lord*, ed. C. F. H. Henry. Grand Rapids, Mich.: 1966.

NIEBUHR, REINHOLD. *Beyond Tragedy: Essays on the Christian Interpretation of History*. New York: 1937.

NIEBUHR, REINHOLD. *Faith and History: A Comparison of Christian and Modern Views of History*. New York: 1949.

NIEBUHR, REINHOLD. *Moral Man and Immoral Society*. New York: 1932.

NIEBUHR, REINHOLD. *The Irony of American History*. New York: 1952.

OTT, HEINRICH. "Rudolf Bultmann's Philosophy of History," *The Theology of Rudolf Bultmann*, ed. C. W. Kegley. New York: 1966.

RICOEUR, PAUL. "Christianity and the Meaning of History," *History and Truth*. Evanston, Ill.: 1965.

RUST, ERIC. *The Christian Understanding of History*. London: 1947.

RUST, ERIC. *Towards a Theological Understanding of History*. New York: 1963.

TILLICH, PAUL. *The Interpretation of History*. New York: 1936.

VOEGELIN, E. *Order and History*. 6 vols. Baton Rouge, La.: 1956.

10 History and Historicism

As the preceding chapters have shown, the speculative philosophy of history is a result of attempts made by not only philosophers but also by historians and sociologists to discover the meaning of history as a whole. These speculative systems assume, for the most part, that there is some ultimate meaning in history which can be explained in terms of some historical law. This belief, usually coupled with some form of historical inevitability (either theistic or naturalistic), is often called "historicism."[1]

[1] There is another and quite different sense of historicism which will be encountered in Volume Two. This is the view, associated with such think-

The speculative philosophy of history, historicism, or, as it has sometimes been called, "metahistory" has been widely attacked by representatives of many disciplines. Some critics have pointed out that the search for the ultimate meaning of history is not and should not be the concern of the historian. It is one thing to speak of the meaning of a particular event or set of events; it is quite another thing to talk about the meaning of history as a whole. The phrase, "the ultimate meaning of history," includes as a part of its meaning the ultimate destiny of human existence. Thus, when one searches for the meaning of history in this sense, he is actually not looking for what *has* happened in the past; he is searching for what *will* (or what *must*) happen in the future. Since the historian is only concerned with the past, the critic of historicism contends, it is quite wrong to confuse speculative systems of history with the legitimate work of historians. Alan Bullock has accused "metahistorians" of misunderstanding the proper task of the historian. Bullock argues [2] that the purpose of the historian is not to derive a metaphysical system from history (i.e., not to present generalities about past and future) but to narrate what happened in the past. Such generalizations lead to oversimplification and inaccuracy in handling the facts of history.

Historicists have also been challenged on other grounds. Some speculative philosophers of history have confused trends in history with laws controlling history. Some have generalized about the various units of history (societies, cultures, or civilizations) without setting forth any clear criteria to identify these units. The laws of history historicists have proposed are often vague and sometimes trivial enough to be empty truisms. Speculative systems of history thrive on unclarified concepts like "force," "class," "dialectic," etc. Perhaps the most outspoken critic of historicism in this century has been Karl R. Popper. His books, *The*

---

ers as Dilthey, Croce, and Collingwood, that all ideas are rooted in some historical context and are therefore limited and relative. Historicists (in this second sense) also maintain that history must use different logical techniques from those used in the physical sciences. Failure to keep these two types of historicism distinct can lead to confusion.

[2] Alan Bullock, "The Historian's Purpose: History and Metahistory," *History Today*, 1951.

Open Society and Its Enemies and *The Poverty of Historicism*, argue that historicist principles have been used in support of totalitarian political systems.

In a recent article, Berkley Eddins points out that speculative theories of history result from two different concerns, the theoretical and the practical.[3] Viewed as a theoretical enterprise, a speculative philosophy of history is an attempt to make sense of history as a whole. As the result of a more practical concern, it is an attempt to show, given the way things are, the best course of action for men to follow. Marx's philosophy of history, to take just one example, has both theoretical (i.e., the movement of history toward the classless society) and practical (i.e., the plea for the proletariat to overthrow capitalism) aspects. Eddins believes that many critics of the speculative philosophy of history forget that these two aspects must be evaluated on different grounds.

Maurice Mandelbaum has criticized the search for a principle that will explain the ultimate direction of historical change.[4] He doubts that the historian will ever have sufficient data to establish any pattern of the past; and even if we were to grant that a particular pattern has held in the *past,* what justification would there be for believing that this pattern would continue to hold in the *future?* Mandelbaum also argues that by their very nature, speculative approaches to history are value charged and thus suffer from a greater degree of subjectivity than a strictly historical understanding of the past.

In spite of its obvious defects, however, most critics of historicism are willing to admit that it does serve some purpose. Mandelbaum sees the speculative systems of history as a fulfillment of man's need to place himself and his society in the context of a larger whole. These systems have also served a social function by providing men with a message about human value and destiny during periods of social and political crisis.[5] In a discussion of what he calls "the major predicament of all historical study," Georges Florovsky states,

---

[3] Berkley Eddins, "Speculative Philosophy of History: A Critical Analysis," *The Southern Journal of Philosophy,* Spring, 1968.
[4] See Mandelbaum's essay in this chapter and his article, "A Critique of Philosophies of History," *The Journal of Philosophy,* 1948.
[5] See Mandelbaum's article cited in n. 4.

No historian can, even in his limited and particular field, within his own competence, avoid raising ultimate problems of human nature and destiny, unless he reduces himself to the role of a registrar of empirical happenings, and forfeits his proper task of "understanding." In order to understand, just historically, for instance, "The Greek Mind," the historian must, of necessity, have his own vision . . . of the whole range of problems with which the "Noble Spirits" of Antiquity were wrestling, in conflict with each other and in succession. A historian of philosophy must be, to a certain extent, a philosopher himself. Otherwise he will miss the problems around which the quest of philosophers has been centered. . . . Thus, contrary to the current prejudice, in order to be competent within his proper field of interpretation, a historian must be responsive to the whole amplitude of human concerns.

In his contribution to this chapter, M. C. D'Arcy also recognizes the defects of speculative approaches to history. But he suggests that they still have some value. There is still need, he argues, to see the past on a level higher than that of individual facts. Where there is too much concentration on the facts, the historian may not see the forest for the trees. "What he lacks in thoroughness of detail," the philosopher of history "makes up for by seeing relations and interconnections which are outside the province of the professional historian." While it is true, D'Arcy concludes, that historicists do not give us history, still using some of the art of the poet or the dramatist, they do give us another type of knowledge of the past.

MAURICE MANDELBAUM
SPECULATIVE PHILOSOPHY OF HISTORY: A CRITIQUE *

The term "the philosophy of history" is a vague one. Taken in its broadest sense it involves every concern which philosophers may have with the knowledge of history. It is not, however, in this broad sense that we shall at present use the term. In a narrower sense the philosophy of history refers to the attempts

* Reprinted from *The Problem of Historical Knowledge* by Maurice Mandelbaum by permission of the Liveright Publishing Corporation. Copyright 1938 by Liveright Publishing Corporation.

which have been made by historians, sociologists, and philosophers to interpret the meaning or significance of the historical process as a whole. These attempts are characterized by an appeal to the empirically discerned facts of history; they represent the search for an ultimate message which can be found in the historical process as a whole. In this they are distinguished from those "universal histories" which are really compendia of historical knowledge, and make no attempt to reveal a message which the historical process as a whole contains. They are also distinguishable from "pragmatic histories," which find particular lessons applicable to present dilemmas in specific portions of the past. The philosophers of history survey the "trend" of the past, seeking to derive philosophically significant knowledge from such surveys. This type of inquiry into universal history is that which since the time of Herder has been called "the philosophy of history." [1]

It is obvious that the doctrine of historical pluralism which was put forward in the last chapter leads to a discussion of the philosophy of history, for historical pluralism seems to deny the very possibility of the philosophy of history taken in this sense. If there is an ultimate pluralism in history the attempt to decipher the message which is contained in "the historical process as a whole" is futile. And yet we find that philosophers, sociologists, and historians have occupied themselves with attempts to construct philosophies of history. Unless we can demonstrate that all such attempts are by their very nature invalid theoretical constructions, we shall not have given a satisfactory defense of the doctrine of historical pluralism. Let us therefore examine the basis upon which any philosophy of history must rest.

It will be recalled that in the preceding chapter we offered no concrete objection to the attempts which have been made to establish a *complete* monism with respect to the historical process, apart from pointing out that such a monism would render the historian's enterprise incapable of any measure of fulfillment. We concerned ourselves wholly with historical monisms which were less ambitious in scope. At this point, however, it be-

[1] That which is sometimes called the philosophy of history is really general sociology: an attempt to discover the laws or principles of historical development. (Cf., Rickert *Probleme der Geschichtsphilosophie*, p. 5.)

comes necessary to examine the grounds on which any complete form of monism might be established.

The root conception out of which all historical monisms have grown is to be found in the principle of teleological development. As we have had previous occasion to note, the conception of a development is applicable only to those series of events in which there is an inherent nontemporal order of a specific type, in which, as we may say, the last element contains the fruition of that which in the first element has its beginning. In a developmental series of events change proceeds not merely in a definitely determined order, but in a definite direction. Where this directional line is broken we say that the development has been cut off. Now such a term as development cannot readily be applied to every series of events in the historical process. It is a matter of empirical fact that historical events often do change their directional lines; the last aspect in a process of historical change often seems to contain something quite different from that which the first aspect began. Thus, in order to validate the conception of development in empirical historical investigations some further element is needed. This element the conception of teleology supplies.

By means of coupling the conception of teleology with that of development, it is possible to hold that every series of historical events is developmental in character. For if the nature of the last element in a series of events determines the nature of the earlier elements, then the direction of the series as a whole is thereby fixed once and for all. The events in the series then take on a more unified character, and the pluralism which seems to be demanded by the nature of historical events tends to disappear. This disappearance soon becomes final. For every series of events can be considered as a part of some other series of events which is larger in scale, and the teleological development which characterizes that series then becomes part of a larger teleological development. Ultimately, then, the whole of the historical process comes to be regarded as a teleological development, and historical monism is adopted.

It is in this fashion that the application of the concept of teleological development to historical events leads to historical monism. It is well to examine what justification can be found for regarding history as a teleological development.

We have already pointed out that there seems to be no empirical basis for holding that every historical series of events possesses a uniform direction. It likewise seems impossible to hold that every historical event is teleologically determined. The only empirically verifiable point at which teleology enters into the nature of historical events is to be found in the influence of human volition on those events. But human volition cannot account for the whole of the historical process; it must have materials upon which to work, and these materials are not manufactured by it. At every point at which human volition comes into play in history we find that limits are set to its influence, and that the nature of any event which it partially determines is also partially determined by countless other factors which are not expressly volitional in character. Thus we may say that so far as empirical evidence is concerned there seems to be no reason why we should hold that every historical event is either developmental or teleological in character.

Another attempt to justify the view that historical events always exemplify a teleological development is to be found in certain analyses of the nature of historical understanding. It has often been claimed that the concept of teleological development is fundamental to the historian's grasp of the past; that only in viewing events in a teleological light can the past be rendered intelligible. It is therefore claimed that history as we know it must represent past events as teleological developments. To this contention a twofold reply can be given. In the first place, we have just pointed out that history as we know it does not seem to show that events possess this characteristic. In the second place, on the basis of an examination of actual historical knowledge, as well as on the basis of the arguments advanced by such persons as Rickert and Troeltsch, we have come to the conclusion that historical understanding does not impose itself upon its materials, but rather follows where these lead. The whole of the present analysis of the nature of historical knowledge may thus be taken as an answer to this attempted justification of the concept of teleological development in history.

A third type of defense for teleology in history has also been offered. It has often been claimed that the apparently pluralistic character of historical events is an illusion forced upon us by a shortsighted empiricism. It is suggested that if we take a longer view of historical events, refusing to allow ourselves to become bogged down in trifling details, the historical process as a whole will reveal itself to be teleological and developmental in character. It is by means of this ostensibly empirical method that philosophies of history are constructed.

Their creators who seek to trace the course of the historical process in the large lay claim to an empirically sound method. Undaunted by the repeated failures of sociologists, historians, and philosophers to uncover any acceptable view of the historical process as a whole, these adventurers grasp at every new attempt as containing the possibility of a solution to their problem. It will be our task to show that the problem is essentially insoluble.

In the first place it should be noted that when the philosopher of history draws a distinction between what is true of the historical process in the large, and what is true of the small-scale events in that process, he immediately forfeits his right to claim that the process as a whole must be monistically conceived. It must be granted that teleological development may not be equally obvious through the whole range of the historical process, but one should be suspicious of any attempts at historical construction which find teleology only in large-scale events. It would seem far more likely that if the historical process were truly characterized by teleological development, we should find instances of such teleology scattered indiscriminately through the whole scale of historical events. In this respect the historical teleology of an Augustine is far more convincing than the teleological developments which are traced by Hegel.

The philosopher of history who draws a distinction between the discernible teleology of large-scale events and the hidden teleology which is supposedly none the less present in the minutiae of the historical process is very likely to accept a bifurcation between historical research and historical synthesis.[2] For

[2] Cf., Hegel's classification of "the methods of treating history" in the Introduction to his *Philosophy of History*.

him "synthesis" is the ultimate goal of historical inquiry, since this synthesis uncovers the true teleological development of history. At first glance the most surprising fact to be found in those historical syntheses upon which philosophies of history are based is the exaggerated stress which they place upon the problems of periodization. In Comte as in Hegel the question of periodization comes to the forefront and almost dwarfs other historical problems by virtue of the magnitude of its all-encompassing framework. However, when one reflects upon the relation which periodization bears to the problem of teleological development, this emphasis upon the periods of history becomes readily understandable.

In dealing with the problem of periods of history, we have already had occasion to point out that periods are delimited with respect to some comparatively long-enduring event which appears to be of great significance. We found that the periods of history are not to be considered as unitary historical entities which embrace all of the historical phenomena of a given time, but, rather, that they are particular abstractions from the historical process as a whole, and have reference only to certain areas of that process at the time in question. It will be well to apply these findings to the periodization which is to be found in the philosophies of history.

If we ask why it is that philosophies of history, which aim to trace teleological development in the historical process, should concentrate their attention upon problems of periodization, we find an answer ready at hand. When we say that a period is delimited by some *long-enduring event of importance* the clue to this answer is already given. For what can so easily define the importance of a long-enduring event as its place in a teleological development? It is a traditional failing of a mind which is not historically oriented to examine the importance of any event merely in terms of its relationship to succeeding events of the same scale. To a degree, it is also characteristic of the nonhistoric mind to confine this discussion of importance to the relationship which the event in question bears to events which are generically similar to it. Thus, when asked to define the importance of the Protestant Reformation, the layman is likely to confine his answer to its supposed influence on modern European freedom of thought, an event quite similar both in scale and in generic nature to that which he understands by the Reformation. The historian, as we well know, would give no such facile answer. But philosophers of history are not conspicuous for their historical orientation; all too frequently they share the layman's tendency to confine their estimates of historical importance to tracing the relationship which one event bears to other events of the same scale and kind. This leads them to a demarcation of historical periods in terms of teleological development. For it will be seen that if we judge the importance of a historical event by what it has contributed to other events which are fundamentally similar to it, we cannot fail to have before us a picture which gives the illusion of a teleological development. Each period having been demarcated with reference to its contribution to a future period, the historical process as a whole takes on a deceptively monistic appearance.

Now, it might be objected that we have failed to take into account the fact that in some philosophies of history certain periods are held to contribute nothing to the teleological development of the process as a whole, and yet that even these blank periods fall within the purview of the philosophers of history. This, however, fails to touch the crucial point in our argument. If there are any philosophies of history in which a "period" is held to be blank, the principle of periodization is adopted without reference to the period in question. It is only held to be a period because it represents a chronological gap in the teleological development which is in question. Thus, in the prevalent commonsense periodization of history (which, strangely enough, is an intellectualistic one) the so-called Middle Ages (usually referred to as the Dark Ages), represent a chronological gap in a teleological development of "free inquiry." The periodization is undertaken on the basis of the positive character of Greek and Modern thought, and the Middle Ages are seen as contributing nothing to history.

In Hegel's philosophy of history the aspect of teleological development is everywhere evident. It is not only specifically formulated in the Introduction to his *Philosophy of History,* but it is evident in the actual historical studies which he undertook in the fields of philosophy and fine art. In Comte, who with Hegel most clearly represents the tendency of a philosopher of history to proceed by periodization, a similar emphasis on a unitary or teleological development can be discovered. The periods which Comte finds represented in the historical process are periods of relative "enlightenment"; they are periods ascribed to the history of social and moral thought. We see in the transitions from religious to metaphysical, and from metaphysical to scientific thought, a pure line of development. To be sure, Comte's positivism would not allow him to adopt an explicitly teleological view of this development, yet it might be contended [3] that there is a strong teleological ingredient within it. Whether or not this is the case, we can see that Comte's periodization of history rests upon his acceptance of a developmental standpoint which binds the periods he has singled out into an apparently monistic unity.

These illustrations, drawn from widely known attempts at periodization, show the degree to which the conception of a unitary or teleological development enters into those attempts. As a consequence it is not to be wondered at that in their attempts to establish monism on an empirical ground, philosophers of history should focus their attention on those large-scale events which they designate as periods of history. It remains for us to show by means of concrete argumentation what was already implicit in our treatment of historical periods: that no teleological periodization of history can establish historical monism.

We have already pointed out that every so-called period represents but a segregated portion of the historical process at any given time. Thus teleological periodization of history does not demonstrate that the historical process as a whole is teleological. With this in mind let us examine Comte's view of "the three stages of development."

Comte held that all thought goes through three stages of development; these stages he termed theological, philosophical, and scientific. By means of this law he sought to unify all historical phenomena. Yet such a law, it will readily be seen, cannot possibly suffice as a basis for historical monism. For even if Comte were correct in his contention that "the whole social

---

[3] Cf., Comte, *Positive Philosophy*, Vol. II, p. 265. Also Troeltsch, *Der Historismus und seine Probleme*, pp. 427 ff.

mechanism is ultimately based on opinions,"[4] no law which abstracts out of the historical process merely one set of determining factors can ever do justice to that process as a whole. The historical process does not consist merely in thought-factors, no matter what formative significance we may attach to them. Opinions may determine certain aspects of economic, political, and artistic forms, but the actual existence of these forms is something over and above the opinions which may have helped to determine their nature. Thought does not spin social forms out of itself, it operates on those forms which are already given in the historical process to which it itself belongs. Thus, no law of the development of thought can be held to unify all that is included within the historical process. The periodization of history from the standpoint of the development of thought is merely one possible periodization of the historical process. No matter how accurate it may be, and no matter how teleological in character it may appear, it cannot serve to establish historical monism.

Furthermore, we can point out that any periodization of the historical process represents an abstraction from that process not merely with reference to the types of phenomena which it includes, but also with reference to the scope of its survey. As is well known, Comte followed Condorcet in his willful exclusion of non-European elements from the survey of history. Such an exclusion (which is all too common) makes it impossible to argue for a complete monism of the historical process on empirical grounds. And even in philosophies of history such as Hegel's in which non-European elements are introduced, other gaps are always present. These gaps are usually to be found in so-called prehistory, in the omission of contemporary primitive civilizations,[5] and in the failure to include the complete history of any one geographical sector within that survey. In the case of Hegel's philosophy of history this appears particularly clearly; the teleological development of history finds a place for one era of each nation's history, and all other eras of that history are excluded.[6] Here again we see that the periodization of history is an abstraction from the historical process, and, thus, that a historical syn-

---

[4] Quoted by J. B. Bury, *The Idea of Progress*, p. 292.
[5] On these points cf., Hegel's *Philosophy of History*.
[6] Cf., Hegel, *Grundlinien der Philosophie des Rechts*, #347.

thesis based upon periodization cannot be used to establish historical monism.

A second major objection to the attempt to establish historical monism through the apparently teleological character of historical periods follows closely upon this first objection. For it will be seen that every abstraction from the historical process as a whole, every focusing of attention upon some one aspect of that process, follows from an original value-charged choice. This we have already had occasion to note with reference to the historian's choice of his subject matter. It applies equally well to the choice made by the philosopher of history with respect to the principle of his periodization. Comte chose, for definite and specifically assignable reasons, to periodize history with respect to social and moral ideas; von Below contends that history should be periodized with reference to political events.[7] This value-charged element in the philosophy of history has been ably indicated by Troeltsch,[8] and it demonstrates the essential subjectivity of every attempt to prove historical monism through an appeal to the teleological development which can be discovered in the sequence of "the great historical periods."

A third objection can be found in the fact that every philosopher stands in the midst of the historical process itself. It is impossible to hold that history represents a teleological development unless one knows (or believes that one knows) what the end of that process will be. But no empirical survey of the past can demonstrate the future to the philosopher of history. It therefore becomes impossible to ground historical monism upon an empirical appeal to the apparent teleology of past periods of history. In order to establish historical monism upon a teleological view of the periods of history it is therefore necessary to transcend one's temporal standpoint. In this Augustine and the entire Christian philosophy of history again represent a sounder approach to the problem of historical monism. For in Augustine and his followers we find an appeal to the nontemporal realm of God as the basis of historical monism. In addition, the belief that the world was soon coming to an end seemed to justify a complete periodization of history. The necessity of attaining a non-

[7] G. v. Below, *Über die Periodisierung*, p. 18.
[8] It is almost the *leitmotif* of *Der Historismus und seine Probleme*.

empirical, transcendent point of view before one can regard the historical process as a teleological development has long been noted by analysts of the idea of progress. But what holds of the conception of progress holds equally well of any unitary or teleological view of development. For the conception of progress is just such a view, save that it explicitly embodies the standpoint that this development represents the attainment of increased value. We may therefore say that in so far as historical monism rests upon the conception of teleological development it can only be established through some nonempirical (transcendent) approach. Thus we conclude our third and final argument against historical monism.

We have now seen that historical monism cannot be established through a direct empirical approach, nor through analyzing the nature of historical understanding, nor through an appeal to the great synthetic surveys of periods in the history of civilization. With ultimate metaphysical arguments concerning historical monism we cannot here concern ourselves. It is sufficient for us to have shown that philosophies of history in the commonly accepted meaning of the term cannot be constructed upon any empirical basis. And this, in fact, suffices to dispose of the traditional philosophies of history, for if historical monism can only be proved by means of a nonhistorical (transcendent) approach, the whole theoretical significance of empirical attempts to construct philosophies of history disappears. In that case every philosophy of history becomes a form of apologetics based upon a belief in the omnipotence and omnipresence of the forces of Providence or Progress. With such apologetics the historian, as historian, need not be concerned. . . .

M. C. D'ARCY, S. J.
HISTORY AND HISTORICISM *

History . . . provides us with knowledge in a manner different from that of science. By the unremitting efforts of scholars,

* Reprinted from *The Meaning and Matter of History* by M. C. D'Arcy with the permission of Farrar, Straus & Giroux, Inc. Copyright © 1959 by Martin Cyril D'Arcy.

much of the past is now within the grasp of every schoolboy. Historians using the accepted canons of judgment for deciding what is certain, probable, and/or still a matter of opinion, have freed us from ignorance and prejudice. But if history can now be taken for granted, what of the so-called philosophy of history or "historicism," as it has been named? As a branch of knowledge it is comparatively a newcomer. The historicists point to writers in the distant past and in the Middle Ages who can be regarded as forerunners or naïve philosophers; as a separate and autonomous study, however, it is modern, and it is not too easy to discover what precisely is meant by it, what it includes and what it excludes. One answer to this last problem might be to take conspicuous historicists, such as Vico, Hegel, Spengler, and Toynbee, and try to find out what they have in common. By the "philosophy" of history is meant not philosophy in the sense of the philosophy of science, where philosophy and "nature" have the same meaning. The chief experiences and activities of man fall under certain headings, the theoretical and practical, his moral and religious and political and social activities, and his creation of art forms and love of beauty. An inquiry into the nature of these experiences and activities constitutes philosophy. History, as we have seen, deserves a special place amongst these activities, and it is, perhaps, because this story of man as man, the passage from barbarism to culture, the rise and fall of so many civilizations, the movement which, it is to be hoped, will be prolonged into a future, that we are forced to ask what kind of unity can be found in this strange story. Opposites are found in it: necessity and freedom, design and accident, progress and frustration. In subordinate studies, such as economics and sociology, would-be scientific laws can be extracted out of the material conditions and forces, and these play their part in history. Again the efforts of man have clearly some aim above the satisfaction of mere animal cravings and immediate pleasures, but they are so confused and obscure that the word "progress" tells us very little. Almost always in the past, before the distinction between the secular and the religious became fixed, writers turned for explanations to religion, to the influence of the gods and of fate. Now that the sciences are considered self-sufficient and the supernatural is felt to be an intruder, the question arises what status or function religious ideas should have in a philosophy of history. The writers on the subject fall into three camps; those who turn to physical laws, be they biological or economic, those who see in man's own efforts a meaningful drama with a beginning and an end, and those who look beyond man to destiny or divine Providence. Some of the writers in this last category draw near to those of the first, because fate and, for instance, the materialistic conception of history both rely on laws of necessity to which man is bound. Within the religious view there are again striking differences, not only, for example, between Buddhism and Christianity but, as we shall see, within Christianity itself.

If a philosophy of history is to include theology and the supernatural it cannot easily be fitted into the usual corpus of philosophical subjects, which range from ethics to metaphysics. The old distinction which St. Thomas Aquinas made between knowledge based on reason and knowledge given to us by authority from Revelation will have to be ignored. The excuse is that as religion is supposed to throw light upon the purposes and the destiny of man we should be ready to consider any light which it may throw on a subject which is so directly concerned with the history and progress of man. As combining ethics and religion its subject matter should be closer to moral philosophy than to metaphysics, though, it must be said, such was not the view of Hegel. It is unfortunately typical of the confusions in this subject that those who have pronounced upon it should differ even as to the nature of what they were writing about. To Hegel history is the very tissue of metaphysics. Toynbee undoubtedly set out to combine the empirical methods of historical research with a metaphysical and religious pattern in his mind. Dr. Pieter Geyl is more modest. He criticizes Toynbee for being too ambitious, and says that we study history, (1) in order to enrich our own civilization "by the reanimation of old methods of existence and thought"; (2) to cultivate a certain kind of understanding, which in its way may be as fruitful as the natural historian's understanding of the processes of nature; and (3) to put our own world and its problems into perspective, so that we may regard them with greater patience and wisdom. Hegel and Toynbee have here been brought down to earth, and in fact, apart from one dangerous implication of a possible parallel between the processes of history and those of nature, Geyl confines himself to a commonsense view of the value of knowing the past. As to the parallel with nature, even this is derided by Alexander Herzen. "Who," he exclaims, "will find fault with nature because flowers bloom in the morning and die at night, because she has not given the rose or the lily the hardness of flint? And this miserable pedestrian principle *we* wish to transfer to the world of history." "History," for him, "is all improvisation, all will, all enterprise. There are no frontiers, there are no timetables, no itineraries."

Nowell-Smith, in the paper already quoted, gives us a hint about the methods of philosophical historians which may be useful. In distinguishing between science and history he refers to Toynbee, and he accuses him of using a "method recognizably like the scientific method." It is a wrong method because it is one of generalization, the recourse to laws of which particular cases are exhibited as instances. Historians cannot follow this method because history does not repeat itself; there have been many revolutions in history, and they may be said to have a family likeness, but each has its own individual traits and the actors in each have to be treated as individuals and not as types. Now this may be an adequate account of what the historian has to do, but the philosopher of history would, I suspect, claim that the formal object of his study differs from that of the historian in that he is looking at history as a whole and he is trying to find there certain laws or tendencies, repetitions in the rise and fall of nations, constant aims and conditions of progress and decay. He will be rash, if, like Toynbee, he tries to justify his work by identifying himself with the historian and then claiming that his results are the result of purely empirical methods. The historian retorts by detailed criticism and by picking holes in the too easy generalizations of the philosopher. No one who takes in his sweep twenty or more civilizations can be deadly accurate in all his details. It would seem a mistake, therefore, for the philosopher of history to pretend to be like the historian in all respects. He must, as Nowell-Smith points out, imitate the methods of the scientist and work with generalizations. He has something in common with the sociologist and the economist, for they seem to belong to a mixed genre which is partly historical and partly scientific. They deal with a certain aspect of human activity. In so far as the activity is human it is free and unpredictable, but as tied to human products and human productions there are sequences and uniform regularities which can be formulated. If the worst comes to the worst the research student can turn to statistics. Now the philosopher of history has at times followed in the wake of the sociologist with the result that his results look to be almost scientific, and of course very much mistaken. In fact he has to find out the correct way of working, if indeed there be a correct way and not a blind alley.

If we free ourselves from the cramping empirical theories which have been prejudicing both the historians and many writers about the nature of history, we may be able to place a little more accurately the position of the philosophy of history in the map of philosophy. History, as I have argued, does more than attend to successions of events or to particulars within this succession. It is free to look for causes, for motives and purposes, and relying upon a common human nature it can succeed in making sense out of a flurry of human actions. To do this the historian relies upon a power of the mind to discern a unity and a theme, and he is greeted with applause when out of a series of events or the policies or actions of some leader, king, or statesman or soldier he can make an intelligible whole. Now in addressing himself to this task the historian brings into play not only the power to weigh evidence and select the relevant facts; he must also use his imagination, possess sympathy, and have something like the talent of the artist. So near, indeed, is the historian to the artist that it has been debated by historians themselves whether they are not nearer to the artist than to the scientist. Let us admit that in the writing of history artistry must be present, but that, nevertheless, it serves as a helpmate and not as the principal agent. The facts must always in the last resort control the views of the historian, and he has no excuse if he neglects them because they are there to be known and made significant. But in a philosophy of history the field is so wide that facts can be a hindrance; the trees are unending. The philosopher here cannot ignore facts; he must use his imagination and delight in the personal and in the particular. At the same time he has to convey these facts on to a loftier site from which he can reassemble them in more general terms and then compare the generalizations to see if they make sense. His story begins to have a Miltonic splendor. Both the nature of the material and the form of selection separate it from history proper, though it still deserves the name of history. History, as we have seen, has its own appropriate way of reaching truth; a way which is different from that of science, and none the worse for that. The philosophy of history has a close connection with history, and the writer of it must, so far as he is able, keep to facts, select what is relevant, use his imagination, and look for an explanation which approximates to truth. But he might do well to claim that as with the historian in relation to the scientist, so he in relation to the historian should stake out his separate territory. This will deliver him from much of the criticism directed at him by the historians. His aim is not to deal with the episodes of history, to burrow into a tiny piece of ground; his eye is fixed on the whole visible surface. What he lacks in thoroughness of detail he makes up for by seeing relations and interconnections which are outside the province of the professional historian.

The historian without knowing it has always envied those who played at being philosophers and held in high repute the work of a Thucydides or on a larger scale the works of a Grote or a Mommsen, a Lecky or Acton. The gift of seeing relations and analogies, of bringing together into one pattern what looked at first sight dissimilar and isolated is one of man's highest gifts, one supremely possessed by the poet. It is the artist and the poet in conjunction with historical insight which makes the philosopher of history and gives him a separate rank and office. Poetry has its own justification as art, but, as has been widely recognized, it can, especially in the form of epic or drama, throw light upon the actions of past men and women. The proper recognition of this has led to a new assessment of what is called myth, which used to be dismissed as fiction. Now we are told that myth is more like to reality as lived through the imagination than to fiction; it is a manner of describing what lies behind the dry facts as noted by the perceiving mind, and it is the recurrent way in all civilizations for giving expression to the innate hopes and desires of man, and to his sense of the past. Poetry and myth, therefore, are enlisted by the philosopher of history to describe the truth he is seeking. Perhaps even more pertinent to the philosopher of history is the view now widely held that human experience can be presented through types of symbols and images. There is a mysterious analogy which runs through the varying levels of human experience, of which the simplest examples are "left and right," "high and low," "up and down." Material symbols serve for spiritual realities, and, so the psychologists tell us, there are fundamental symbols which contain a wealth of meaning, so that when they appear in religious or poetic form in other civilizations the historian is initiated into the ideas and into the ritual of behavior of the people who use them. How valuable this can be is seen in the modern approach to the writings of the Near and Middle East, in past history. During one period of Biblical criticism, for instance, it was almost taken for granted that the early books contained more fiction than truth. This view, however, has lost currency now that we have become more familiar with the way in which the minds of more primitive peoples worked, and not only of the more primitive but of those also with different traditions from our own. Greek philosophy and the rise of the physical sciences have helped to determine our method of approach to history. We have placed our confidence in the clear and distinct ideas provided by deductive and inductive methods and concepts and hypotheses. We now see that without the use of such methods, other peoples have employed symbols and images, parables and stories, not for the sake of what we would call storytelling, but to bring out the significance of the past. This way of historytelling was to them the more apposite in that the history was inextricably bound up with religion and theology; in other words it was a simple philosophy or theology of history. The Bible begins with the origin of man and rapidly sketches the long stretch of time before the history takes more definite shape in the election of Abraham and the varied fortunes of the chosen people. Besides the use of images and symbols the Biblical writers employ what has come to be called an apocalyptic and eschatological form. We still have difficulty in interpreting the meaning of some of this literature, but we now have the advantage of knowing what to seek, namely a pattern of history as definitely intended to narrate truth as the Bayeux Tapestry.

A philosophy of history as it has developed within the last two centuries will not be the same as Biblical history or an ancient epic. It will gain by leaning on accredited history and, in so far as is compatible with its aims, by relying on historical methods. But it may claim to have an *"esprit"* and a formal object which gives it a status of its own. While in its generalizations it approaches the sciences closer than history, and while it draws nearer to history than to science in its method of studying the past, it is not afraid to use as an ally the poetic imagination as manifested in images, symbols, and analogies. For this reason perhaps a better name for it would be epic or gnomic history. By withdrawing from the camps both of the sciences and of history, it frees itself from burdens which would crush it. No philosopher of history can know the data of the whole of the past in the same way in which a historian ought to know the small area of history about which he writes; nor again does he seek for the kind of scientific truth which the chemist or the anatomist requires. If criticized for failing to follow or reach the standards demanded by these sciences, he can answer that the critics have been making a "category mistake"; they are asking him to do what he never set out to do, to furnish what is not necessary for him. Mythopoeic truth is nearer to what he seeks. He must, like the historian, use interpretation; he must be intent on discovering intelligible wholes or patterns, and he can take over from the historian a group of intelligible wholes about which most historians will be agreed. With these he now looks for a greater unity, for a system which will bring these separate wholes into order. His aim is gained when he can produce a pattern or drama which makes such good sense that the reader of it is persuaded to say, "There must be some truth in this."

The growing criticism of Arnold Toynbee's *A Study of History* shows that the tide is flowing against philosophies of history. Sir Isaiah Berlin's lecture on *Historical Inevitability* provides some of the reasons why they are unacceptable to the philosopher and historian alike. It is, however, in Professor Pieter Geyl's *Debates with Historians* that the ambiguity of Toynbee's position is abundantly shown as well as the misunderstanding which can arise between historian and historicist. Geyl has included in his book four chapters of attack, and by the time he is reviewing the last volumes of Toynbee his patience is changing into restrained fury. As a result he reveals not only the grounds for his dislike of those who, like Spengler, Sorokin, and Toynbee, attempt to make a system out of history, but also the correct attitude which he believes a historian ought to adopt. The impression, however, which he leaves on at least one reader is that both he and Toynbee should revise their claims and arguments.

Geyl admits that there is "an ingrained habit of the human mind—and indeed it is a noble ambition—to try to construct a vision of history in which chaos, or apparent chaos, is reduced to order." This attempt consists in making the historical process conform to a line or rhythm or movement with definable and intelligible laws which enable the observer to predict something of the future. "It used," he says, "to be fashionable in the eighteenth and nineteenth centuries to do this in a spirit of optimism." Nowadays it is the past which is looked upon nostalgically, and the historical process is thought to be composed of recurring cycles. Spengler, for instance, pictured civilizations as "independent and mutually impenetrable entities"; they were like living organisms which had their periods of youth, middle age, and decay. He relied on his imagination, on flashes of intuition, and drew conclusions from dogmatic generalizations. Sorokin, on the other hand, divides civilizations into two types, the ideational and the sensate. The first is spiritual and lasting; the second is mainly physical a process of becoming, which has the usual stages from birth to death. Where he differs from Spengler is in his attention to facts, or rather to statistics. He compiles vast quantities of figures, and from these data he fills in his picture of the civilizations. Toynbee, in his turn, found Spengler "most unilluminatingly dogmatic and deterministic," and felt that there was room "for English empiricism." He, therefore, claims that his work is based on an empirical investigation. It is this claim which rouses Geyl's ire. "Had he really examined history with an open mind, merely formulating the theses supplied him by the observed facts, phenomena, developments, he could never have printed that imposing announcement of the division into so many parts in the opening pages of his first volume, nor could he in his references, as early as 1934, indicate what he was going to say about various chief problems in part 9 or in part 13, in 1950 or

1960.* He has been, in fact, selecting just what suited him. His method is vitiated by subjectivism, and apart from truisms there are a series of laws and parallels which are of no practical value because they are artificial."

The root of Geyl's objections to Toynbee and other historicists is that they do not write history. He points out that Toynbee assumes the reality of his multiple civilizations, that he gets himself into difficulties over freedom and determinism, at one moment insisting on indeterminism in history, and at the next preparing to draw the horoscope of the future; but these are incidental failings compared with the basic error that he sits so loose to historical evidence, that "he soars above the ground of history where we others plod," and that he expects of "history what history cannot possibly give—certainty." The historian must always hold large generalizations in suspicion, and be slow to use parallels and analogies. Toynbee's view is bound to be one-sided and subjective, for "a large view or interpretation like this one cannot possibly be proved by history, nor do I believe that it is derived from a study of history. . . ." It is true that the historian is not just a recorder of facts. "The facts are there to be used. Combinations, presentations, theories are indispensable if we want to understand. But the historian should proceed cautiously in using the facts for these purposes. It goes without saying that he should try to ascertain the facts as exactly as possible; but the important thing is that he should remain conscious, even then, of the element of arbitrariness, of subjectivity, that necessarily enters into all combinations of facts, if only because one has to begin by selecting them; while next, one has to order them according to an idea which must, in part at least, be conceived in one's own mind."

In asserting that large views, such as Toynbee's, can neither be proved from history nor derived from a study of history, Geyl rules out all philosophies of history. What his criticism proves is that Toynbee should not have claimed to rest his case entirely on empirical methods. That Toynbee has done so is a pity, and, I

---

* This argument, of course, depends upon the assumption that Toynbee had not gathered his facts and planned the work before announcing what he intended to do.

think, a mistake. It is not because he is as omniscient in every period of his story as the specialist historian is in his particular field that his work has stirred admiration. That admiration is aroused because he satisfied quite a different demand of the mind. What that demand is is seen in the interest shown in books with general themes, such as "The Spirit of Our Day," "The Decline of the West," or in talks and discussions on the wireless. A recent discussion on the Home Service of the BBC, called "The Divided Inheritance," produced verdicts on the "present-day football mentality," "lack of a common background," "the breakup of homelife." A commentator voiced general opinon and interest when he said that "it is good to air a problem," and to hear experts, even though such discussions never come to a clear and unanimous conclusion. There is a type of subject about which an expert or a wise man can enlighten us without overwhelming us with facts or even proving his point. Such a type of subject appears in great drama, in early epical stories, in the first attempts of historians before they have learnt that history and the philosophy of history are separate pursuits. If, to suggest the impossible, Toynbee's *A Study of History* had been written two thousand or a thousand years ago, it would now be ranked amongst the great works of the past. Critics would talk of its insights into human nature, the genius shown in his illustrations, the sweep of his knowledge and the unity of his theme. He would be compared with Herodotus and Eusebius and St. Augustine. In fact most of those who became famous in the past for their story of human affairs tended to satisfy this universal demand for light upon the baffling record of man's failures and successes. Plutarch's *Lives* have never ceased to appeal, because he made character count so much. Voltaire encouraged the belief in a rise from barbaric habits to humanism, and Gibbon only partially concealed under the name of history a great story or drama of morals. Toynbee finds in Challenge-and-Response the clue to history, and Geyl dismisses it as a truism and shows how variously and with what care it must be applied to any particular historical phase. But those who have been taught to find in the trilogy of Aeschylus on the legendary story of the house of Atreus that sin brings suffering and suffering wisdom do not feel that this apothegm is just a truism. It is a form of knowledge, a step forward in wisdom, the kind of wisdom which belongs to a study of man in relation to his destiny.

Aristotle made this point when he insisted that we must cut our coat of knowledge according to the cloth, that our knowledge of human actions must differ from that of physical reality. Hence in morals we advance in wisdom when we see that virtue is a mean between two extremes, but the knowledge is not like a physical measuring rod. Similarly in the philosophy of history the kind of knowledge we can obtain is different from the scientific or strictly historical; it answers an undying desire to have some intimation about how human life proceeds. Deep down there is a fixed conviction that there is a meaning and a pattern, and any insight into it is felt to be valuable. This is why the sage figures so often in ancient literature and why the great legends and sagas were welcomed as throwing a dark light upon the human condition. Hence it is that Geyl, while legitimately rejecting Toynbee's own claims for his work, is not on that account justified in his skepticism about the possibility of any philosophy of history. His skepticism recoils upon himself as a historian, for he admits that the historian has to be selective, subjective, and that the idea according to which he orders his facts, "must, in part at least, be conceived in one's own mind." I do not see why being "conceived in one's own mind" should be an obstacle to truth, seeing that every truth, even the most obvious, must be conceived in one's own mind. Nor again does selection necessarily make a view "subjective" in a bad sense or bar the way to true knowledge. As we have seen, history can be defended, and as a form of interpretation the knowledge of it can, in a way different from scientific knowledge, be sufficiently certain. The philosopher of history, too, uses interpretation and uses his own norms. He is not bound to accept the rules laid down by Geyl; he looks at history and relies upon history, but he also has something of the art of the poet and the dramatist, or, perhaps, a special kind of poetic art, like that described for us by David Jones in the Introduction to his *Anathemata*. "The particular quarry that the mind of the poet seeks to capture is a very elusive beast indeed. Perhaps we can say that the country to be hunted, the habitat of that quarry, where the 'forms' lurk that he's after, will be found to be part of vast, densely wooded, inherited and entailed domains. It is in that 'sacred wood' that the spoor of these 'forms' is to be tracked." The poet, however, is both less and more free than the historian-hunter; for the poet "may feel something with regard to Penda the Mercian and nothing with regard to Darius the Mede. In itself that is a limitation; it might be regarded as a disproportion; no matter, there is no help—he must work within the limits of his love. There must be no mugging up, no 'ought to know' or 'try to feel'; for only what is actually loved and known can be seen *sub specie aeternitatis.*" By his love the poet is tied, but he is free to ignore what he does not love. Not so with the philosopher of history. He must hunt in the "vast, densely wooded . . . domains," and it is his duty to "mug up" facts in the hope that they may stir in him some love or appreciation. He must keep nearer to the earth than the poet in the expectation that he may become familiar with the alphabet of history and in the end discover some of the sentences which compose it. Whether he can succeed or not the quest is an alluring one and it continues to excite hunters, even though the bystanders may warn them that the quarry is as mythical as the Holy Grail.

BIBLIOGRAPHY

BECK, R. N. and LEE, D. H. "The Meaning of Historicism," *American Historical Review,* 1954.

BERLIN, ISAIAH. *Historical Inevitability.* Oxford: 1954.

BULLOCK, ALAN. "The Historian's Purpose: History and Metahistory," *History Today,* 1951.

COLLINGWOOD, R. G. *The Idea of History.* Oxford: 1946.

DANTO, A. C. *Analytical Philosophy of History.* Cambridge: 1968.

DAWSON, C. *The Dynamics of World History.* New York: 1957.

DRAY, W. *The Philosophy of History.* Englewood Cliffs, N.J.: 1964.

GEYL, P. *Debates with Historians.* New York: 1958.

GEYL, P., Toynbee, A., and Sorokin, P. *The Pattern of the Past: Can We Determine It?* Boston: 1949.

GEYL, P. *The Use and Abuse of History.* New Haven: 1955.

MANDELBAUM, M. "Some Neglected Philosophic Problems Regarding History," *The Journal of Philosophy,* 1952.

BIBLIOGRAPHY

MANDELBAUM, M. "A Critique of Philosophies of History," *Journal of Philosophy*, 1948.

MANDELBAUM, M. *The Problem of Historical Knowledge*. New York: 1967.

POPPER, K. *The Open Society and Its Enemies*. London: 1945.

POPPER, K. *The Poverty of Historicism*. London: 1957.

STOVER, R. *The Nature of Historical Thinking*. Chapel Hill, N.C.: 1967.

WALSH. W. H. "Meaning in History," *Theories of History*, ed. P. Gardiner. New York: 1959.